MW00527379

ILLUSTRATED
BIBLE HISTORY

ILLUSTRATED
BIBLE HISTORY

OF THE
OLD AND NEW TESTAMENTS

FOR THE USE OF CATHOLIC SCHOOLS

By IGNATIUS SCHUSTER, D.D.

THIRTY-SECOND EDITION
WITH ILLUSTRATIONS BY PHILIP SCHUMACHER,
TWO COLORED MAPS, AND
A GLOSSARY OF PROPER NAMES BY THE
REV. H. J. HECK

TAN BOOKS AND PUBLISHERS, INC.
Rockford, Illinois 61105

NIHIL OBSTAT

Innocentius Swoboda, O.F.M.

Censor Librorum

IMPRIMATUR

Sti. Ludovici, die 21. Augusti, 1950

✠*Joseph E. Ritter*

Archiepiscopus

Originally published by B. Herder Book Co., St. Louis, Missouri, U.S.A.

Thirty-second edition 1959

The typography in this book is the property of TAN Books and Publishers, Inc. and no reproductions therefrom are permitted according to law.

PRINTED IN U.S.A.

TAN BOOKS AND PUBLISHERS, INC.
P.O. Box 424
Rockford, Illinois 61105

1974

CONTENTS

FIRST PART

HISTORY OF THE OLD TESTAMENT

FIRST EPOCH

FROM ADAM TO ABRAHAM.

SECOND EPOCH

ELECTION AND GREATNESS OF THE ISRAELITES.—FROM ABRAHAM TO MOSES. (2000 TO 1500 B. C.)

SECOND PART

HISTORY OF THE NEW TESTAMENT

FIRST SECTION

HISTORY OF JESUS CHRIST

HIS BIRTH AND INFANCY

SECOND SECTION

The Acts of the Apostles

FIRST PART.

History of the Old Testament.

FIRST EPOCH.
From Adam to Abraham.

CHAPTER I.

The Creation of the World.

The heavens show forth the glory of God, and the firmament declareth the work of His hands.—*Ps. 18, 1.*

IN the beginning God created heaven and earth. The earth was void and empty, darkness was on the face of the deep, and the Spirit of God moved over the waters. God said: "Be light made," and light was made. This was the first day.

2. On the second day God said: "Let there be a firmament made amidst the waters; and let it divide the waters from the waters." And it was so. God called the firmament Heaven.

3. On the third day God said: "Let the waters that are under the heaven be gathered into one place; and let the dry land appear." And it was so done. God called the dry land, Earth; the gathered waters, Seas. He also said: "Let the earth bring forth the green herb and such as may seed, and the fruit tree yielding fruit after its kind." And it was so done.

4. The fourth day God said: "Let there be lights made

in the firmament of heaven, to divide the day and the night, and let them be for signs, and for seasons, and for days and for years." And it was so done. God made the sun, moon and countless stars, and set them in the firmament of heaven, to shine upon the earth, and to rule the day and the night.

THE CREATION OF THE WORLD.

5. The fifth day God said: "Let the waters bring forth the creeping creatures having life, and the fowl that may fly over the earth under the firmament of heaven." And God created fish and birds of every kind, and He blessed them, saying, "Increase and multiply."

6. The sixth day God said: "Let the earth bring forth the living creature in its kind: cattle and creeping things, and beasts of the earth according to their kinds." And it was so done. At last God created man, and gave him dominion over all the rest. And God saw all the works that He had made, and they were very good. The seventh day God rested, and He blessed that day and made it holy.

QUESTIONS.

1. What did God create in the beginning? In what condition was the earth at first? What moved over the waters? What was then made? 2. What was made on the second day? 3. What did God say on the third day? What did God call the dry land? The waters? What else did God then create? 4. What did God say on the fourth day? 5. What did God say on the fifth day? 6. On the sixth day? What did God give to man? What did God do on the seventh day?

CHAPTER II.

Creation and Fall of the Angels.

O ye angels of the Lord, bless the Lord; praise and exalt Him above all forever.—*Dan. 3, 58.*

BESIDES the visible world, God also created an invisible world, namely, innumerable spirits called Angels. They were all good, happy, and endowed with excellent gifts of nature and of grace; but they did not all continue in that state, for, being possessed of a free will, a great many of them abused it, lost the grace of God, and became wicked.

2. They rebelled against God—Lucifer, their leader, saying: "We shall be like unto the Most High; we will place our throne above the stars."

3. Then there was a great strife in heaven. Michael and the other angels who had remained faithful to God, fought against the bad and rebellious spirits, whose chief is now called Satan, or the Devil. The bad angels were conquered and cast from heaven down to hell. The angels who remained faithful were rewarded with everlasting happiness. They forever see the face of God in heaven.

QUESTIONS.

1. Besides the visible world, what did God create? In what state were the angels first? Did they all continue in that happy state? 2. What did they do? What did Lucifer, their leader, say? 3. What was there then in heaven? Against whom did Michael and the other good angels fight? Who were conquered, and

how were the bad angels punished?   How were the good angels rewarded?

CHAPTER III.

*Creation of the First Man. — Paradise. — The First Com-
mandment. — Creation of Eve.*

He that liveth forever, created all things together.   God only shall
be justified, and He remaineth an invincible king
forever.—*Ecclus., 18, 1.*

WHEN God created man, He said: "Let us make man to our image and likeness, and give him dominion over all animals and over the whole earth." He then formed a human body of the slime of the earth, breathed into his face the breath of life, and man became a living soul. At the same moment God added to the nature of man many favors, and, especially, sanctifying grace. Thus was made the first man, who was named Adam, that is to say, man taken from the earth. By his nature man was the image of God; by grace he was the likeness of God.

2. By a special effect of His goodness the Lord God created, expressly for man, a garden of pleasure, called Paradise. There were in it all sorts of beautiful trees, covered with delicious fruit; and in the middle of the garden stood the tree of life, and the tree of knowledge of good and evil. A river, divided into four branches, watered the whole garden.

3. It was in this garden of delights that God placed man, that he might cultivate it for his own pleasure and occupation. God then commanded man, saying: "Of every tree of Paradise thou shalt eat, but of the tree of knowledge of good and evil thou shalt not eat; for in what day soever thou shalt eat of it, thou shalt die the death."

4. Adam was still alone on the earth. Hence God said: "It is not good for man to be alone; let us make him a help like unto himself." Then God caused all the animals to come before Adam, that he might give to each its name. But

for Adam there was not found a help like unto himself; therefore, casting a deep sleep upon Adam, God took one of his
ribs and formed of it a woman. When Adam awoke, God
brought to him his wife; and Adam rejoiced to see another
being like himself. He called her Eve, that is, Mother of
the Living.

QUESTIONS.

1. What did God say when He created man? How did He create
man? What was the first man called? How is man the image of
God, and how the likeness of God? 2. What did God, in His special
goodness, create expressly for man? What was in the garden, and
what stood in the middle of it? 3. What commandment did God
give to man? 4. What did God say, seeing Adam still alone on the
earth? Why did God cause all the animals to come before Adam?
How did God create a helpmate for Adam? What did Adam call
her?

CHAPTER IV.

The Fall of our First Parents.

He is a liar, and the father thereof.—*John, 8, 44.*

OF all the animals that God had placed upon the earth,
none was more cunning than the serpent. Hence the
devil, who was envious of the happiness of our first parents,
made use of him in order to seduce them.

2. Eve, prompted by curiosity, approaching the forbidden
tree, saw a serpent near it. He began to speak, and said to
her: "Why has God commanded you, that you should not
eat of every tree of Paradise?" Eve answered: "Of the
fruit of the trees of Paradise we do eat; but of the fruit of the
tree which is in the midst of Paradise, God has commanded
us that we should not eat, and that we should not touch it,
lest, perhaps, we die."

3. The serpent said to the woman: "No, surely you shall
not die if you eat of the fruit of that tree; but, rather, your
eyes shall be opened, and you shall be as gods, knowing good
and evil."

4. Hearing this, Eve gave way to pride, and she saw that the fruit was good to eat and pleasant to behold. She took and ate of the fruit, and gave to her husband, and he also ate. Thus was the first sin committed.

5. At the same time they lost sanctifying grace, which was the life of their soul; they lost the immortality of their body: their eyes were opened, and they saw with shame that they

THE FALL OF OUR FIRST PARENTS.

were naked. In their shame and confusion they began to sew fig-leaves together, in order to cover their nakedness.

6. But soon they heard the voice of God calling them, and they hid themselves among the trees. And God said: "Adam, where art thou?" And Adam answered: "I heard Thy voice, and I was afraid, because I was naked, and I hid myself." And God said: "Who has told thee that thou art naked? Hast thou eaten of the forbidden fruit?" Adam replied: "The woman whom Thou gavest me to be my companion gave me of the fruit, and I did eat." And the Lord

said to the woman: "Why has thou done this?" She replied: "The serpent deceived me, and I did eat."

7. Then God said to the serpent: "Because thou hast done this thing, thou art cursed among all the beasts of the earth. Upon thy breast thou shalt go, and dust shalt thou eat all the days of thy life. I will put enmity[1] between thee and the woman, and thy seed and her seed; she shall crush thy head, and thou shalt lie in wait for her heel." This referred to the Savior, who was one day to destroy the power of Satan. The woman mentioned is the Blessed Virgin Mary.

8. To Eve God said: "In sorrow and pain shalt thou bring forth thy children. Thou shalt be subject to thy husband, and he shall have dominion[2] over thee."

9. And to Adam He said: "Because thou has harkened to the voice of thy wife, and hast eaten of the tree, whereof I commanded thee that thou shouldst not eat, cursed is the earth in thy work; with labor and toil shalt thou eat thereof all the days of thy life. Thorns and thistles shall it bring forth to thee. In the sweat of thy face thou shalt eat bread, till thou shalt return to the earth, out of which thou wast taken; for dust thou art, and into dust thou shalt return."

10. How great is the mercy of God, that He promised a Redeemer to our sinful parents. How hateful must sin be to God, since He pronounces so terrible a curse on those favored creatures whom He had so recently blessed. When God had pronounced the sentence of banishment and death on Adam and Eve; when He had commanded the elements to oppress them in divers ways, He drove them out of Paradise, and placed before the gate Cherubim, with flaming sword, turning every way, to guard the way leading to the tree of life.

QUESTIONS.

1. Of what animal did the devil make use, in order to seduce our first parents?　2. What did the serpent say to Eve when she saw him at the tree?　What did Eve reply?　3. What did the serpent then say?　4. What did Eve do?　What did Adam do?　What was thus committed?　5. What change then took place in Adam and

[1] EN'MITY, strife, warfare.　　　　[2] DOMIN'ION, power, control.

Eve?   What did they do to cover their nakedness?   6. What did
they do when God called them?   What did Adam say?   What did
God say?   What did Adam reply?   What did the Lord say to the
woman?   What did she reply?   7. What did God say to the serpent?   In what words did God promise a Redeemer?   8. What did
God say to the woman?   9. What did He say to Adam?   10. When
God banished Adam and Eve from Paradise, whom did He place at
the entrance to guard the way to the tree of life?

CHAPTER V.

Cain and Abel.

By the envy of the devil, death came into the world.—*Wis. 2, 24.*

ADAM and Eve had many children; the first two were
Cain and Abel. Cain was a husbandman, or tiller of
the earth; Abel was a shepherd. Abel was just, but the
works of Cain were evil. Now, it happened one day that
they offered a sacrifice to God in gratitude for the benefits
He had bestowed upon them.

2. Abel offered the firstlings of his flock, and Cain, fruits
of the earth. The Lord regarded Abel and his gifts with
favor, but for Cain and his offerings He had no regard. Seeing this, Cain was exceedingly angry, and his countenance
fell.

3. And the Lord said to Cain: "Why art thou angry, and
why is thy countenance fallen? If thou do well, shalt thou
not receive? but if ill, shall not sin forthwith be present at
the door?" Keep away from sin. But Cain did not heed
the Lord.

4. One day he said to his brother: "Let us go forth
abroad." Abel, suspecting no evil, went out with him; and
when they were in the field, Cain rose up against Abel, his
brother, and slew him. The Lord said to Cain: "Where is
thy brother Abel?" Cain replied in an insolent manner:
"I know not; am I my brother's keeper?"

5. And the Lord said to him: "What hast thou done?

The voice of thy brother's blood crieth to me from the earth. Now, therefore, cursed shalt thou be upon the earth, which hath opened her mouth and received the blood of thy brother at thy hand. When thou shalt till it, it shall not yield to thee its fruit. A fugitive and a vagabond shalt thou be upon the earth."

6. And Cain, in despair, said to the Lord: "My iniquity is greater than that I may deserve pardon. Behold! Thou

DEATH OF ABEL.

dost cast me out this day from the face of the earth. Every one, therefore, who findeth me will kill me." The Lord said to him: "No, it shall not be so; but whosoever shall kill Cain shall be punished sevenfold." And He set a mark upon Cain, that whosoever found him should not kill him. And Cain went out from the face of the Lord, and dwelt as a fugitive on the earth.

7. Abel, who offered a sacrifice pleasing to God, is a figure of Christ, whose sacrifice of the Cross was infinitely pleasing

to God. In the conduct of Cain we see the awful consequences of envy. Had he promptly suppressed in his heart the first emotion of envy, he never would have stained his hands and his soul with his brother's blood, which cried to heaven for vengeance.

QUESTIONS.

1. Who were the first two children of Adam and Eve? What was Cain? What was Abel? 2. What offerings did Cain and Abel make to God? Why did they offer a sacrifice? Were the sacrifices of the two brothers equally well received? What happened then? 3. What did the Lord say to Cain? Did Cain heed the words of God? 4. What did Cain say to Abel? What happened when they walked out together? What did the Lord say to Cain? What did Cain reply? 5. What did the Lord then say? 6. What did Cain, in despair, say to the Lord? What did the Lord reply? 7. Of whom is Abel a figure? What do we see in the conduct of Cain?

CHAPTER VI.

The Deluge.

The wicked shall be destroyed from the earth, and they that do unjustly shall be taken away from it.—*Prov. 2, 22.*

ADAM lived nine hundred and thirty years. He had many sons and daughters, to whom he announced the Law of God and the coming of the Redeemer. His immediate descendants also lived to a very great age. Mathusala, the oldest of them, lived nine hundred and sixty-nine years. The people became very numerous. Some were herdsmen and lived in tents; others built cities and became mechanics and musicians. The descendants of the pious Seth, whom God had given to Adam instead of Abel, were good, feared God, and hence were called the children of God. Henoch, one of the children of God, was noted for his faith and piety, and was taken up alive into heaven. The descendants of Cain, however, turned away from God, were wicked, and were called the children of men.

2. Unhappily, the children of God began to associate with

the children of men, and soon they themselves became wicked. Then God said that men must not live so long, seeing that they have become corrupt in their ways. "His days shall be one hundred and twenty years."

3. The wickedness of men went on increasing, and their thoughts were continually bent upon evil. Seeing this, God said: "I will destroy man, whom I have created, from the face of the earth." But amongst these wicked men there was one just and virtuous man, who was called Noe. Noe

THE DELUGE.

found favor with the Lord, and to him the Lord said: "Make thee an ark of timber planks; thou shalt make little rooms in the ark, and thou shalt pitch it within and without, with bitumen. The length of the ark shall be three hundred cubits, and the breadth of it fifty cubits, and the height of it thirty cubits.

4. "Thou shalt make a window in the ark, and a door in

its side, and thou shalt divide the ark into lower, middle and third stories. Behold, I will bring the waters of a great flood upon the earth, to destroy all flesh wherein is the breath of life. But I will establish my covenant[1] with thee. Thou shalt enter into the ark, thou and thy sons, and thy wife, and the wives of thy sons with thee.

5. "And of every living creature, of all flesh, thou shalt bring two of a sort into the ark, that they may live with thee. Thou shalt take unto thee of all food which may be eaten, and thou shalt lay it up with thee." Noe did all that the Lord had commanded him to do. He spent a hundred years in building the ark, during which time he preached penance to the people.

6. But men heeded not the warning. They ate, drank, and were married just as before, without a thought of the terrible punishment that was to come upon them. Then the Lord said to Noe: "Go in, thou and all thy house, into the ark; and after seven days I will cause rain to fall upon the earth for forty days and forty nights, and I will destroy every substance that I have made, from the face of the earth."

7. Noe entered into the ark, with all his family, taking with him all that the Lord had commanded him; and the Lord shut him in on the outside. And, when the seven days were passed, the fountains of the great deep were broken up, and the flood-gates of heaven were opened, and the rain fell upon the earth for forty days and forty nights. The waters continued to increase till they rose fifteen cubits above the highest mountains. Thus every living being was destroyed, that moved upon the earth, both of fowl, of cattle, of beasts and all men. Noe only remained, and they that were with him in the ark.

8. The ark is a figure of the Church; for, as no one escaped the waters of the deluge,[2] except those that were in the ark, so no one shall escape the deluge of fire on the last day, save

[1] COV'E-NANT, a bargain, an agreement.

[2] DEL'UGE, a great flood, or overflowing of the earth by water.

those who are in the Catholic Church, the true ark of salvation.

QUESTIONS.

1. How long did Adam live? Mathusala? What were the descendants of Seth called? What became of Henoch? 2. Did the children of God always remain good? What did God then say? Were the wicked men converted? Seeing that they were not converted, what did God say? 3. Was there no just man on the earth? What did the Lord tell Noe to do? 4. What did the Lord establish with Noe? Whom and what did He tell him to take into the ark? 5. How long was Noe building the ark? Did Noe warn the people of the threatened danger? 6. Did they heed the warning? What did God then say to Noe? 7. What happened after Noe and his family entered into the ark? 8. Of what is the ark a figure?

CHAPTER VII.

Noe's Offering—His Children.

Bless ye the God of heaven; give glory to Him in the sight of all that live, because He hath shewed His mercy to you.—*Tob. 12, 6.*

NOW God remembered Noe, and sent a wind upon the earth. This moved the waters, and after a hundred and fifty days they began to abate. At length the ark rested upon a mountain in Armenia,[1] called Mount Ararat, and the tops of the hills began to appear. Noe perceived this with great joy, for he had been now three hundred and fifty days shut up in the ark.

2. In order to see whether the waters had subsided[2] on the earth, he opened the window and sent forth a raven, which did not return. He next sent forth a dove; but she, not finding a spot whereon to rest her foot, returned to the ark. After seven days he again sent forth the dove. She came back to him, in the evening, carrying in her mouth a bough of an olive tree, with green leaves. Noe, therefore, understood that the waters had abated from off the face of the earth.

[1] AR-ME′-NIA, a country in Asia.
[2] SUB-SI′-BED, fallen, become lower.

3. He stayed in the ark yet other seven days, and he sent
forth the dove again, which did not return to him. God then
said to Noe: "Go out of the ark." So Noe went out of the
ark with his wife, his sons and their wives, together with all
the living creatures which he had placed in it. Filled with
gratitude towards the Lord, who had so wonderfully preserved him, he built an altar to the Lord and offered on it a
sacrifice of clean animals.

4. The sacrifice of Noe was pleasing to the Lord. He

NOE'S OFFERING.

blessed Noe and his sons, and said to them: "Increase and
multiply, and fill the earth." God made a covenant with
Noe that He would never again destroy the earth with water.
The rainbow which we see in the clouds is the sign of this
covenant between God and the earth. The sons of Noe were
Sem, Cham and Japhet. Now Noe began to cultivate the
earth. He planted a vineyard, and drinking of the wine, he
fell asleep, and was uncovered in his tent.

5. Cham, seeing his father in this condition, spoke of it in a jesting way to his brothers. They, however, filled with a chaste and holy fear, put a cloak upon their shoulders, and, going backwards so as not to look upon him where he lay, covered their father's nakedness. And Noe, awaking and hearing what had happened, said: "Cursed be Chanaan; a servant of servants shall he be unto his brethren." But he blessed Sem and Japhet. Children should learn from this example not to mock or ridicule their parents.

QUESTIONS.

1. How long was it before the waters began to abate? Where did the ark rest? 2. What did Noe send from the ark, to see if the waters had subsided? Did the raven return? What did Noe then send forth? What did the dove bring back in her mouth? 3. Did the dove return to the ark the third time? What did Noe do on leaving the ark? 4. Was Noe's sacrifice pleasing to the Lord? What covenant did the Lord make with Noe? What sign did God give? What were the sons of Noe called? What did Noe plant? What happened when Noe had drunk of the wine of his vineyard? 5. What did Cham do? What did his brothers do? When Noe awoke and heard what Cham had done, what did he then say?

CHAPTER VIII.

The Tower of Babel.

Except the Lord build the house, they labor in vain that build it.
—*Ps. 126, 1.*

THE descendants of Noe soon multiplied, and again became as wicked as men had been before the deluge. Now, they were unable to live any longer together, and they said: "Come let us make a city and a tower, the top whereof may reach to heaven; and let us make our name famous before we be scattered abroad in all the lands." But God frustrated[1] their foolish design. He said: "Let us confound their tongue, that they may not understand one another's speech."

2. Till then there had been but one language spoken

[1] FRUS-TRA'-TED, thwarted, prevented.

amongst men. So the Lord scattered them from that place into all the lands, and they ceased to build the city. Therefore, the city was called Babel, which signifies confusion, because there the language of the whole earth was confounded.

3. The children of Sem remained in Asia, and from them descended the Israelites, the chosen people of God. Most of the descendants of Cham settled in Africa, while those of Japhet took up their abode in Europe. Thus were different

THE TOWER OF BABEL.

nations founded. The more men multiplied on the earth, the more wicked they became. Instead of adoring the true God, they began to adore a multitude of false gods.

4. Some worshiped the sun, moon and stars; others worshiped men and beasts, and even the works of their own hands. To these false divinities[1] even human victims were offered, and sometimes innocent children, who were made to

[1] DI-VIN'-I-TIES, gods.

endure the most cruel torments. Such is the consequence of abandoning the worship of the true God.

QUESTIONS.

1. Did the descendants of Noe remain good? What did they say? What did God do? What did He say? 2. What was the tower called? 3. Where did the children of Sem remain? What people descended from them? Where did most of the descendants of Cham settle? Where did the children of Japhet take up their abode? What happened when men multiplied upon the earth? What did they adore instead of the true God? 4. What victims were offered to these false gods?

SECOND EPOCH.

The Age of the Patriarchs.—Election and Greatness of the Israelites.—From Abraham to Moses. (2000 to 1500 B. C.)

CHAPTER IX.

Call of Abram.

As God hath called every one, so let him walk.—*I. Cor., 7, 17.*

A MONGST the multitude of the wicked there was one just and upright man. He was called Abram. The Lord chose him, that, through him and his posterity,[1] the true faith and hope in the promised Redeemer might be preserved and propagated[2] on the earth. He said to him: "Go forth out of thy country and from thy kindred, and out of thy father's house, and come into the land which I will show thee, and I will make of thee a great nation. I will bless thee and magnify thy name, and thou shalt be blessed; and in thee shall all the kindred of the earth be blessed."

2. The father of Abram had gone to settle in Chaldea,[3] and had taken up his abode at Haran, with his relatives; but, as idolatry[4] had at last made its way even into that family, the Lord called Abram forth from amongst his kindred. Abram believed the word of God, and instantly set out for Chanaan, taking with him Sarai, his wife, and Lot, his nephew, and his servants and his herds of cattle. After a long journey he arrived in the land of Chanaan,[5] and came to Sichem. He was then seventy-five years old.

[1] POS-TER'-ITY, descendants, those who come after. [2] PROPA-GA'-TED, extended, carried from place to place. [3] CHAL-DEA (pr. Kaldee'-a), a country of ancient Asia. [4] I-DOL'-A-TRY, the worship of false gods. [5] CHA'-NAAN (pr. Ka'-nan), a country in Asia, now called Palestine, or Holy Land.

3. Chanaan, on account of its beauty and fertility, was called a land flowing with milk and honey. There the Lord again appeared to Abram, and said to him: "To thy seed will I give this land." Abram, wishing to show his gratitude, raised in that place an altar to the Lord. Henceforth Chanaan was also called the Promised Land. Gratitude to God for past favors is the most certain means of obtaining new ones.

QUESTIONS.

1. What just man was found amongst the multitude of the wicked? Why did the Lord choose Abram? What did He say to him? 2. Where did the father of Abram go to settle? Why did the Lord call Abram forth from amongst his kindred? Whom and what did Abram take with him? 3. What was Chanaan called? Why was it so called? What did the Lord say when He again appeared to Abram? What did Abram do to show his gratitude? What was Chanaan also called?

CHAPTER X.

Abram's Love of Peace.

Blessed are the peacemakers, for they shall be called the children of God.—*Matt. 5, 9.*

GOD blessed Abram, and increased his herds and those of Lot in such a manner that the pasture in that country was not sufficient for them. On this account a strife arose between the herdsmen of Abram and those of Lot. And Abram said to Lot: "Let there be no quarrel, I beseech thee, between me and thee, and between my herdsmen and thy herdsmen; for we are brethren. Behold, the whole land is before thee: depart from me, I pray thee. If thou wilt go to the left hand, I will take the right; if thou choose the right hand, I will pass to the left."

2. Lot chose the fertile country about the Jordan,[1] and dwelt in Sodom. Abram dwelt in Hebron, and built there an

[1] JOR'-DAN, a river of Judea.

altar to the lord. Some time after this, strange kings having come into the land, began to rob and plunder the cities of Sodom and Gormorrha,[1] took Lot captive, and seized all his substance. As soon as Abram heard that Lot had been taken captive, he, with three hundred and eighteen well-armed men, his servants, pursued the kings, overtook them, res-

MELCHISEDECH'S OFFERING.

cued Lot from their hands, and brought him back with all his possessions.

3. As Abram returned victorious, Melchisedech,[2] king of Salem,[3] and the King of Sodom, went out to meet him. Melchisedech, being a high priest of the Most High, offered to the Lord a sacrifice of bread and wine, as a sacrifice of praise and thanksgiving, for Abram and his servants. He blessed him and said: "Blessed be Abram by the Most High God,

---

[1] Sod'-om and Gomor'rha (pr. Go-mor'-ra), at that time cities of Asia. [2] Mel-chis'-edech (pr. Mel-kiz'-e-dek). [3] Sa'-lem, means City of Peace; it was afterwards called Jerusalem.

who created heaven and earth; and blessed be the Most High God, by whose protection the enemies are in thy hands." Abram gave him the tithes[1] of the booty. The king of Sodom then said to Abram: "Give me the persons, and the rest take to thyself." But Abram would accept no reward. Melchisedech was a figure of the eternal High Priest, Jesus Christ. His sacrifice was a figure of the sacrifice of the Mass.

QUESTIONS.

1. Why did a strife arise between the herdsmen of Abram and Lot? What did Abram say to Lot? 2. Where did Lot go to dwell? Where did Abram dwell? Who came into the land and began to rob and plunder? What did they do to Lot? What did Abram do when he heard what had befallen Lot? 3. Who met Abram when he returned victorious? Who was Melchisedech? What did he offer to the Lord? Of whom was Melchisedech a figure? Of what does his sacrifice remind you?

CHAPTER XI.

Abraham's Faith and Hospitality.—Circumcision.

The just man liveth by faith.—*Rom. 1, 17.*

AFTER these things the word of the Lord came to Abram in a vision, saying: "Fear not, I am thy protector, and thy reward exceeding great." On a certain night, Abram was called by a voice from heaven, which said: "Look up to heaven and number the stars, if thou canst. So shall thy seed be." Abram believed, and his faith, together with his good works, justified him before God.

2. The Lord again appeared to him, when he was ninety-nine years of age, and said to him: "I am the Almighty God. Walk before me and be perfect." Neither shall thy name by called any more Abram, a high father, but Abraham, father of the multitude, because I have made thee a father of many nations. I will establish My covenant between Me and thee: All the male kind of you shall be circumcised. Sarai,

---

[1] TITHES, the tenth part.

thy wife, shall be called Sara, and she shall bear thee a son, whose name thou shalt call Isaac.[1]

3. As Abraham was one day, about noon, sitting at the door of his tent, he saw three men approaching. He ran to meet them, bowed down before them, and invited them to rest in his tent and partake of some refreshment. Calling Sara, his wife, he told her to make some cakes of the finest flour. He caused the best calf of his herds to be killed for the entertainment of the unknown visitors. Butter, milk and honey were also placed before them, Abraham himself waiting upon his guests.

4. After the meal, when they were about to depart, one of the strangers said to Abraham that after a year he would return, and that Sara, his wife, would have a son. Then Abraham understood that the Lord God Himself, accompanied by angels, was his guest. Kindness and courtesy to strangers should be praised and encouraged, since God rewarded so richly the hospitality of Abraham. Circumcision[2] was a figure of the Sacrament of Baptism.

QUESTIONS.

1. What promise was made to Abraham by a voice from heaven? What justified Abraham before God? 2. What does Abraham signify? What covenant did the Lord make with Abraham? What token did He give him? 3. What happened when Abraham was one day sitting at the door of his tent? 4. What promise did one of the strangers make to Abraham? What did God so richly reward? Of what is circumcision a figure?

CHAPTER XII.

Destruction of Sodom and Gomorrha.

He shall rain snares upon sinners: fire and brimstone and storms shall be the portion of their cup.—*Ps. 10, 7.*

ABRAHAM went part of the way with the strangers, who were going to Sodom. As they journeyed along to-

---

[1] ISAAC (pr. I'zak). [2] CIRCUM-CIS-ION (pr. cir-kum-sizh'-un), a Jewish rite.

gether, the Lord said to Abraham: "The cry of Sodom and Gomorrha is multiplied, and their sin is become exceedingly grievous." He told him that He would destroy the two cities. Abraham was struck with fear; for, although the men amongst whom he lived were wicked, he loved them as neighbors.

2. At last, drawing near to the Lord, he said: "Wilt Thou destroy the just with the wicked? If there be fifty just men in the city, shall they perish withal? and wilt Thou not spare that place for the sake of the fifty just, if they be therein?" The Lord replied: "If I find in Sodom fifty just men within the city, I will spare the whole place for their sake." And Abraham said: "Seeing I have once begun, I will speak again to my Lord, whereas I am but dust and ashes. If there be five less than fifty just persons in the city, wilt Thou destroy it?"

3. And the Lord said to Abraham: "I will not destroy it if I find five and forty." Abraham continued to plead in this manner, till at last the Lord said to him: "I will not destroy it for the sake of ten." Then the Lord disappeared, and Abraham returned to his tent.

4. The ten just men were not found in Sodom, and the two angels were sent to destroy it. They reached Sodom in the evening, and found Lot sitting at the gate of the city. Lot invited them into his house, and the angels said to him: "Arise, get you out of this place, for the Lord will destroy it." Lot went that night to two young men who were to marry his daughters, and told them to arise and go forth, for the Lord would destroy the city.

5. But they thought that he spoke in jest. At the first dawn of day the angels pressed Lot to depart, saying: "Take thy wife and thy two daughters, lest you also perish with the wicked city." And, as Lot still lingered, they took him by the hand, and, as it were against his will, led him and his family out of the city, warning them all not to look back under pain of death.

6. Lot's wife, however, looked back, and was instantly changed into a pillar of salt. The sun had just risen when Lot entered the neighboring city of Segor. Then the Lord rained down from heaven fire and brimstone, and utterly destroyed those two wicked cities, with all their inhabitants.

7. On the site where these cities once stood is now the Dead Sea, a sulphurous lake which infects the air around, and is carefully shunned by man and beast. A terrible ex-

DESTRUCTION OF SODOM.

ample of the curse which great crimes draw down from heaven on those who commit them.

QUESTIONS.

1. What did the Lord tell Abraham as they journeyed together? 2. What did Abraham say to the Lord? 3. For how many just men did the Lord promise to spare Sodom? 4. Were the ten just men found in the city? Who were sent to destroy it? Whom did the angels find sitting at the gate? What did they say to Lot? 5. At the dawn of day what did the angels press Lot to do? Seeing that he still lingered, what did

they do? What did they tell him and his family not to do? 6. What was the punishment of Lot's wife? What did the Lord then do to these two wicked cities? 7. What sea is now on the site of those cities?

CHAPTER XIII.

Birth of Isaac, and Abraham's Sacrifice.

The mind of the just studieth obedience.—*Prov. 15, 28.*

SARA gave birth to a son, as the Lord had promised. He was named Isaac, and circumcised on the eighth day. Abraham loved this son very tenderly, and the Lord wished to see whether he loved his son more than God. When the boy had grown up, the Lord said to Abraham: "Take thy only-begotten son Isaac, whom thou lovest, and go into the land of vision, and there thou shalt offer him for a holocaust[1] upon one of the mountains which I will show thee."

2. Abraham instantly arose, and by night saddled his ass, taking with him two young men and Isaac his son. And when he had cut the wood for the holocaust, he went to the place which God had shown him. On the third day he came in sight of Mount Moria, where he was to sacrifice his son; and he said to his servants: "Stay you here with the ass; I and the boy will go with speed as far as yonder, and, after we have worshiped, will return to you."

3. Then he took the wood for the holocaust and laid it upon the shoulders of Isaac. He himself carried in his hands fire and a sword. As they went along Isaac said: "My father." And Abraham answered: "What wilt thou, son?" "Behold," said the son, "fire and wood: where is the victim for the holocaust?" Abraham replied: "God will provide Himself a victim for a holocaust, my son." So they went on together.

4. When they reached the top of the mountain, Abraham

[1] HOL'-O-CAUST, a victim, every part of which is consumed by fire.

erected an altar, placed the wood upon it, bound his son and
laid him on the altar. Then he put forth his hand and took
the sword to sacrifice his son. But behold! an angel from
heaven cried out to him, saying: "Abraham, Abraham."
And he answered: "Here I am." And the angel said:
"Lay not thy hand upon the boy, neither do thou anything
to him. Now I know that thou fearest God, and hast not
spared thy only-begotten son for My sake."

ABRAHAM'S SACRIFICE.

5. Abraham lifted up his eyes and saw behind him a ram
sticking fast by his horns in the bushes; him he took and
offered, instead of his son. The angel of the Lord spoke
again to Abraham, saying: "By My own self have I sworn,
saith the Lord, because thou hast done this thing, and hast
not spared thy only-begotten son for My sake, I will bless
thee, and I will multiply thy seed as the stars of heaven and
as the sand that is by the sea-shore. And in thy seed shall
all the nations of the earth be blessed, because thou hast

obeyed My voice." Then Abraham returned home with his son.

6. The seed, or person in whom all nations shall be blest, is the same that was promised in Paradise; it is the Savior who was descended from Abraham, and who redeemed mankind from sin and hell. Isaac, carrying the wood on which he himself was to be sacrificed, is a true figure of Christ carrying His cross. Abraham is a grand model, which parents ought to imitate. They should love their children much, but not so much as to transgress,[1] for their sake, the laws of God.

QUESTIONS.

1. What was Abraham's son named? What did the Lord do in order to see whether Abraham loved his son more than God? 2. Did Abraham obey? What did he do? What did he say to his servants? 3. What did he lay on the shoulders of Isaac? What took place as they went along? 4. What did Abraham do when they reached the top of the mountain? What did the angel say from heaven to Abraham? 5. What did Abraham sacrifice instead of his son? What did the angel again say? 6. Who is the seed in whom all nations shall be blest? Of whom is Isaac a true figure? Why? For whom is Abraham a grand model?

CHAPTER XIV.

Isaac Marries Rebecca.

He that trusteth in the Lord shall be set on high.—*Prov. 29, 25.*

NOW Abraham was advanced in years, and the Lord had blessed him in all things. He, however, wished, before his death, to see his son wedded to a virtuous wife. But, as the daughters of the land were wicked, he said to his old servant Eliezer: "Go to my own country and kindred, and take a wife thence for my son Isaac; but take care not to take one of the daughters of the Chanaanites, among whom I

---

[1] TRANS-GRESS, to break, to violate.

dwell." The servant promised to observe faithfully all that Abraham had commanded him.

2. He then took ten camels of his master's herd, loaded them with rich presents, and set out for Haran, where Nachor, the brother of Abraham, dwelt. Arriving there, he let his camels rest near a well outside the city. It was in the evening, the time when the young women were wont to come out to draw water from the well. Then he prayed fervently within himself that heaven might prosper his undertaking:

3. "O Lord, I beseech thee, show kindness to my master Abraham. Behold, I stand nigh the spring, and the daughters of the inhabitants of the city will come out to draw water. Now, therefore, the maid to whom I shall say: 'Let down thy pitcher that I may drink,' and she shall answer: 'Drink, and I will give thy camels drink also,' let it be the same whom Thou hast provided for Thy servant Isaac; and by this I shall understand that Thou hast shown kindness to my master." He had not yet ended his prayer when Rebecca, a beautiful and modest maiden, came out, carrying a pitcher.

4. She went down to the spring, filled the pitcher, and was returning, when Eliezer ran to meet her, and said: "Give me a little water to drink out of thy pitcher." She answered him kindly: "Drink, my lord." And quickly she let down the pitcher upon her arm, and gave him drink. And when he had drunk, she said: "I will draw water for thy camels, also, till they all drink." Then, pouring water into the troughs, she let the camels drink.

5. After they had drunk, the servant presented her with golden ear-rings and bracelets, saying to her: "Whose daughter art thou? Tell me, is there any place in thy father's house to lodge?" She answered: "I am the daughter of Bathuel, the son of Nachor. We have a good store of both straw and hay, and a large place to lodge in."

6. Then Eliezer bowed down and adored the Lord, saying:

"Blessed be the Lord of my master Abraham, who hath not taken away his mercy and truth from my master, and hath brought me the straight way into the house of my master's brother." He was then invited to the house, and bread was set before him, but he refused to eat until he had delivered his message. When he had stated the object of his coming, Laban, the brother of Rebecca, and Bathuel, her father, answered: "The word hath proceeded from the Lord: we cannot speak any other thing but His pleasure. Behold! Rebecca is before thee: take her and go thy way, and let her be the wife of thy master's son, as the Lord hath spoken."

7. Then the servant bowed down to the ground, adored the Lord, and, bringing forth vessels of silver and gold, with garments of the finest texture, presented them to Rebecca. He also presented rich gifts to her brother and mother. Then, full of joy, he partook of the refreshments offered him. Next morning, after Rebecca had received the blessings of her parents and brother, she set out with her maidens for her destined home, and, on arriving there, became the wife of Isaac. Abraham lived several years after Isaac's marriage. He died, aged one hundred and seventy-five years, and was buried by his son at Hebron, where Sara, his wife, had been buried before.

QUESTIONS.

1. What did Abraham desire to see before his death? What did he say to his servant? 2. What did Eliezer then do? 3. What was his prayer at evening by the well? Who came out just then from the city? 4. What did Eliezer say when he met her? What did Rebecca reply? What did she do? 5. With what did Eliezer then present her? What did he ask her? What was Rebecca's answer? 6. What did Eliezer then say? What did he refuse to do? When he stated to the father and brother of Rebecca the object of his coming, what did they answer? 7. What did the servant then do? What happened next morning? Whose wife did Rebecca become? How long did Abraham live? Where was he buried?

CHAPTER XV.

Esau and Jacob.

The father's blessing establisheth the house of the children.—*Ecclus. 3, 11.*

ISAAC and Rebecca remained twenty years without children. At length God heard their prayer, and gave them two sons. The first-born, Esau, was red and hairy, and of a rough, harsh temper. Jacob, the second, was smooth in appearance and gentle in his bearing. Esau became a skillful hunter and a husbandman. Jacob was a plain man, and dwelt in tents.

2. Isaac loved Esau, and ate with pleasure the game that he had killed. Rebecca, on the other hand, loved the mild and gentle Jacob. She loved him the more because an angel had revealed to her in a vision that he, instead of Esau, had found favor with God. One day Jacob was cooking a mess of pottage, when Esau, coming home from the field faint with hunger, said to his brother: "Give me of this pottage, for I am hungry."

3. Jacob said to him: "Sell me thy first birthright." Esau replied: "Lo! I die of hunger: what will the first birthright avail me?" Jacob answered: "Swear, therefore, to me." Esau swore, and sold his birthright. And, taking bread and the mess of pottage, he ate and drank and went away, making little account of having sold his birthright.

4. Now, Isaac was old and had lost his eyesight. One day he called Esau, his son, and said to him: "My son, thou seest I am old, and I know not the day of my death. Take thy arms, thy quiver and bow, and go abroad; and when thou hast taken something by hunting, make me savory meat thereof, as thou knowest I like, and bring it that I may eat, and my soul may bless thee before I die." Esau promptly obeyed the command of his father, and went to the fields to hunt.

5. Rebecca had overheard the words of Isaac, and fearing that, contrary to the will of God, Esau might be preferred to Jacob, she said to him: "Now, my son, follow my counsel. Go to the flock and bring me two of the best kids, that I may make of them meat for thy father, such as he gladly eateth; so that, after having eaten it, he may bless thee before he die."

6. Jacob hastened to the flock and brought two kids. Rebecca prepared them as though they were game, and then clothed Jacob in Esau's best garments, and covered his neck and hands with the skin of the kids, and sent him to his father with the meats she had prepared.

7. Isaac asked: "Who art thou, my son?" Jacob answered: "I am Esau, thy first-born; I have done as thou has commanded; arise, sit, and eat of my venison, that thy soul may bless me." Isaac said again: "Come hither, that I may feel thee, my son, and may prove whether thou be my son Esau, or no." Jacob then drew near to his father, and Isaac, touching him, said: "The voice, indeed, is the voice of Jacob, but the hands are the hands of Esau." And he gave him his blessing.

8. Scarcely had Jacob gone out when Esau came with the game he had taken and cooked for his father. "Arise, my father, and eat," said he. Isaac, in surprise, asked him: "Who art thou?" and he answered: "I am thy first-born son, Esau." And Isaac saw that Jacob had deceived him. Then Esau roared out with a great cry, saying: "He hath already taken from me my birthright, and now he hath robbed me of my father's blessing!"

9. Then he said to his father: "Hast thou kept no blessing for me?" And, as he continued to cry out and lament, Isaac, moved with compassion, said to him: "In the fat of the earth, and in the dew of heaven from above, shall thy blessing be. Thou shalt live by the sword, and shalt serve thy brother; but the time shall come when thou shalt shake

off and loose his yoke from thy neck." From this time Esau hated his brother.

QUESTIONS.

1. Who were the two sons of Isaac and Rebecca? What was the difference between the two brothers? What did Esau become? What did Jacob prefer? 2. Which of his sons did Isaac love? Which did Rebecca love? Why did Rebecca love Jacob? What happened one day when Jacob was cooking a mess of pottage? 3. What did Jacob say to Esau? What did Esau reply? Did Esau make much account of having sold his birthright? 4. What did Isaac, being old and blind, say one day to Esau? 5. What did Rebecca say to Jacob when Esau was gone? Why did she tell Jacob to deceive his father? 6. Did Jacob obey his mother? What did he do? 7. What did his father ask him when he brought in the kids? What did Jacob reply? What did Isaac say again? What did he say after touching Jacob? What did he then give him? 8. Who came in then? What did Esau say to his father? What did Esau cry out? 9. What did Isaac then say to him, being moved with compassion?

CHAPTER XVI.

Jacob's Flight and His Sojourn with Laban.

Have confidence in the Lord; in all thy ways think on Him, and He will direct thy steps.—*Prov. 3, 5 and 6.*

ESAU was very angry because he had lost the blessing. He resolved to kill Jacob. Rebecca knew the evil intentions of Esau, and saw that the life of Jacob was in danger. She, therefore, called Jacob and said to him: "My son, flee to Laban, my brother, and dwell with him till the wrath of thy brother hath passed away." Jacob at once set out.

2. As he went on, it happened that night overtook him on an open plain. Being tired from the journey, he lay down on the ground and slept, having a stone for a pillow. In his sleep he saw a ladder standing upon the earth, the top touching heaven; and by it the angels of God ascended and descended.

3. The Lord was leaning upon the ladder, and said to him: "I am the Lord God of Abraham, thy father, and the God of Isaac. The land wherein thou sleepest, I will give to thee and to thy seed. And thy seed shall be as the dust of the earth; and in thee and thy seed all the tribes of the earth shall be blessed." And when Jacob awoke from sleep he said: "Indeed, the Lord is in this place, and I knew it not.

JACOB'S VISION.

How terrible is this place! This is no other but the house of God and the gate of heaven."

4. As soon as the morning dawned he took the stone upon which his head had lain during the vision, and set it up as a monument; he also poured oil upon it, in honor of God, and changed the name of the place from Luza to Bethel, that is to say, the house of God. He also made a vow, saying: "If God shall be with me, and I shall return prosperously to my father's house, the Lord shall be my God; and of all things that Thou shalt give me, I will offer tithes to Thee."

5. This being done, he continued his journey, and, having come to a well near which three flocks of sheep were lying, he addressed the shepherds who were tending their flocks, saying: "Brethren, whence are you?" They answered: "Of Haran." He then asked them if they knew Laban, the son of Nachor. They replied: "We know him: and behold! Rachel his daughter cometh with his flock."

6. When Rachel drew near, Jacob met her in a friendly manner, and rolled the stone from the mouth of the well, so that her flock might drink. He informed Rachel that he was the son of Rebecca, her father's sister. She joyfully ran home and announced the glad tidings to her father, who, coming out, embraced Jacob and then conducted him to his house.

7. Jacob remained twenty years with Laban, tending his flocks with great care and fidelity. But Laban tried, by various unjust means, to withhold from Jacob a part of the hire to which he was justly entitled. Nevertheless, God blessed Jacob, and he became rich in flocks, and herds, and servants.

8. The mysterious ladder which reached from earth to heaven is a figure of Christian churches, in which the angels bear up our prayers to heaven, and return to us laden with graces. The seed in whom all nations of the earth shall be blessed is the Savior of the world, who was first promised in Paradise, then to Abraham, again to Isaac, and now to Jacob.

QUESTIONS.

1. Why did Esau hate Jacob? What did he resolve to do? What did Rebecca advise Jacob to do? 2. What happened to Jacob on the way? What did he see in sleep? 3. Who leaned upon the ladder? What did the Lord say? What did Jacob say when he awoke? 4. What did he set up as a monument? What did he call that place? 5. Whom did Jacob meet at a well? What did Jacob do on meeting Rachel? 6. Of what did Jacob inform Rachel? Who then came out to meet Jacob? Whither did Laban conduct him? 7. How long did Jacob remain with Laban? 8. Of what is the mysterious ladder a figure? What is said of our churches? Who is the seed promised to Jacob?

CHAPTER XVII.

Jacob Returns Home, and is Reconciled with His Brother.

Loving one another with the charity of brotherhood.—*Rom. 12, 10.*

WHEN Laban saw that Jacob had become very rich, he began to envy him, and ceased to regard him with favor. Then God said to Jacob: "Return into the land of thy fathers. I will be with thee." Jacob rose up without delay, and set out with all he possessed. He had reached the banks of the river Jordan, when he began to fear on account of his brother. He sent messengers before him to say to Esau: "Let me find favor in thy sight."

2. The messengers returned, saying to Jacob: "Esau cometh with speed to meet thee, with four hundred men." Then Jacob was sore afraid, and he thus prayed: "God of my fathers, O Lord, who saidst to me, 'Return to thy land,' I am not worthy of the least of all Thy mercies, and of Thy truth which Thou hast fulfilled to Thy servant. With my staff I passed over this Jordan, and now I return with two companies. Deliver me from the hand of my brother."

3. During the night an angel appeared to Jacob, with whom he wrestled till morning. And Jacob said to the angel: "I will not let thee go, except thou bless me." The angel said to him: "Henceforth thy name shall not be called Jacob, but Israel," that is to say, one who has wrestled with God. He then divided his children, his servants, and his flocks into companies, and, putting himself at the head of one of them, he advanced to meet his brother, bowing seven times to the ground before him.

4. But Esau, rejoiced to see his brother Jacob, ran to meet him, and embraced him with many tears. Then, perceiving the children, he asked: "Whose are those?" Jacob replied: "They are the children which God hath given me." And, he made a sign to them and they all advanced and bowed down before Esau. Jacob then presented Esau with several flocks.

5. But Esau refused them, saying: "I have plenty, my brother; keep what is thine for thyself." Jacob insisted, and said: "I beseech thee, take the blessing which God hath given me." Then Esau yielded to his prayer, and Jacob, full of gratitude for the protection of God, continued his journey, and arrived in the land of Chanaan, where his aged father dwelt. Isaac was happy that his son had returned, and lived after this about twenty years. Finally, enfeebled by age, he died one hundred and eighty years old. Esau and Jacob buried him at Hebron.

QUESTIONS.

1. What did Laban do, seeing that Jacob had become rich? What did God say to Jacob? Why was Jacob seized with fear when he had reached the banks of the Jordan? What message did he send to Esau? 2. What was Jacob's prayer when he heard that his brother was coming to meet him? 3. Who appeared to Jacob during the night and wrestled with him? 4. What did Esau do when he saw his brother coming? 5. Where did Jacob arrive soon after? Whom did he find there?

CHAPTER XVIII.

Joseph Sold by His Brethren.

By the envy of the devil, death came into the world; and they follow him that are of his side.—*Wis. 2, 24 and 25.*

JACOB had twelve sons, and he loved Joseph above all the others, because he was young and very good. And Jacob made him a coat of divers colors. One day, when the brothers were all tending their flocks, some of them committed a most wicked crime. Joseph, being shocked and angry, told his father, on his return home, what he had seen.

2. From that time forward his brothers hated Joseph, and could not speak to him kindly. Joseph had once a remarkable dream, which he thus related to his brothers: "Hear my dream: I thought we were binding sheaves in the field, and my sheaf arose, as it were, and stood, and your sheaves, standing about, bowed down before my sheaf."

3. His brothers replied: "Shalt thou be our king? or shall we be subject to thy dominion?" And they hated him more than before. Joseph dreamed, also, that the sun, the moon and eleven stars worshiped him. His father rebuked him, saying: "What meaneth this dream? Shall I, and thy mother, and thy brethren, worship thee upon the earth?"

4. But Jacob thought within himself that perhaps God had destined Joseph for great things. One day, when the sons of Jacob had gone, with their flocks, to Sichem, Jacob said to Joseph: "Go and see if all things be well with thy brethren and the cattle." He obeyed, and went in search of them.

5. When they saw him afar off, they said: "Behold, the dreamer cometh. Let us kill him and cast him into some old pit, and we will say some evil beast hath devoured him: and then it shall appear what his dreams avail him." Reuben the eldest of the brothers, hearing this, sought to deliver Joseph out of their hands, and said to them: "Do not take away his life, nor shed his blood, but cast him into this pit." This he said because he wished to restore the boy to his father.

6. When Joseph drew near to his brothers they forthwith stripped him of his coat of divers colors, and cast him into the pit, in which, happily, there was no water. Then they sat down to eat bread, and saw some foreign merchants passing by, with camels carrying spices, balm and myrrh into Egypt.

7. Juda then said to his brothers: "What will it profit us to kill our brother? It is better that he be sold, and that our hands be not defiled, for he is our brother." The others agreed, and, the merchants having come up, they drew Joseph out of the pit and sold him for twenty pieces of silver. Joseph wept and besought them to have pity upon him, but in vain. The merchants took him away with them into Egypt.

8. Reuben, being absent at the moment, knew nothing of

this wicked bargain. On going to the pit into which Joseph had
been cast, and not finding him there, he rent his garments in
despair, saying: "The boy doth not appear, and whither shall
I go?" The other brothers remained quite unconcerned.

JOSEPH SOLD BY HIS BRETHREN.

9. Having killed a kid, they dipped Joseph's coat in the
blood and sent it to their father, saying: "This we have
found; see if it be thy son's coat or no." The father, knowing the coat, said: "It is my son's coat; a wild beast hath
devoured Joseph." Then he rent his garments, and, putting
on sackcloth, mourned his son a long time.

10. His children gathered around and strove to soothe his
grief, but he would not be comforted, saying: "I will go
down to my son into the grave mourning." Jacob thus
expressed his belief in the immortality of the soul. Joseph
was here, as in some other circumstances of his life, a figure of
Christ. Joseph was sold by his brethren; our Lord by one

of His apostles.   Joseph forgave his brethren; Jesus prayed
for His enemies.

QUESTIONS.

1. How many sons had Jacob? Which of them did he love more than
the others? What sort of coat did Jacob have made for Joseph? 2. Why
did the other brothers hate Joseph? What remarkable dream had Joseph?
3. What else did he dream? 4. What did Jacob think within himself?
5. When Jacob sent Joseph to some distance from home, to see if all
were well with his brethren, what did they say when they saw him
coming? 6. Which of the brothers sought to deliver Joseph from the
hands of the others? What did Reuben say to them? What did they
do to Joseph? Whom did the brothers see passing by? 7. What did
Juda then say? To whom was Joseph then sold? For how much? 8.
Did Reuben know of this wicked bargain? What did he say when he
went to the pit and did not find Joseph there? 9. What did the other
brothers then do? What did Jacob say when he saw Joseph's coat? 10.
What did he say when he would not be comforted? Of whom is Joseph
a figure? Why?

CHAPTER XIX.

Joseph in the House of Putiphar.

Fear God and depart from evil.—*Prov. 3, 7.*

ON arriving in Egypt, the merchants sold Joseph to
Putiphar, the captain of the royal guard.   And the
Lord was with Joseph, blessing him in all he did; wherefore he found favor in the sight of his master, who gave him
charge of all his household.   And the Lord blessed the house
of the Egyptian[1] for Joseph's sake, and multiplied his riches.
But after some time Joseph was severely tried in his new home

2. The wife of Putiphar urged him to commit a most grievous sin.   But Joseph would not consent, and said: "Behold,
my master hath delivered all things to me.   How, then, can
I do this wicked thing, and sin against my God?"   But even
this decided refusal did not prevent the wicked woman from

[1]EGYPTIAN (pr. E-gip'-shan).

renewing her attacks on Joseph's virtue, and every day she importuned him anew. But Joseph would not listen to her.

3. Now, it so happened that Joseph was one day alone in the house, attending to some business, when the woman took hold of the skirt of his cloak and renewed her shameful proposal. But Joseph fled, leaving his cloak in her hands. The woman, seeing herself thus slighted, began to hate Joseph, and accused him to her husband of attempting the very crime which she had tried in vain to induce him to commit.

4. Putiphar, believing his wife too easily, caused the innocent young man to be cast into prison. The chaste Joseph is, in his firm resistance to temptation, a model for all young people. This history teaches us, also, that in this world the good have sometimes to suffer unjustly, but that if they remain patient and pray for their enemies, as Joseph, then their suffering will soon be turned into joy.

QUESTIONS.

1. To whom did the merchants sell Joseph? Did he find favor in his master's sight? What did the Lord bless for Joseph's sake? 2. Who urged Joseph to commit a grievous sin? What did Joseph say when he refused? 3. What happened one day when Joseph was alone in the house? What did Joseph do? What did the woman begin to do, seeing herself thus slighted? Of what did she accuse Joseph to her husband? 4. What did Putiphar do? For whom is the chaste Joseph a model? How must we behave towards our enemies?

CHAPTER XX.

Joseph in Prison.

The Lord your God trieth you, that it may appear whether you love Him.—*Deut. 13, 3.*

JOSEPH was now pining in prison, amongst criminals. But even here God did not abandon him, but caused him to find favor in the sight of the keeper of the prison, who gave him charge of all the prisoners. Amongst these were the chief butler and the chief baker of Pharao, accused of treason against their king. After some time they both, on the same night, had a dream. which perplexed[1] them and made them sad.

2. Joseph, perceiving their sadness, asked them, saying: "Why is your countenance sadder to-day than usual?" They answered: "We have dreamed a dream, and there is nobody to interpret it to us." Joseph said to them: "Doth not interpretation[2] belong to God? Tell me what you have dreamed."

3. The chief butler first told his dream: "I saw before me a vine, on which were three branches, which, by little and little, sent out buds; and afterwards the blossoms brought forth ripe grapes. And the cup of Pharao was in my hand, and I took the grapes and pressed them into the cup which I held, and I gave the cup to Pharao."

4. Joseph answered: "This is the interpretation of the dream: The three branches are yet three days, after which Pharao will restore thee to thy former place, and thou shalt present him the cup as before. Only remember me, when it shall be well with thee, and do me this kindness, to put Pharao in mind to take me out of this prison."

5. Then the chief baker, seeing that Joseph had so wisely interpreted the dream, said: "I also dreamed a dream, that I had three baskets of meal upon my head; and that in one basket, which was uppermost, I carried all kinds of pastry, and that the birds ate out of it."

6. Joseph said to him: "This is the interpretation of the dream: The three baskets are yet three days, after which Pharao will take thy head from thee and hang thee on a cross, and the birds shall tear thy flesh." The third day after this was the birthday of Pharao.

7. At the banquet he remembered the chief butler and chief

---

[1] PER-PLEX'ED, puzzled.

[2] INTERPRETATION, the act of explaining what is unintelligible or not understood.

baker. The former he restored to his place; the latter he caused to be hanged upon a gibbet. The chief butler rejoiced in his good fortune, but thought no more of Joseph.

QUESTIONS.

1. In whose sight did Joseph find favor when in prison? Who were amongst the prisoners? 2. What did Joseph ask them? 3. What did the chief butler dream? 4. What interpretation did Joseph give of that dream? 5. What was the chief baker's dream? 6. What did Joseph say was the meaning of the chief baker's dream? 7. What happened at the banquet three days after, on Pharao's birthday? Did the chief butler remember Joseph when rejoicing in his good fortune?

CHAPTER XXI.

Joseph's Exaltation.

Behold, thus shall the man be blessed that feareth the Lord.—*Ps. 127, 4.*

AFTER two years, Pharao had a dream. He thought he stood by the river Nile, out of which came seven cows, very beautiful and very fat; and they fed in marshy places. After them came, also, seven others that were lean and ill-favored, and they devoured the fat ones. Then the king awoke. He slept again, and dreamed another dream, in which he saw seven ears of corn growing upon one stalk; and the ears were full and fair.

2. After these came up seven other ears, thin and blighted, devouring all the beauty of the former. Pharao awoke a second time, and, morning having come, he sent for all the soothsayers and wise men of Egypt, and related to them his dreams. But no one was found who could interpret them.

3. Then the chief butler remembered Joseph, and was sorry that he had so long forgotten him. He told the king that there was in the prison a Hebrew youth who had interpreted dreams for him and for the chief baker, and that all had come to pass just as he said.

4. The king's curiosity being excited, he ordered the youth to be brought before him. Then he addressed him, saying: "I have dreamed dreams, and there is no one that can expound them. Now, I have heard that thou art very wise at interpreting them." Joseph answered: "God alone can give Pharao a prosperous answer." Pharao then related what he had seen.

5. Having heard the dreams, Joseph said: "God hath shown to Pharao what He is about to do. The seven beautiful kine, and the seven full ears, are seven years of plenty; the seven lean and thin kine, and the seven blasted ears, are seven years of famine. There shall come seven years of great plenty in the whole land of Egypt, after which shall follow other seven years of so great a scarcity that all the abundance before shall be forgotten; for the famine shall consume all the land, and the greatness of the scarcity shall destroy the greatness of the plenty.

6. "Now, therefore, let the king provide a wise and industrious man, who shall gather into barns the fifth part of the fruit of the seven years of plenty, so that it be ready against the seven years of famine." This counsel was pleasing to Pharao, and he said to his courtiers: "Can we find such another man, that is full of the spirit of God?" Then the king said to Joseph: "Can I find one wiser and one like unto thee? Thou shalt be over my house, and at the commandment of thy mouth all the people shall obey. Only in the kingly throne will I be above thee."

7. Then the king, having made Joseph ruler over all the land of Egypt, took the ring from his own hand and placed it on that of Joseph. He put on him, also, a robe of silk, and a chain of gold around his neck, and caused him to be seated in a triumphal chariot next to his own, and to be proclaimed governor of Egypt. He also changed his name, and called him Savior of the World. Joseph was thirty years old when he was made ruler of Egypt.

8. The life of Joseph teaches us clearly that the ways of

God are wonderful. His brothers hated him, and this hatred of theirs brought him to Egypt; and this was the first step to his greatness. The wife of Putiphar hated him, and her hatred brought him into prison; and this was the next step to his greatness, for in prison he became acquainted with the

JOSEPH IN THE CHARIOT.

chief butler of the king. But if Joseph had murmured against Providence, or had cursed his enemies, God would not have placed him on the throne of Egypt.

QUESTIONS.

1. What dreams had Pharao? 2. For whom did he send to expound them? Could they expound them? 3. Whom did the chief butler then remember and speak of to the king? 4. Who was then brought before the king? What did the king say to Joseph? What was Joseph's answer? 5. How did Joseph interpret the king's dreams? 6. What did the king then say to the courtiers? 7. What did he make Joseph? How old was Joseph when he became ruler of Egypt? 8. How did the enemies of Joseph help to bring about his greatness? How did Joseph act when he was afflicted?

CHAPTER XXII.

The Sons of Jacob go into Egypt.

Revenge is Mine, and I will repay them in due time.—*Deut. 32, 35.*

THE seven years of plenty came, as Joseph had foretold. There was great abundance everywhere. And Joseph gathered the surplus of the grain every year, and stored it up in the granaries. But after the years of plenty the seven years of scarcity set in, and famine prevailed in all the countries. The people of Egypt cried to the king for bread, but he answered them: "Go to Joseph, and do all that he shall say to you."

2. Joseph opened all the granaries, and sold to the Egyptians. Likewise the people from other countries came to Egypt to buy corn. At last the famine reached Chanaan, and Jacob, having heard that there was wheat in Egypt for sale, sent ten of his sons with money to buy food. But Benjamin, the youngest, he kept at home, fearing lest some evil might befall him on the way.

3. The ten sons of Jacob arrived safely in Egypt, and seeing Joseph, they bowed down before him, not knowing that he was their brother. But he at once recognized them, and remembered the dreams he had dreamed. He wished to know whether they were now sorry for their sin; so he spoke to them as if they were strangers to him, and said: "You are spies."

4. They answered: "It is not so, my lord, but we have come to buy food. We, thy servants, are twelve brethren, the sons of one man in the land of Chanaan. The youngest is with our father; the other is not living." Joseph then cast them into prison three days. On the third day he brought them out, and said: "If you be peaceable men, let one of your brethren be bound in prison, and go ye your ways, and carry the corn that you have bought into your

houses; and bring your youngest brother to me, that I may find your words to be true, and you may not die."

5. Then they said one to another: "We deserve to suffer these things, because we have sinned against our brother, seeing the anguish of his soul when he besought us and we would not hear; therefore is this affliction come upon us." They thought that Joseph did not understand them, for he spoke to them through an interpreter. But he understood all that they said, and his heart was moved to pity, so that, turning aside from them, he wept.

6. But, in order to see if their repentance was sincere, he returned to them and ordered Simeon to be bound before their eyes. Then he commanded his servants to fill their sacks with wheat, and put each man's money secretly in his sack, and give them, besides, provisions for the journey. This being done, they loaded their asses with the corn and returned home.

7. They related to their father all that had happened, and, on opening their sacks, every man found his money tied in the mouth of his sack. Seeing this, they were troubled and afraid. And Jacob said to them: "Ye have made me childless. Joseph is not living, Simeon is kept in bonds, and Benjamin ye will take away. My son shall not go down with you, for if any evil befall him you will bring my hairs in sorrow to the grave."

QUESTIONS.

1. What did Joseph do when the seven years of plenty came? When the famine years came, and the people of Egypt cried to the king for bread, what did he say to them? 2. What did Joseph do then? Who sent his sons from Chanaan to Egypt to buy corn? Which of his sons did Jacob keep at home? 3. What did the ten sons of Jacob do when they were presented to Joseph? What did Joseph then remember? What did he ask his brothers, and of what did he accuse them? 4. What did they say in reply? What did Joseph say? 5. What did the brothers say one to another? Did Joseph understand them? 6. What did he do in order to see if their repentance was sincere? What did he command his servants to do? 7. What did Jacob say to his sons when they told him what had happened?

CHAPTER XXIII.

Benjamin's Journey to Egypt.

Stretch out thy hand to the poor, that thy expiation and thy blessing may be perfected.—*Ecclus. 7, 36.*

BUT after some months the corn which the sons of Jacob had brought from Egypt was consumed, and the famine still continued. Therefore Jacob said to his sons: "Go again into Egypt and bring us a little food." Juda told his father that the governor had forbidden them to come back to Egypt unless they brought Benjamin with them. And Juda added: "Send the boy with me, that we may set forward, lest both we and our children perish. I take the boy upon me; require him at my hand."

2. So Jacob consented to let Benjamin go. And he told his sons to take some of the best fruits of the country as presents to the governor of Egypt, and also to return the money which they had found in their sacks, lest, perhaps, it was done by mistake. Then he prayed that God might prosper their journey and make the governor of Egypt favorable to them, and send back with them Simeon and Benjamin.

3. Then they went down to Egypt and stood before Joseph. When Joseph saw them, and Benjamin in their midst, he commanded his steward to conduct them to his house and prepare a banquet. The steward obeyed. But the brothers, on finding themselves in the governor's house, were seized with fear, and said one to another: "Because of the money which we carried back the first time in our sacks, we are brought in, that he may bring upon us a false accusation, and by violence make slaves of us."

4. Therefore they went to the steward at the door, and said: "We cannot tell who put that money in our bags." But he said to them: "Peace be to you; fear not." And he brought Simeon out to them. Joseph now having entered the house,

they bowed down before him and offered their gifts. He kindly saluted them in return, and asked if their aged father was yet living.

5. They told him that their father lived and was in good health. Then Joseph, seeing Benjamin, inquired if that was their youngest brother. They answered: "He is our youngest brother." Then Joseph said: "God be gracious to thee, my son;" and, going out, he wept, for his heart was deeply touched at the sight of his young brother. Having dried his tears and washed his face, he returned to his brethren and ordered food to be placed before them. Then they were ordered to sit before him, and he placed them according to their age, the first-born first, and the youngest last. All received gifts, but Benjamin received five times more than the rest. And they wondered very much.

QUESTIONS.

1. What did Jacob say to his sons when the corn brought from Egypt was consumed and the famine continued? What did Juda tell his father.? 2. What did Jacob tell his sons to take with them to Egypt? 3. What did Joseph tell the steward when he saw Benjamin with the others? What did the brothers, being seized with fear, say to one another? 4. How did Joseph receive them? What did he ask them? 5. What did Joseph do on seeing Benjamin? How did he place them at table?

CHAPTER XXIV.

Joseph's Silver Cup.

It is good for me that Thou hast humbled me, that I may learn Thy justifications.—*Ps. 118, 71.*

JOSEPH showed this preference for Benjamin in order to see if his brothers had overcome their former envious feelings. He wished to know, also, whether they really loved their youngest brother, or whether they would sacrifice him, also, to the spirit of jealousy.

2. Hence he commanded the steward to fill their sacks with

corn, and to put each one's money in the top of his sack; but to place in the mouth of Benjamin's sack Joseph's own silver cup. This was done, and the brothers set out on their journey.

3. But they had scarcely gone forward a little way when Joseph sent his steward after them, who, overtaking them, accused them of stealing his master's cup. He said: "Why have ye returned evil for good?" Struck with terror, and angry at being suspected of theft, the brothers replied: "With whomsoever the cup shall be found, let him die, and we will be the bondsmen of my lord." The steward replied: "Be it according to your words."

4. They immediately took down their sacks and opened them, and when the steward had searched them all, beginning with that of the eldest, he found the cup in Benjamin's sack. The brothers, rending their garments, loaded their asses again and returned to the city. And, falling down before Joseph, they said: "Behold, we are all bondmen to my lord." But Joseph answered: "God forbid! He that stole the cup, he shall be my bondman, and go you away free to your father."

5. Then Juda told Joseph how much it had cost their father to part with Benjamin. They would rather die, all of them, he said, than to return to their aged father without his youngest son. Juda, moreover, offered to remain and be the governor's slave till death, if he would allow Benjamin to go back safe to his father. This proposal showed how sincere was the repentance of the sons of Jacob for their former crime.

QUESTIONS.

1. What was Joseph's object in showing a marked preference for Benjamin? 2. What did he, therefore, command his steward to do? 3. Whom did Joseph send after the brothers? Of what did the steward accuse them? What did the brothers reply? 4. In whose sack was the cup found? What did the brothers then do? What did Joseph answer? 5. What did Juda then tell Joseph? What did Juda offer to do? What did this proposal show?

CHAPTER XXV.

Joseph Makes Himself Known to His Brethren.

Be ye kind, one to another: merciful, forgiving one another.—
Eph. 4, 32.

JOSEPH could no longer restrain himself, and, therefore, he commanded his officers and servants to retire. Then, with tears and sobs, he said: "I am Joseph. Is my father

JOSEPH EMBRACING BENJAMIN.

yet living?" His brothers could not answer him, being struck with exceeding great fear. But Joseph said mildly to them: "Come nearer to me. I am Joseph, your brother, whom ye sold into Egypt. Fear nothing, for God sent me before you into Egypt, for your preservation."

2. Then he said: "Make haste and go ye up to my father, and say to him: Thus saith thy son Joseph: Come down

to me; linger not; and thou shalt dwell in the land of Gessen; and thou' shalt be near me, thou and thy sons." Then, falling upon the neck of Benjamin, he wept, and Benjamin wept also in like manner. Then he embraced all his brethren, and wept over each of them, after which they were emboldened to speak to him.

3. The news went abroad in the king's court: The brethren of Joseph are come. And Pharao, with all his family, was glad. He told Joseph to invite his father and his brethren to come to Egypt. Joseph gave his brothers chariots, and provisions for the way. He ordered two robes to be given to each of them, but to Benjamin he gave five robes of the best, with three hundred pieces of silver. Besides, he gave them rich presents for their father, and warned them not to be angry in the way.

QUESTIONS.

1. What did Joseph, unable to restrain himself any longer, command his officers and servants to do? What did he say, with tears and sobs? What did he afterwards say, telling his brothers to draw near? 2. What did he tell them to do? 3. When the news went abroad that Joseph's brethren had come, what did Pharao do? What did Joseph give to his brothers? What did he give to Benjamin? What warning did he give them?

CHAPTER XXVI.

Jacob Goes Into Egypt.

Honor thy father and thy mother, that thou mayst be long-lived upon the land, which the Lord thy God will give thee.—*Exod. 20, 12.*

WHEN Joseph's brethren returned to their father, they told him: "Joseph thy son is living, and he is ruler in all the land of Egypt." But Jacob did not believe them, until they showed him the chariots and all the presents that Joseph had sent. Then he awoke, as it were, from a deep sleep; his spirit revived, and he said: "It is enough for me if Joseph my son be yet living. I will go and see him before I die."

2. And he set out for Egypt, with his whole family and all his possessions. When he had reached the confines of Chanaan he offered a sacrifice to God, who spoke to him in a vision of the night, saying: "Fear not; go down into Egypt, for I will make a great nation of thee there, and will bring thee back again from hence."

3. Consoled by the vision, Jacob continued his journey, and arrived in Eygpt. Juda went on in advance to apprise Joseph of his father's approach. Joseph immediately made ready his chariot, and went up to meet his father. As soon as he saw him coming he descended from his chariot and embraced him, weeping.

4. And Jacob said to Joseph: "Now I shall die with joy, because I have seen thy face and leave thee alive." Joseph presented his father to Pharao, who asked him: "How many are the years of thy life?" Jacob answered: "The days of my pilgrimage are a hundred and thirty years, few and evil, and they are not come up to the days of the pilgrimage of my fathers." Then Jacob, having blessed the king, retired. And Joseph gave his father and his brothers possessions in the land of Gessen, the most beautiful and fertile part of Egypt.

QUESTIONS.

1. What did Joseph's brethren tell their father on their return? Did Jacob believe them? What did he say when he awoke as from a sleep? 2. What did he do then? What did Jacob do when he reached the confines of Chanaan? 3. What did Joseph do when told by Juda that his father was approaching? What did he do when he saw his father? 4. What did Jacob say to Joseph? What did Pharao ask Jacob? What did Jacob tell the king? Where did Joseph give his father and brothers possessions?

CHAPTER XXVII.

The Last Words of Jacob.

Children, hear the judgment of your father, and so do, that you may
be saved.—*Ecclus. 3, 2.*

JACOB lived seventeen years in Gessen. When the day of
his death approached, Joseph, with his two sons, Ephraim and Manasses, went to visit him. Jacob kissed the
boys, blessed them, and prayed that the angel who had delivered him from evil during life might protect the sons of
Joseph. To Joseph he said: "Behold, I die, and God will
be with you, and will bring you back into the land of your
fathers."

2. Then, his children and grandchildren having assembled
around his couch, he blessed them all. To Juda he gave a
special blessing. "Juda," said he, "thy hand shall be on
the neck of thy enemies. The sons of thy father shall bow
down to thee, *and the scepter shall not be taken away from
Juda till He come that is to be sent, and He shall be the expectation of nations."*

3. Then, having told them to bury him with his fathers in
the land of Chanaan, he died. When Joseph saw this he fell
upon his father's face, weeping and kissing him. He then
ordered the body to be embalmed.

4. And Pharao commanded that all Egypt should mourn
Jacob for seventy days. When the time of mourning was
passed, Joseph, accompanied by all the ancients of the house
of Pharao, set out for the land of Chanaan, and buried the
remains of his father at Hebron. Now, Jacob being dead, the
brothers feared that Joseph would remember the wrong they
had done him, and therefore they came to him and begged
forgiveness. Joseph received them kindly, saying: "You
thought evil against me, but God turned it into good."

5. Joseph lived one hundred and ten years, and saw his
children's children to the third generation. When his end

drew nigh, he said to his brethren: "God will visit you after my death, and will make you go up out of this land, to the land which He swore to Abraham, Isaac and Jacob. Carry my bones with you out of this place." He then died, and they embalmed him and laid him in a coffin.

6. The words of Jacob to his son Juda refer to the Savior, who was expected by the nations, and who was descended from Juda. The patriarch Joseph is a figure of St. Joseph, the foster father of Christ. The one was ruler of Egypt; the other is the protector of the Catholic Church.

QUESTIONS.

1. How long did Jacob live in Gessen? Who went to visit him when the day of his death approached? Whom did he pray to protect Joseph's sons? What did he say to Joseph? 2. To whom did Jacob give a special blessing? What did he prophesy for him? 3. What did Jacob then tell his sons to do for him? What did Joseph do? What did he order to be done? 4. What did Pharao command? What did Joseph do when the time of mourning was past? 5. How long did Joseph live? When his end drew nigh, what did he say to his brethren? 6. What did Jacob promise to Juda? Of whom was Joseph a figure?

CHAPTER XXVIII.

Job's Patience.

Whom the Lord loveth He chastiseth.—*Heb. 12, 6.*

IN the time of the patriarchs there lived in Arabia a man whom God wished to give to all mankind, and for all time, as a perfect model of patience. This man's name was Job. He had seven sons and three daughters. He owned seven thousand sheep, three thousand camels, five hundred yoke of oxen, five hundred she-asses, and had a great number of servants.

2. On this account, and still more because of his singular piety, he was held in high esteem among the people of the east. One day the Lord said to Satan: "Hast thou considered my servant Job, that there is none like him in the earth?" Satan, answering, said: "Doth Job fear God in

vain? Thou hast blessed the work of his hands, and his
possessions hath increased on the earth. But stretch forth
Thy hand and take away his possessions, then Thou shalt see
that he will murmur against Thy providence."

3. Then the Lord said to Satan: "All that he hath is in
thy hand; only put not forth thy hand upon his person." So
it came to pass that on one occasion, when the sons and daughters of Job were feasting in the house of their eldest brother,
a messenger came to Job, exclaiming: "The oxen were
plowing, and the asses feeding beside them, and the Sabe-
ans rushed in and took all away, and slew the servants with
the sword, and I alone have escaped to tell thee."

4. While he was yet speaking, another messenger came to
tell Job that fire fell from heaven, which struck the sheep and
the shepherds, and that he alone had escaped. Whilst he
was yet speaking there came a third messenger, who announced to Job that the Chaldeans had taken away his camels and slain the servants, all but himself.

5. Then came a fourth messenger, who, entering in, said to
Job: "Whilst thy sons and daughters were eating and drinking in the house of their elder brother, a violent wind came
on a sudden from the side of the desert, and shook the four
corners of the house, and it fell and crushed thy children, and
they are dead, and I alone have escaped to tell thee."

6. Then Job rose up and rent his garments, and, having
shaved his head, fell down upon the ground and worshiped,
saying: "The Lord gave and the Lord hath taken away. As
it hath pleased the Lord, so it is done. Blessed be the name
of the Lord." In all these things Job sinned not by his lips,
nor spoke he any foolish thing against God. And the Lord
said to Satan: "Hast thou considered my servant Job, that
there is none like him in the earth?" Satan replied: "All
that a man hath he will give for his life; but put forth Thy
hand, touch his bone and his flesh, and then Thou shalt see
if he will not curse Thee."

7.   The Lord said: "Behold, he is in thy hand, but yet
save his life." So Satan struck Job with a most grievous
ulcer from the sole of the foot even to the top of his head.
And Job sat on a dung-hill and scraped the ulcerated matter
with a potsherd.[1]   Then his wife came, not to comfort, but
rather to tempt him, for she mockingly said: "Bless God
and die."

8. But Job said to her: "Thou hast spoken like one of the

JOB AND HIS COMFORTERS.

foolish women. If we have received good things at the hand
of God, why should we not receive evil?"   Again, in all
these things Job did not sin with his lips or his heart.   Now,
when his three friends heard of the evils that had befallen
him, they came to visit him.

9.   When they saw him afar off they knew him not, and,
crying out, they wept, and rending their garments, they
sprinkled ashes on their heads.   They sat with him on the

[1] POT'-SHERD, a piece or fragment of a broken pot.

ground seven days and seven nights, and no man spoke to him a word; for they saw that his grief was very great.

10. But when Job at length began to complain of the excess of his misery, they reproached him, saying that secretly he must have been a great sinner, or the just God would not have afflicted him in so grievous a manner. But Job loudly and firmly asserted his innocence, and consoled himself with the hope of the resurrection of the body, saying: "I know that my Redeemer liveth; and in the last day I shall rise out of the earth; and I shall be clothed again with my skin, and in my flesh I shall see my God, whom I myself shall see, and not another. This my hope is laid up in my bosom."

11. When they had finished their reproaches, the Lord revealed Himself in a whirlwind to Job, and mildly reproved him, because in defending his innocence he had spoken some imprudent words. God's wrath, however, was kindled against the three friends, and He commanded them to offer a holocaust for themselves, whilst Job should pray for them. And the Lord looked graciously on Job's humility, and granted his prayers in behalf of his friends. The Lord rewarded Job's faith and patience by healing his body and restoring to him double what he had lost. And new sons and daughters were born unto him.

12. Job, practising virtue while happy and wealthy, was admired by the angels, but he was not yet feared by the devils; but when he remained free from sin even in the depths of misery and affliction, then the devils began to tremble before him. From this we learn that wrong patiently endured for God's sake is the highest virtue. The friends of Job knew not that at times God sends afflictions even to His saints, to make them more holy and to give them greater glory in heaven. Job also said that he would not live to see the Savior promised to Adam, to Abraham, to Isaac and to Jacob, but that he would see Him on the day of the general

resurrection. From Job we may also learn how pleasing to God and how powerful is the intercession of the saints.

QUESTIONS.

1. Who lived in Arabia in the time of the patriarchs? What was this man's name? 2. Why was Job held in high esteem by all who knew him? What did the Lord say one day to Satan? What did Satan answer? 3. What did the Lord then say? What happened whilst the children of Job were feasting at the house of their elder brother? 4. What did another messenger come to tell Job? What did a third messenger tell him? 5. A fourth? 6. What did Job then do? What did Satan again say to the Lord? 7. What did Satan do, having the desired permission? What did Job's wife do and say? 8. What reply did Job make? 9. What did the friends of Job do? 10. What did they do when Job complained? 11. How was Job's faith rewarded? 12. When was Job admired by the angels, and when feared by the devils? What is the highest virtue? What truth did the friends of Job not know? What did Job say about the Redeemer? What does this history teach with regard to the intercession of the saints?

THE AGE OF MOSES.

From the Year 1500—1450 B. C.

CHAPTER XXIX.

The Birth of Moses.

He that dwelleth in the aid of the Most High, shall abide under the protection of the God of Jacob.—*Ps. 90, 1.*

GOD had made two promises to the patriarchs, Abraham, Isaac and Jacob: first, that they should be the fathers of a great nation; second, that the Savior would be a descendant of theirs. The first promise was now fulfilled. In the space of two hundred years the descendants of Jacob in Egypt had become a great people. In the meantime a new king had arisen, who said to the Egyptians: "Behold, the children of Israel are stronger than we. Come, let us oppress them, lest they join with our enemies and depart out of the land."

2. Now, the Egyptians hated the children of Israel, and mocked them and made their life bitter with hard works in brick and clay. And the king placed overseers over them, to oppress them with labor. But the more they were oppressed the more numerous they became. The king, seeing this, issued a decree that all the male children born of Hebrew parents should be cast into the river; hoping, by this means,

FINDING OF MOSES IN THE BULRUSHES.

either to destroy the Hebrew people, or at least to prevent them from increasing in numbers.

3. Now, it came to pass that a Hebrew mother bore a son, and seeing that he was very beautiful, she hid him for three months. At the end of that time, not being able to keep him any longer, she laid the babe in a basket of reeds and placed it in the sedges by the river's bank. The sister of the child

stood a little way off, to see what would happen. And behold, at that time the daughter of Pharao went down to bathe
in the Nile.

4. Seeing the basket amongst the bulrushes on the river
bank, the princess sent one of her maids to bring it to her.
On opening it they saw within it a lovely infant, crying pite-
ously. She had compassion on it, and said: "This is one of
the babes of the Hebrews." The child's sister then taking
courage, drew near and asked: "Shall I go and call to thee
a Hebrew woman to nurse the babe?" She answered, "Go."
The maid went and called her mother.

5. When the mother came, the princess said to her: "Take
this child and nurse him for me, and I will give thee thy
wages." The woman took the child and nursed him. And,
when he had grown up, he was brought to Pharao's daughter, who adopted him as her own, and called him Moses,
which means rescued from the waters. Moses, saved in his
infancy from the cruelty of Pharao, is a type of Jesus, rescued, also, in His infancy from the power of Herod.

QUESTIONS.

1. What two promises had God made to the patriarchs, Abraham,
Isaac and Jacob? How was the first promise fulfilled? What did
a new king of Egypt tell the Egyptians? 2. What did the king do to
the Israelites, or Hebrews? Seeing that this did not prevent the
Hebrews from increasing in numbers, what decree did the king issue?
3. What did a Hebrew mother do? Who stood a little way off, to see
what would become of the child? Who went down just then to the
river to bathe? 4. What did the princess do on seeing the basket?
What did she say on seeing the babe? What did the child's sister do
then? What did the princess tell her? 5. What did the princess say
to the mother when she came? To whom did the mother give him back?
What did the princess call him? Of whom is Moses, rescued from the
cruelty of Pharao, a figure?

CHAPTER XXX.

The Flight of Moses.

We beseech you, brethren, rebuke the unquiet, support the weak.
—*Thess. 5, 14.*

MOSES was reared at the court of Pharao, and instructed in all the learning of Egypt. But when he was grown up and saw the misery of his brethren, the Hebrews, he resolved to help them. For he would rather be afflicted and despised with the people of God, than live in the palace of a wicked king. He left the splendor of the court, and openly declared himself a friend of the Israelites.

2. The king, hearing this, sought to kill him; but Moses fled to the land of Madian.[1] On his way he sat down by a well, and behold, the seven daughters of Jethro came to draw water for their flocks. But, when the sheep stood near the troughs, some shepherds rushed in and rudely drove away the flock. Thereupon Moses arose, defended the maidens, and watered their sheep.

3. Then the seven sisters went home, and their father asked: "Why have ye returned sooner than usual?" They answered: "A man of Egypt drove away the shepherds, and gave our sheep to drink," Jethro asked again: "Where is he? Call him, that he may eat bread." So Moses entered the house and swore to dwell with Jethro, and remained for forty years, and married Sephora, one of the daughters of Jethro.

4. Moses, despising the splendor of Egypt in order to comfort the Jews, is a figure of the Son of God, who came down from heaven, was born in a stable, and laid in a manger, to redeem us from the flames of hell.

[1] Ma'-dian, or Me'-dia, a province of ancient Asia, bordering on Egypt.

QUESTIONS.

1. In what was Moses instructed? What did he resolve to do when he was grown up? As whose friend did he openly declare himself? 2. Who sought to kill him? Whither did he fly? Who came to a well to water their father's flock? Who drove their sheep away? Who defended the maidens? 3. What did Jethro ask his daughters when they had returned home? What did they reply? What did Jethro tell them to do? How long did Moses stay there, and whom did he marry? 4. Of whom is Moses a figure?

CHAPTER XXXI.

The Burning Bush.

I can do all things in Him who strengtheneth me.—*Phil. 4, 13.*

NOW, Moses fed the sheep of Jethro, his father-in-law. One day he drove his flock into the desert, and came as far as Mount Horeb. There the Lord appeared to him in a flame of fire, which issued from the midst of a bush. Moses saw that the bush was on fire and was not burnt. He said: "I will go near to see why the bush is not burnt." As Moses drew near the Lord cried out to him from the burning bush: "Moses, Moses!" and he answered: "Here I am." And God said: "Come not nigh hither. Put off the shoes from thy feet; for the place whereon thou standest is holy ground. I am the God of thy father, the God of Abraham, the God of Isaac, and the God of Jacob."

2. Moses, in awful reverence, hid his face, and dared not look at God. And the Lord said to him: "I have seen the affliction of My people in Egypt, and I am come to deliver them out of the hands of the Egyptians, and to bring them out of that land into a land that floweth with milk and honey." The Lord further told Moses that he should go to Pharao to demand the liberation of the children of Israel.

3. Moses answered: "Who am I that I should go to Pharao, and should bring forth the children of Israel out of Egypt?" The Lord said: "I will be with thee." Moses

declared that the people would not believe him; but would
ask who had sent him. Then God said to Moses, "I AM
WHO AM. Thus shalt thou say to the children of Israel:
'HE WHO IS hath sent me to you'." Moses answered and
said: "They will not believe me, nor hear my voice; but
they will say, 'The Lord hath not appeared to thee'." Then
God asked Moses: "What is that thou holdest in thy hand?"
Moses answered, "A rod." The Lord then told Moses to

MOSES AT THE BURNING BUSH.

cast his rod upon the ground. He threw it upon the ground,
and the rod was turned into a serpent, so that Moses fled
from it in terror.

4. But the Lord called him back, saying: "Take it by the
tail." Moses did so, and the serpent became again a rod.
The Lord told Moses to work this, and some other signs, before the Israelites, and they would believe. But Moses still
objected, saying that he was not eloquent, but that his speech
was slow and hesitating.

5. Then the Lord said to him, "Who made man's mouth? or who made the dumb and the deaf, the seeing and the blind? Did not I? Go, therefore, and I will teach thee what thou shalt speak." Moses answered: "I beseech Thee, Lord, send whom Thou wilt send." The Lord, being angry at Moses, said: "Aaron, thy brother, is eloquent; speak to him, and put My words into his mouth; he shall speak in thy stead to the people." So Moses returned to Egypt; and Aaron, his brother, inspired by the Lord, came forth to meet him.

6. Moses repeated to his brother all the words of the Lord. Then they went together to assemble the children of Israel; and Aaron spoke to them that the Lord had looked upon their affliction. And Moses wrought the sign of the rod, and other miracles. Whereupon the people believed; and, falling down, they adored the Lord.

7. As the people of Israel would not have believed that God had sent Moses to free them from slavery, but for the miracles he wrought; so we should not receive any one as sent by God, in a special manner, except he prove his mission by signs and miracles.

QUESTIONS.

1. What was the occupation of Moses? Whither did he drive his sheep one day? How did the Lord appear to him there? What did the Lord call to Moses from the burning bush? What did the Lord say? 2. What did Moses do? What did the Lord say to him? 3. What did Moses answer? 4. What did God tell Moses to do with the serpent? 5. What did God say to Moses when he told Him that his speech was slow? Who met Moses on his return to Egypt? 6. What did Moses repeat to Aaron? Whom did they assemble? 7. What do we learn from the mission and the miracles of Moses?

CHAPTER XXXII.

The Ten Plagues of Egypt.

According to thy hardness and impenitent heart, thou treasurest up to
thyself wrath, against the day of wrath and revelation
of the just judgment of God.—*Rom. 2, 5.*

MOSES and Aaron went to Pharao and demanded in the name of God, that he should allow the people of Israel to go out into the desert to offer sacrifice to the Lord. Pharao proudly answered: "Who is the Lord that I should hear his voice, and let Israel go? I know not the Lord, neither will I let Israel go." And from that day forth he ordered the overseers and taskmasters to oppress the Israelites more and more by putting them to still harder work.

2. The Lord told Moses and Aaron to appear again before Pharao. They did as the Lord commanded, and Aaron cast his rod before Pharao, and it was turned into a serpent. Pharao called the magicians and they, by enchantments and certain secrets, also turned their rods into serpents; but Aaron's rod devoured their rods. But the heart of Pharao remained hardened, and he would not let the people go. Then the Lord sent ten plagues upon the Egyptians.

3. Next morning Aaron went, by the command of God, to the bank of the Nile and struck the river with his rod, and instantly it was turned into blood. Thereupon the fish died, the water was corrupted, and the water of all the streams and ponds in Egypt was changed into blood. And the Egyptians dug new wells round about the river; for they could not drink the water of the river. Even then the heart of Pharao did not relent.

4. After seven days, Aaron stretched forth his hand over the rivers, and streams, and pools of Egypt, and immediately a multitude of frogs came forth from the waters, and covered the whole land of Egypt. They entered the houses and the ovens, and covered the tables and the beds, and spared nei-

ther the hut of the peasant nor the palace of the king. Then
Pharao, being frightened, called for Moses and Aaron, and
said to them: "Pray ye the Lord to take away the frogs
from me, and from my people, and I will let the people go to
sacrifice to the Lord." Moses did as the king desired, and
the frogs disappeared.

5. But when Pharao saw that the frogs were gone, he hardened his heart again. Then Aaron was commanded by God
to strike with his rod the dust of the earth; and instantly
myriads of gnats arose and tormented both men and beasts
throughout all Egypt. All the dust of the earth was turned
into gnats. But Pharao's heart remained obdurate.

6. Then the Lord sent a very grievous swarm of flies into
the houses of Pharao and his servants, and the whole land
was corrupted by them. Then Pharao's heart began to fail,
and he said to Moses and Aaron: "I will let you go to sacrifice to the Lord your God in the wilderness; but go no farther. Pray for me." But when God, at the prayer of Moses,
had banished the flies, Pharao's heart grew hard again, and
he refused to let the people go.

7. Then God sent a plague on the cattle, which destroyed
the best part of the flocks and herds of the Egyptians, but
spared those of the Israelites. Still Pharao would not sub-
mit. Then Moses was ordered by God to take handfuls of
ashes from the chimney and sprinkle it in the air in the presence of Pharao. Forthwith the Egyptians were covered with
boils and swelling blains. But even this did not soften Pharao's heart.

8. Then again Moses stretched forth his rod towards
heaven, and the Lord sent down thunder and hail, and lightning running along the ground; and the hail, mixed with fire,
drove on and smote every herb of the field and every tree of
the country, and killed every man and beast that were in
the open fields. None of it fell, however, in the land of Gessen, where the children of Israel dwelt. Pharao called Moses

and Aaron, and said: "I have sinned this time also. Pray ye the Lord that the thunder may cease, and that I may let you go." But when, at the prayer of Moses, the hail had ceased, the king broke his promise, and his heart became exceedingly hard.

9. Then the Lord sent a burning wind, which blew all that day and night; and in the morning the locusts came, and they covered the whole face of the earth and wasted all things, devouring the grass of the earth and whatever fruits the hail had left; and there remained not anything that was green, either on the trees or in the herbs, in all Egypt. Therefore, Pharao in haste called Moses and Aaron, saying: "Forgive me my sin this time also, and pray to the Lord your God, that He take away from me this death." Moses prayed to the Lord, and the Lord sent a very strong wind from the west, which took the locusts and threw them into the Red Sea. This time, again, Pharao hardened his heart.

10. Then Moses stretched forth his hand towards heaven. and there came a horrible darkness in all the land of Egypt for three days. No man saw his brother, nor moved himself out of the place where he was. But where the children of Israel dwelt, there was light. Then Pharao called Moses and Aaron, saying: "Go, sacrifice to the Lord—let your sheep only and your herds remain." Moses answered: "All the flocks shall go with us." Thereupon the king hardened his heart again, and would not let the people go. Moreover, he said to Moses: "Get thee from me. In what day soever thou shalt come in my sight, thou shalt die." Moses replied. "I will not see thy face any more."

QUESTIONS.

1. What did Moses and Aaron demand of Pharao? What did Pharao proudly answer? What did he order the overseers and taskmasters to do? 2. What did the Lord tell Moses to do? What did the Lord then tell Moses and Aaron to do? 3. What happened when Aaron struck the water with his rod? Did Pharao then relent? 4. What happened when, after seven days, Aaron stretched out his hand over the waters? What did Pharao, being frightened, ask Moses and Aaron to do? What did he promise to do? 5. What did God then command Aaron to do? Was Pharao's heart changed by this prodigy? 6. What was the next plague? Pharao's

heart beginning to fail him, what did he resolve to do? When God,
at the prayer of Moses, had banished the flies, what happened? 7.
What plague did God then send? What was Moses ordered to do
when Pharao remained obdurate? Did this soften Pharao's heart?
8. When Moses raised his rod towards heaven, what did the Lord
send down? Where did none of the hail fall? 9. How did the locusts
come and disappear? 10. What did Pharao say after the darkness
was taken away? What did Pharao say to Moses?

CHAPTER XXXIII.

The Paschal Lamb.—Departure from Egypt.

The house of the wicked shall be destroyed, but the tabernacles of
the just shall flourish.—*Prov. 14, 11.*

THE Lord spoke again to Moses: "Yet one plague more
will I bring upon Pharao and Egypt, and after that he
will let you go and thrust you out." Now, Moses was a very
great man in the land of Egypt, in the sight of Pharao's
servants and of all the people.

2. Moses, therefore, spoke to all the people: "Thus saith
the Lord: At midnight I will enter into Egypt; and every
first-born in the land of Egypt shall die, from the first-born
of Pharao, who sitteth on his throne, even to the first-born of
the handmaid that is at the mill, and all the first-born of the
beasts; and there shall be a great cry in all the land of Egypt,
such as neither hath been before, nor shall be hereafter. But
with all the children of Israel there shall be no death nor
mourning, that you may know how wonderful a difference
the Lord maketh between the Egyptians and Israel. And all
these thy servants shall come down to me, and shall worship
me, saying: 'Go forth, thou and all the people that is under
thee.' After that we will go out."

3. After this, Moses and Aaron spoke to the children of
Israel, telling them of the Lord's command to kill, in every
family, a lamb without blemish, on the fourteenth day of
the month, and to sprinkle the door-posts with the blood of
the lamb. The Lord also commanded that on the same night

they should eat the flesh of the lamb with unleavened bread and wild lettuce. They should, moreover, have their loins girt, and shoes on their feet, and staves in their hand; for that it was the passage of the Lord, and that on that night His angel would slay every first-born of the Egyptians.

4. The Israelites did as they were commanded, and at midnight, the fourteenth day of the month, the destroying angel

EATING THE PASCHAL LAMB AND MARKING THE DOOR-POSTS.

visited every house in Egypt and slew every first-born, from the king's own to the first-born of the captive woman in prison. But the houses of the Jews he did not enter; for the doors thereof were sprinkled with the blood of the lamb. And a fearful cry arose from all the land of Egypt, because there was death in every house.

5. And Pharao arose in the night, and, struck with terror, he besought Moses and Aaron to go with the Israelites, and take with them their herds and all they possessed. "Go," he said, "and, departing, bless me." The Egyptians them-

selves pressed the people to go forth speedily, saying: "We shall all die." Then the people of God rose up in haste, while it was yet night, and began their journey, taking the unleavened bread with them. Moses also carried the bones of Joseph with him.

6. The descendants of Jacob had lived in Egypt four hundred and thirty years. Leaving Egypt, they numbered six hundred thousand men, besides women and children. Moses commanded the people, saying: "Remember this day in which, with a strong hand, the Lord brought you forth out of this place, that you eat none but unleavened bread." He also told them to sanctify unto the Lord every firstborn, because the Lord had spared their first-born children on the night on which He slew every first-born of the Egyptians.

7. The paschal lamb was a figure of Jesus, who died on the cross for the sins of men. As the destroying angel dared not to enter the houses of the Jews that were sprinkled with the blood of the lamb, so the devil has no power over those Christians that receive worthily the body and blood of our Lord in holy communion. In Pharao we behold the sad picture of a man grown old in sin. When oppressed by calamity he seemed to repent, but as soon as the danger was past he fell back into his pride and hardness of heart.

QUESTIONS.

1. After Pharao had seen these awful signs, what did he do? What did Moses tell him? What did Pharao order Moses to do? What did Moses reply? 2. What message did he give from God? 3. What did the Lord tell Moses and Aaron to command the people of Israel to do? 4. What took place at midnight? 5. What did Pharao, struck with terror, beseech Moses and Aaron to do? 6. How long did the descendants of Jacob live in Egypt? How many did the children of Israel number on leaving Egypt? What did Moses tell the people? Of what is the paschal lamb a figure? 7. How may the blood of the paschal lamb be compared to holy communion? Of whom is Pharao a sad picture?

CHAPTER XXXIV.

Passage of the Red Sea.

Our God is our refuge and strength: a helper in troubles.—*Ps. 45, 2.*

NOW, God Himself conducted the Israelites in their march, going before them by day in a pillar of cloud, by night in a pillar of flame. They at length reached the shores of the Red Sea, where they pitched their tents. Suddenly Pharao repented of having allowed the Israelites to go, and he pursued them with chariots and horsemen, and with his whole army; and he overtook them at nightfall near the Red Sea.

2. When the Israelites saw the Egyptians behind them, they were seized with fear, and cried to the Lord for help. Moses, however, calmed and encouraged them, saying: "The Lord will fight for you." At the same time the pillar of cloud which had gone before them, went back and stood between their camp and the army of the Egyptians. Moreover, the cloud gave light to the Israelites, but it made the night darker for the Egyptians, so that they could not see nor stir for the rest of the night. Then Moses, commanded by God, stretched his rod over the sea, and immediately the waters divided and stood like a wall on either side, leaving a dry road between for the children of Israel to pass over. And the children of Israel went in through the midst of the sea.

3. At the dawn of day the Egyptians pursued them into the midst of the sea. But suddenly a great tempest arose and overthrew their chariots and horsemen. And the Lord said to Moses: "Stretch thy hand over the sea;" and behold! the divided waters came together again, swallowing up Pharao and his whole army, so that not even one of the Egyptians escaped.

4. Thus did the Lord, by a splendid miracle, deliver the

Hebrews that day from the Egyptians. And the people feared the Lord and believed in Him, and in Moses, His servant. The passage of the Red Sea is a figure of the Sacrament of Baptism. There was no other way left the Israelites to escape from Pharao and enter the land of promise, save through the waters of the Red Sea; so is there no way to escape from the power of the devil and to enter heaven, except through the waters of baptism. In the death of Pharao

DROWNING OF THE EGYPTIANS.

and his army we have an example of the divine justice. Pharao and his servants had made a law to drown the Hebrew babes in the Nile. In punishment for this cruelty he and his army were swallowed up by the waves of the sea.

QUESTIONS.

1. Under what forms did God guide the Israelites through the desert? Where did they at length arrive, and pitch their tents? What did Pharao do? ͦ What did the Israelites do, seeing the Egyptians be-

hind them? What did Moses assure them? What did Moses then do, commanded by God? 3. What happened to the Egyptians when they pursued the Israelites into the midst of the sea? 4. Of what is the passage of the Red Sea a figure? How does the justice of God shine forth from the death of Pharao and his army?

CHAPTER XXXV.

The Miracles Wrought in the Desert.

Thou didst feed Thy people with the food of angels, and gavest them bread from heaven prepared without labor, having in it all that is delicious, and the sweetness of every taste.—*Wis. 16, 20.*

AFTER the people of God had crossed the Red Sea, Moses ordered them to go on towards the wilderness. They marched three days through the wilderness, and found no water. Finding some at last, they could not drink it because it was bitter. The people murmured against Moses, saying: "What shall we drink?" Moses prayed, and the Lord showed him a tree, which, when cast into the water, rendered it sweet. And, when they had gone far into the wilderness, the people began to murmur still more, seeing that there was no food, and they wished that they had remained and died in Egypt, asking Moses why he had brought them out into the wilderness to die. Instead of punishing them for their want of confidence, God, full of mercy and goodness, promised to give them food in abundance.

2. He sent them, accordingly, in the evening, quails in vast numbers, sufficient for all the children of Israel to eat; and in the morning a delicious white food fell from heaven. When the Israelites saw the bread, which looked like hoarfrost, they exclaimed, "Manhu," which signifies, "What is this?" Moses informed them that it was the bread which the Lord gave them. He then told every one to gather of it as much as he needed.

3. They did so, and found it pleasant to eat, tasting like flour mixed with honey. On the day before the Sabbath they

gathered a double quantity, as none fell on the Sabbath. This manna was their food for forty years, until they reached the confines of Chanaan. Some time after these events they encamped in another part of the desert, where again there was no water.

4. Here, also, they murmured against Moses, and blamed him for having brought them out of Egypt. Then Moses reproved them for their want of confidence in God; and ad-

MOSES STRIKING THE ROCK.

dressing the Lord in prayer, he asked what he should do. The Lord commanded him to strike a rock on the side of Mount Horeb with his rod. Moses did so, and a stream of pure water burst forth from the rock, so that all the people and the cattle could quench their thirst at will. At this time the Amalekites marched against the chosen people. Moses sent Josue with a number of picked men against them. During the battle Moses prayed on the top of the hill. As long as his hands were uplifted, the Israelites remained victorious; but when, through fatigue, he let them sink, they lost. Hence Aaron and Hur upheld his hands until the enemy was put to flight.

5. The tree which sweetened the water of the desert was a figure of the cross, which sweetens the sufferings of this life. The manna which daily fell from heaven, and sustained the Israelites for forty years in the desert, was a figure of Christ in the Holy Eucharist, who, every day during the Holy Mass, descends from heaven to nourish our souls for life everlasting. The waters which flowed from the rock, when struck by Moses, signify the graces which flow so abundantly for us from the Sacraments of the Church.

QUESTIONS.

1. After the Israelites had crossed the Red Sea, whither did Moses order them to go? What did the people begin to do in the wilderness, seeing that there was no water and no food? What did God promise to do for them? 2. What did He send them? What did they say when they saw the bread? What did Moses tell them to do? 3. What did the manna taste like? How long were the Israelites fed on this manna? What happened to the Israelites in another place where they were encamped? 4. What did Moses do when they began again to murmur? What did the Lord command him to do? 5. What does the tree which rendered the water sweet signify? Of what was the manna a figure? What does the water that flowed from the rock signify?

CHAPTER XXXVI.

God Gives the Ten Commandments on Mount Sinai.

Keep My Commandments, and do them: I am the Lord.—*Lev. 22, 31.*

IN the third month after their departure from Egypt, the Israelites came to Mount Sinai, where they rested and pitched their tents. Moses ascended the mountain, and God appeared to him there. He commanded him to go down to the people and remind them of the wonders He had wrought in their behalf. He told him, moreover, to announce to them that, if they would keep his Law, they should continue to be His chosen people.

2. Moses went down from the mountain and related to the people what the Lord had said. They all cried out with one voice: "All that the Lord hath spoken we will do." Then Moses went up again to the mountain, and the Lord told him that all the children of Israel should sanctify and purify themselves from all defilement that might render them unfit to appear in His presence, and to come, on the third day, to the mountain; but that barriers must be placed around it, so that they might not approach too near and die.

3. The third morning being come, there was thunder and lightning around the mountain, and a thick cloud covered its top. Smoke, mixed with fire, was seen to ascend, the mountain rocked and trembled, while a trumpet sounded very loud, and the people below on the plain feared exceedingly. Then was heard the voice of the Lord, speaking from the cloud that covered the mountain, saying:

4.   I. I am the Lord thy God. Thou shalt not have strange gods before Me. Thou shalt not make to thyself a graven thing, nor the likeness of anything; thou shalt not adore them, nor serve them.

II. Thou shalt not take the name of the Lord thy God in vain.

III. Remember that thou keep holy the Sabbath day.

IV. Honor thy father and thy mother, that thou mayest be long-lived upon the land which the Lord thy God will give thee.

V. Thou shalt not kill.

VI. Thou shalt not commit adultery.

VII. Thou shalt not steal.

VIII. Thou shalt not bear false witness against thy neighbor.

IX. Thou shalt not covet thy neighbor's wife.

X. Thou shalt not covet thy neighbor's goods.

5. The people, trembling and afraid at the foot of the mountain, cried out to Moses: "Speak thou to us, and we will hear; let not the Lord speak to us, lest we die." Moses told them that the Lord had come down to instill fear into their hearts, that they might not sin. And the people stood afar off, but Moses went into the dark cloud, and the Lord gave him further laws, which he wrote down and explained to the people. They answered with one voice: "We will do all the words of the Lord, which He hath spoken." Moses raised an altar at the foot of the mountain, and offered a holocaust to the Lord. And, taking the blood of the victim, he sprinkled the people with it, saying: "This is the blood of the covenant which the Lord hath made with you concerning all these words."

6. As the Old Covenant, or Testament, was consecrated by the sprinkling of the blood of animals, so the New Testament was ratified and sealed by the blood of the Son of God, who said: "This is My blood, of the New Testament."

QUESTIONS.

1. Whither did the Israelites come in the third month after their departure from Egypt? Who appeared to Moses when he ascended the mountain? What did God command Moses to do? 2. What did the people cry out with one voice? What did the Lord tell Moses to do when he went again up to the mountain? 3. What took place when the third morning had come? Whose voice was heard speaking from the mountain? 4. Repeat the ten commandments that God thus gave from the mountain. 5. What did the people, trembling and afraid at the foot of the mountain, cry out? Where did Moses then go? What did the people say? What did Moses do in order to confirm them in this good resolution? With what did he sprinkle the people? 6. How was the Old Testament consecrated, and how was the New Testament ratified and sealed?

CHAPTER XXXVII.

The Golden Calf.

O Lord, rebuke me not in Thy indignation, nor chastise me in Thy
wrath.—*Ps. 6, 2.*

MOSES again ascended the mountain, and remained there forty days and forty nights, conversing with God. And when God had finished speaking with Moses He gave him two tables of stone, on which were written the ten commandments. Now the people, seeing that Moses did not come down from the mountain as soon as they expected, rose up against Aaron, and besought him, saying: "Make us gods that may go before us. For, as to this Moses, the man that brought us out of the land of Egypt, we know not what has befallen him."

2. Hoping to dissuade them from their impious project, Aaron replied: "Take the golden ear-rings from the ears of your wives, and your sons and daughters, and bring them to me." Contrary to all expectation, they brought their rings to Aaron, who, fearing to offer resistance, accepted them, and made a molten calf, and built an altar. And the people exclaimed: "These are thy gods, O Israel, that have brought thee out of the land of Egypt." Next morning they offered holocausts and peace-victims, and began to eat and drink and to dance, after the manner of the Egyptians.

3. Meanwhile, Moses came down from the mountain with the two tables of stone, whereon God Himself had written His commandments. When he heard the shouts of the people, and saw them dance before the golden calf, he dashed the tables to the ground, and broke them at the foot of the mount. Then, laying hold of the calf, he burnt it and beat it to powder.

4. He severely rebuked Aaron for yielding to the wicked desires of the people. Then, standing in the gate of the camp, he said: "If any man be on the Lord's side, let him

join with me." And all the sons of Levi gathered around
him. Then Moses ordered them to take their swords, go
through the camp, and slay every man whom they found
practicing idolatry. They did as they were commanded, and
about twenty-three thousand men were put to death that day.
Next day Moses again ascended the mountain, and earnestly
entreated the Lord for his ungrateful people. But the Lord

MOSES RECEIVING THE TABLES OF THE LAW.

said: "Let me alone, that I may destroy them." Still Moses
insisted, saying: "I beseech Thee, this people hath sinned:
either forgive them this trespass, or, if Thou do not, strike me
out of the book that Thou hast written."

5. The Lord heard his prayer, and ordered him to cut two
other tables of stone. Moses obeyed, and on those tables the
Lord again wrote the ten commandments. But when Moses
came down from the mountain with the tables in his hands,
his face was so radiant with glory that the Israelites were

afraid to come near; hence he veiled his face whenever he spoke to the people. From this terrible punishment inflicted upon the Israelites we may learn what a fearful thing it is to offend God. Moses, the mediator of the Old Covenant, is a figure of Jesus Christ, the mediator of the New Testament. The prayer of Moses for his people teaches us in a striking manner that the intercession of saints has great power to avert the chastisements of God.

QUESTIONS.

1. How long did Moses remain on the mountain, conversing with God? What did the Lord give him? Seeing that Moses did not return from the mountain, what did the people ask Aaron to do? 2. What did Aaron tell them to do, hoping to dissuade them from their impious project? When the earrings were brought, what did Aaron do? What did the people do? 3. What did Moses bring down from the mountain? When he heard the shouts of the people, and saw them dancing round the golden calf, what did he do? 4. What did he do to Aaron? What did he order the sons of Levi to do? How many men were put to death that day? What did Moses do next day? What did the Lord say to him? How did Moses insist? 5. The Lord having heard his prayer, what did He order him to do? What did the Lord write on the two tables of stone? How did Moses appear on coming down from the mountain? How is Moses a figure of Jesus Christ? What does the prayer of Moses teach us in a striking manner?

CHAPTER XXXVIII.

The Making of the Tabernacle.

I have loved, O Lord, the beauty of Thy house, and the place· where Thy glory dwelleth.—*Ps. 25, 8.*

HITHERTO the Israelites had no fixed place of worship, nor, properly speaking, any priesthood. Their patriarchs had offered sacrifice to God now in one place, now in another. In later times the heads of families had exercised the priestly functions; but this state of thing was no longer to exist. Moses, while conversing with the Lord on the mountain, had received from Him the clearest and most defi-

nite directions regarding divine worship, with all the cere-
monies that were to accompany it.

2. Moses, therefore, built a shrine, or tabernacle, that could
be taken apart and carried from place to place. It was a
portable tabernacle, or church, as we would call it, and well
suited to the wandering life of the children of Israel. It was
made of the most precious wood. Its length was thirty, its
breadth ten, and its height also ten cubits. The boards were
overlaid with plates of gold, and furnished with sockets[1] of

THE TABERNACLE.

silver. It was divided into two parts: the fore part, being
larger, was called the Sanctuary; the further part, being
smaller, was called the Holy of Holies.

3. On the inside, he covered the roof and the walls with
rich tapestry, and on the outside with skins and furs. Moreover, to the ceiling of the Holy of Holies, as also to its inner

[1] SOCK'ETS, hollows, to set the boards into.

walls, he fastened a most precious weaving in very brilliant colors, adorned with an embroidery of cherubim and palms and flowers. At the entrance of the Sanctuary was hung a richly-embroidered curtain; and one, more costly still, separated the Sanctuary from the Holy of Holies. In the Holy of Holies he placed the ark of the covenant, which was covered with gold within and without. At its four corners, on the outside, were attached rings of gold, through which bars overlaid with gold were passed, whereby to carry the ark.

4. In the ark he put the tables of the law. As these tables, on which the ten commandments were written, contained the chief heads of the Old Covenant, the ark itself was called the Ark of the Covenant. Later on, there was placed in the ark, also, a vase filled with manna, and the rod of Aaron. He then placed over the ark a cover, or lid, of the purest gold, called the propitiatory,[1] at the ends of which stood two cherubim of beaten gold, looking at each other, and spreading their wings so as to overshadow the propitiatory.

5. In the Sanctuary was a table, overlaid with gold, on which were every day placed the loaves of proposition, made of the finest flour, and unleavened, together with a golden cup filled with wine. On this table, also, stood the seven-branched candlestick, on which were burning, day and night, seven flames fed by the purest oil. Before it stood an altar of incense, whereon the richest spices fumed unceasingly. Moses made a court in front of, and around, the tabernacle, for the gathering of the people; and there he erected the altar of holocausts, of brass, and also a large brazen laver for the priests.

6. When all was completed according to God's command, Moses poured a sacred oil on the tabernacle, and on all it contained, and then a cloud covered the ark of the covenant, and the glory of the Lord filled the tabernacle, and rested be-

---

[1] PROPITIATORY (pr. pro-pish'-ee-a-tory), the lid or cover of the Ark of the Covenant.

tween the two cherubim. As often as Moses had occasion to consult the Lord, he received an answer of the Lord from the propitiatory in the Holy of Holies. As the tabernacle was divided into two parts, so our churches have two parts: one for the priests, called the sanctuary, and another for the faithful, called the body of the church. Hence the tabernacle was a pattern of our Christian churches.

QUESTIONS.

1. How had the patriarchs hitherto offered sacrifice? What had happened in later times? Was this state of things to continue? What did Moses receive from God, while he conversed with Him on the mountain? 2. What did Moses, therefore, build? How was the tabernacle divided? 3. How did Moses adorn the tabernacle inside and outside? What was hung at the entrance of the tabernacle, and before the Holy of Holies? What did Moses place in the Holy of Holies? What was placed outside the ark on its four corners? 4. What did Moses place in the ark? Why was the ark called the Ark of the Covenant? What stood at either end of the cover of the ark? What did the wings of the cherubim shade? 5. What was in the sanctuary? What was every day placed on the table? What was also placed on this table? What did Moses make in front of the tabernacle? 6. When all was completed according to God's command, what did Moses do? What then covered the ark? What filled the tabernacle? Of what is the tabernacle a pattern?

CHAPTER XXXIX.

Laws Regulating Divine Worship.

Blessed are they that dwell in Thy house, O Lord: they shall praise Thee forever and ever.—*Ps. 83, 5.*

BY God's command Moses now prescribed what sacrifices were to be offered, together with the manner of offering them, and the times when they were to be offered. Some of these sacrifices were bloody, others unbloody. The former consisted of sheep, goats and oxen; the latter of flour, fruits, oil and wine. When the thing offered was wholly consumed on the altar, it was called a holocaust, or whole-burnt offering, and represented the highest act of adoration.

2. But when only the fat, as the most delicate part, was

burned, and the rest eaten, it was called either a sacrifice of
thanksgiving for benefits received, or a sacrifice of expiation
for sins committed. Moses also instituted the feasts of the
Lord; for the Lord had told him to establish, first, the feast
of the Pasch, or Passover, in memory of the paschal lamb
eaten by the children of Israel on the night when the first-
born of the Egyptians were slain, and also in memory of their

THE HIGH PRIEST IN HIS VESTMENTS.

deliverance from Egyptian bondage. For seven days they
were to eat unleavened bread while celebrating that feast.

3. Secondly, they were to keep holy, seven weeks after,
the feast of Pentecost, in remembrance of the law given them
on Mount Sinai. On that day they were to bring the first-
fruits of their harvest as an offering to the Lord. Thirdly,
when the harvest was all gathered in, they were to solemnize
the feast of the Tabernacles, during which they were to take
branches of trees and build tents, and dwell in them, so that

their descendants might learn how the Lord had made their fathers dwell in tents in the desert.

4. On these three festivals all the men of Israel were to appear before the Lord in the tabernacle, and later on in the temple. There was also to be a day of expiation, kept as a most solemn fast. On that day the high priest was to sacrifice a calf in atonement for his own sins, and a he-goat for the sins of the people.

5. After the sacrifice, he was to raise the veil and enter into the Holy of Holies, taking with him the blood of the victim and the golden censer; he was then to incense the propitiatory, or cover of the ark, and to sprinkle it and the front of the ark with the blood.

6. Finally, Moses consecrated Aaron as high priest, his sons as priests, and the other men of the tribe of Levi as ministers of the sanctuary, He purified Aaron with water, and clothed him with divers sacred vestments, chief of which was the ephod, a marvelous work of gold and purple and fine linen, the edges of which were ornamented with rich embroidery of gold.

7. He suspended from his neck the rational, on which were twelve stones, each bearing the name of one of the twelve tribes; he placed upon his head the mitre, in the middle of which, in front, was a gold plate with the inscription: "The Holy of the Lord." Finally, he poured oil upon his head and consecrated him. After his sons and the Levites had also been consecrated, Aaron advanced to the altar, and having offered a victim, stretched his hand over the people, and blessed them.

8. And behold! a fire came forth from the pillar of cloud and consumed the holocaust. Seeing which, the people fell prostrate on the ground, praising the Lord. All the public worship of the Israelites was figurative. The bloody sacrifices signified the bloody sacrifice of the cross, which alone truly appeased the divine wrath.

9. The unbloody sacrifices prefigured the unbloody sacrifice

of the mass, by which the fruit of the sacrifice of the cross is constantly applied to us, and which is, at once, a sacrifice of adoration, of thanksgiving, of prayer, and of expiation.   The high priest was a figure of Jesus Christ, who, on the cross, offered Himself to His Eternal Father in a bloody manner, and who daily, at Mass, offers Himself in an unbloody manner at the hands of the priest.

QUESTIONS.

1. What did Moses prescribe by God's command?   Of what kinds were the sacrifices?   Of what did the former consist?   Of what did the latter consist?   When was the sacrifice called a holocaust?   2. When was it a eucharistic sacrifice?   What did Moses also institute? What were these feasts?   3. What were they, secondly, to celebrate? What were they to bring on that day as an offering to the Lord? When were they to celebrate the feast of Tabernacles?   4. What were the men of Israel to do on these three feasts?   What was there also to be?   What was the high priest to sacrifice on that day?   5. What was he to do after the sacrifice?   6. Whom did Moses consecrate as high priest?   Whom as priests?   Whom as ministers of the sanctuary? With what did he clothe Aaron?   7. What did he pour upon his head? What did Aaron do after his sons and the Levites were consecrated? 8. What was all the public worship of the Israelites?   What did the bloody sacrifice signify?   9. What the unbloody sacrifice?   Of whom was the high priest a figure?

CHAPTER XL.

The Spies.

Thou hatest all the workers of iniquity; Thou wilt destroy all that speak a lie.—*Ps. 5, 7.*

IN the second year after their departure from Egypt, the Israelites set out from Mount Sinai, and pursued their march to the desert of Pharan.   Thence Moses sent twelve men, one of every tribe, to explore the land of Chanaan.   He said to them: "Go and view the land, whether it be good or bad; and the people, whether they be strong or weak; and the cities, whether they be walled or without walls."   So the men went up and viewed the land, entering at the south side, and arriving at Hebron.   Thence they proceeded as far as the torrent of the grapes. Here they cut off a branch with its cluster of grapes, and the men carried it upon a pole. After forty days they returned, bringing with them figs, grapes and other rich fruits, as specimens of what the land produced.

2. They told Moses and all the people that the land of Chanaan was good, flowing with milk and honey, as might be seen by these fruits; but that it would be very difficult to conquer that country, as the men were large and strong, and the cities surrounded by walls. They added: "There we saw certain monsters of the sons of Enac, of the giant kind, in comparison of whom we seemed like locusts." Then the people, losing courage and confidence in God, began to murmur against Moses and Aaron, wishing that they had died in Egypt, or in the desert. They exclaimed: "Let us appoint a captain and return to Egypt."

3. In vain did Caleb and Josue, who were of the number of the spies, or explorers, endeavor to appease the anger of the multitude, saying that the land of Chanaan was very good, and that if the men of that country were strong, the Lord would fight for the children of Israel. But the people would not listen to reason. They threatened to put Josue and Caleb to death.

4. Then the glory of the Lord appeared over the ark, and God said to Moses: "How long will this people detract Me? How long will they not believe Me for all the signs that I have wrought before them? I will strike them, therefore, with pestilence, and will consume them." Moses interceded for the people, saying: "Forgive, I beseech Thee, the sin of this people, according to the greatness of Thy mercy."

5. The Lord answered: "I have forgiven according to thy word. But yet all the men that have seen the signs that I have done in Egypt and in the wilderness, and have tempted Me now ten times, shall not see the land. You shall wander forty years in the desert, and faint away and die in the desert; but your children shall possess the land."

6. After pronouncing this sentence on the rebellious Israelites, the Lord struck dead the ten spies who had excited them to sedition. But Josue and Caleb were spared and blessed. From God's dealings with the Israelites on this, as on many other occasions, we may learn that even after the guilt of sin has been remitted, there still remains a temporal punishment to be undergone in one way or another, unless God, by a new act of His mercy, takes it away.

QUESTIONS.

1. Whom did Moses send to explore the land of Chanaan? What did the spies bring with them when they returned? 2. What did they tell Moses and the people? What did the Israelites then begin to do? 3. What did Josue and Caleb say to the people, trying to appease their anger? What did the people threaten to do? 4. What did God then say to Moses? What did Moses say, interceding for the people? 5. What did the Lord answer Moses? What did He promise? 6. What did the Lord do after pronouncing this fearful sentence? What may we learn from God's dealings with the Israelites on this and many other occasions?

CHAPTER XLI.

The Revolt of Core and His Adherents.

He that resisteth the power, resisteth the ordinance of God; and they that resist, purchase to themselves damnation.—*Rom. 13, 2.*

ONE day, whilst the children of Israel were in the wilderness, they found a man gathering wood on the Sabbath day, and they brought him to Moses and Aaron, who put him in prison, to see how he should be punished. But the Lord said to Moses: "Let that man die; let all the multitude stone him without the camp." So it was done. Some time after, two hundred and fifty men, belonging partly to the tribe of Reuben and partly to the tribe of Levi, and having for leaders Core, a Levite, and Dathan and Abiron, both of the tribe of Reuben—all these rose up against Moses and Aaron. They were envious of the high position of Moses and Aaron, and accused them of tyranny and ambition. They said: "All the people are holy; why do ye raise yourselves above the people of God?" Moses, hearing this, and knowing that it was a revolt against God Himself, was much afflicted, and fell flat on his face.

2. He afterwards spoke to the rebellious Levites, and told them: "Is it because God has chosen you to serve near the tabernacle, that you would wish to usurp the dignity of the priesthood also? To-morrow the Lord will make known who they are that belong to Him. Prepare, then, and stand each with his censer on one side, and Aaron will stand on the other."

3. On the following day, when the two hundred and fifty men were to appear before the Lord with their censers, Moses ordered the leaders of the revolt to come forth from their tents. But they impudently replied: "We will not come." Then Moses went himself to their tents, accompanied by Aaron, and told the people to separate themselves from those wicked men, lest they should perish with them. Moses said: "If these men die the common death of men, the Lord did not send me; but if the earth, opening her mouth, swallow them down, and they go down alive into hell, you shall know that they have blasphemed the Lord."

4. Hardly had Moses ended these words, when lo! the earth opened under the feet of these hardened sinners, and swallowed them up, with their tents and all that belonged to them, and they went down alive into hell. At the same time fire came down from heaven and destroyed the two hundred and fifty men who had taken sides with Core, Dathan and Abiron.

5. After this, the Lord spoke to Moses, saying: "Speak to the children of Israel, and take of every one of them a rod, by their kindreds, of all the princes of the tribes, twelve rods, and write the name of every man upon his rod; and lay them up in the tabernacle of the covenant. Whomsoever of these I shall choose, his rod shall blossom." Moses did as the Lord had commanded.

6. Next day, when Moses entered into the tabernacle, he found that the rod of Aaron had budded and blossomed. He then brought out all the rods to the children of Israel, and each one received back his own rod.

7. After all the people had seen that Aaron was chosen by the Lord, Moses was ordered to take Aaron's rod and place it in the tabernacle, that it might serve as a memorial and token of the rebellion of the children of Israel. The awful punishment of Core, Dathan and Abiron ought to show us the folly and wickedness of murmuring against the priests whom God has placed over us.

QUESTIONS.

1. Who rose up against Moses and Aaron?   2. What did Moses, much afflicted, tell the rebels?   3. Whom did Moses order, next day, to be brought forth from their tents?   What did Core, Dathan and Abiron impudently reply?   What did Moses then tell the people to do? 4. This being done, what happened?   What happened to the two hundred and fifty men who had taken sides with Core, Dathan and Abiron?   5. After this, what did the Lord say to Moses?   6. Next day, when Moses entered into the tabernacle, what did he find?   7. After all the people had seen that Aaron was chosen by the Lord, what was Moses ordered to do?   What ought the awful punishment of Core, Dathan and Abiron to show us?

CHAPTER XLII.

The Doubt of Moses.—The Brazen Serpent.

There is no confusion to them that trust in Thee.—*Dan. 3, 40.*

IN the beginning of the fortieth year of their wanderings, the Israelites—the children of those that had died in the desert—suffered from the want of water, and began again to murmur against the Lord. Then the Lord appeared in glory and said to Moses: "Speak to the rock, and it shall yield waters." Then Moses, taking the rod from the tabernacle, assembled the people before the rock, which he was about to strike. Then he raised the rod and struck; but, doubting a little, he struck a second time.

2. That momentary diffidence, which was only a venial sin, and which made Moses strike the rock a second time, was displeasing to the Lord, and He told Moses and Aaron: "Because you have not believed Me, you shall not bring these people into the land which I will give them." Thence the

THE BRAZEN SERPENT.

Israelites removed their camp and came to Mount Hor, where Aaron died, and Eleazar, his son, became high priest. Some time later, the Israelites, tired of their incessant wanderings in the desert began again to murmur against the Lord and Moses. Wherefore fiery serpents were sent amongst them, by whose deadly bite a great number were killed.

3. Then the people, knowing that the serpents had been

sent in punishment of their sins, came to Moses and said: "We have sinned, because we have spoken against the Lord and thee: pray that He may take away these serpents from us." And Moses prayed for the people. Whereupon the Lord said to him: "Make a brazen serpent, and set it up for a sign: whosoever being struck shall look on it, shall live." Moses therefore made a brazen serpent, and set it up for a sign, which healed all those that looked upon it.

4. The brazen serpent was a figure of the Redeemer raised on the cross. He it is who heals the wounds of all who, having been bitten by the infernal serpent, turn to Him with true compunction for sin, and hope in His divine mercy. The waters which flowed from the rock in the wilderness to refresh the Israelites and slake their thirst, were emblematic of the divine graces which flow to mankind through the Sacraments of the Church.

QUESTIONS.

1. From what did the Israelites begin to suffer towards the end of their wanderings? What did the Lord then order Moses to do? What did Moses do? 2. What was displeasing to the Lord? What did He tell Moses? Of what were the Israelites tired? What was sent amongst them when they began again to murmur? 3. What did the people beseech Moses to do? What did God, hearing the prayer of Moses, command him to do? What did He promise? 4. Of what was the brazen serpent a figure? Of what were the waters that flowed from the rock emblematic?

CHAPTER XLIII.

The Prophecy of Balaam.

They will curse and Thou wilt bless.—*Ps. 108, 28.*

AS the Israelites were nearing the promised land, they came to the confines of Moab. Balac, the king of that country, being in very great fear, sent the elders and the nobles of his kingdom, with rich presents, to Balaam, that he might come and curse his enemies. This Balaam believed in the true God; but, at the same time, he practised soothsaying and divination.

2. When the messengers had arrived with their presents, Balaam said: "Tarry here this night, and I will answer whatsoever the Lord shall say to me." And God told him: "Thou shalt not go, nor shalt thou curse the people." So the princes returned to the king. But Balac sent a greater number of nobles, and richer presents, than the first time. Balaam told the messengers again to stay for one night. In that night God came to Balaam and said: "Arise and go; yet so, that thou do what I shall command thee."

3. Then Balaam arose and went to the land of Moab. The king took him to three different mountains, whence he could behold the Israelites in the valley, and ordered him to curse them. But Balaam being each time prevented by God from cursing, blessed them, saying: "How beautiful are thy tabernacles, O Jacob, and thy tents, O Israel! He that blesseth thee shall also himself be blessed, and he that curseth thee shall be reckoned accursed."

4. Then Balac grew angry, and exclaimed: "I had intended to honor thee, but the Lord hath deprived thee of the honor; for I called thee to curse my enemies, and thou, on the contrary, hast blessed them three times." So he ordered him to return to his country. Thereupon the eyes of Balaam were opened and he saw a vision, and his lips were opened and he prophesied[1]: "I shall see Him, but not now; I shall behold Him, but not near. A star shall rise out of Jacob, and a scepter shall spring up from Israel, and shall strike the chiefs of Moab, and shall smite the children of Seth." The prophecy of Balaam refers to the Savior, and the star mentioned is the star which appeared to the three wise men at the birth of Christ.

QUESTIONS.

1. When the Israelites came to the confines of Moab, what did Balac, king of the Moabites, do, being afraid of them? What did

[1] PROPH'-E-SIED, foretold.

Balaam practise, although believing in the true God? 2. What did the Lord tell Balaam in a vision? What did the king do a second time? What did the king do when Balaam went to him? 3. What did Balaam, refusing to curse the Israelites, say? 4. What did Balac, the king, then do and say? What did he order the prophet to do? What did Balaam prophesy? To whom does this prophecy refer?

CHAPTER XLIV.

Parting Advice of Moses.—His Death.

Blessed are the dead who die in the Lord.—*Apoc. 14, 13.*

THE hour had come at last when Moses was to be taken away from his people. Before he died, God commanded him to lay his hands on Josue, in the presence of all the people, so that they might obey him as their ruler. For God had said to Moses: "Thou shalt not pass over this Jordan; but Josue shall bring the people into the land which I swore I would give to their fathers."

2. Then Moses made his farewell discourse to the people in a most touching manner: "Hear, O ye heavens, the things I speak; let the earth give ear to the words of my mouth. Hear, O Israel, the Lord our God is one Lord. Thou shalt love the Lord thy God with thy whole heart, and with thy whole soul, and with thy whole strength. Let none be found among you that consult soothsayers, or observe dreams and omens. These things the Gentiles do; but thou art otherwise instructed. The Lord thy God will raise up to thee a *prophet* of thy nation, and of thy brethren, *like unto me.* Him thou shalt hear."

3. He reminded them of all the wonders which God had wrought in their behalf. He promised them that if they were faithful in observing the commandments of God, they should be blessed in their houses, blessed in their fields, blessed in the fruits of the land, blessed in their cattle, blessed when they came in and when they went out.

4. Then he warned them that if they did not hear the voice of the Lord, and keep His commandments, a curse should come upon them and all that they possessed. Then, having blessed the people, he went up from the plains of Moab to Mount Nebo. From that place the Lord showed him, afar off, the land of Chanaan, which He had promised to his fathers, Abraham, Isaac and Jacob.

5. There Moses died, at the age of one hundred and twenty years; and all Israel mourned him for thirty days. Moses was a figure of Jesus Christ. Like Christ, he proclaimed the law of God, and confirmed his preaching with miracles, prophecies, and a holy life. The prophet of whom Moses speaks is the Savior, who was to give a new law, more perfect than that of Moses.

QUESTIONS.

1. Before Moses died, what did God command him to do? 2. What did Moses then tell the people? What did he warn them never to forget? What did he tell them to do? 3. Of what did he remind them? What did he promise them? 4. What did he tell them would happen if they did not hear the voice of God and keep His commandments? Whither did Moses go up from the plains of Moab, after having blessed the people? What did the Lord show him from Mount Nebo? 5. Of whom was Moses a figure? Why was he a figure of Christ? Who is the prophet mentioned by Moses?

CHAPTER XLV.

Entrance of the Israelites into the Promised Land.

By faith the walls of Jericho fell down.—*Heb. 11, 30.*

AFTER the death of Moses, the Lord spake to Josue: "My servant Moses is dead; arise and pass over this Jordan, thou and the people with thee. I will deliver to you every place that the sole of your foot shall tread upon. No man shall be able to resist thee all the days of thy life." Encouraged by these promises, the people advanced towards the Jordan. When they reached it banks, Josue ordered the priests to take the Ark of the Lord, and go before the people.

2. As soon as the priests, carrying the ark, stepped into the Jordan and their feet touched the water at the bank, the waves that came down from above stood heaped together, and swelling up like a mountain, were seen afar off; but the floods which were beneath, ran down into the sea, until they wholly failed. Then all the people passed over through

THE TAKING OF JERICHO.

the channel that was dried up. They pitched their tents before Jericho. On the following day they celebrated the pasch, and having eaten of the fruits of the earth, the manna ceased to fall.

3. Jericho was a strongly fortified city, capable of offering a long resistance. The children of Israel wished to take it, but they lost courage when they saw the height and strength of the ramparts. But the Lord, seeing their want of confi-

dence, ordered Josue to bring together all the fighting men of Israel, and to march, in deep silence, around the city once a day for six days.

4. But on the seventh day they should go around the city seven times; and at the last time, all the people, on hearing the priests that were before the ark sounding the trumpets, should shout together with a great shout. So it was done. When the seventh day came, they marched silently six times around the city; but at the seventh turn, when the priests sounded the trumpets, all the people shouted, and instantly the walls fell down. Every man went up by the place that was against him; and they took the city.

5. After many hard-fought battles, Josue at length made himself master of all the land of Chanaan. During this time he frequently experienced the especial assistance of God. On one occasion he waged war against the five kings of the Amorrhites. The Israelites conquered and pursued their enemies. But night coming on would soon have put an end to the vcitory. Then Josue spoke to the Lord, in the sight of all the people : "Move not, O sun, towards Gabaon; nor thou, O moon, toward the valley of Ajalon." So the sun stood still in the midst of heaven. There was not, before nor afterward, so long a day.

6. Chanaan was divided among the twelve tribes of Israel. The tribe of Levi alone received no portion, as they lived on the tithes and sacrifices; but they received forty-eight cities in different parts of the country. The descendants of the two sons of Joseph, Ephraim and Manasses, received each a portion of the land. Thus the country was divided among the twelve tribes: Reuben, Simeon, Juda, Zabulon, Issachar, Dan, Gad, Aser, Nephtali, Benjamin, Ephraim and Manasses. Thus were the promises fulfilled which God had made to the patriarchs. When Josue was old, he assembled the people and admonished them to observe the law, and to avoid

intercourse and marriage with the heathens. Josue died at
the age of one hundred and ten years.

7. The promised land was a figure of heaven. As the
Israelites did not obtain possession of Chanaan till they had
toiled and fought and suffered much, so Christians cannot
enter heaven, the true land of promise, unless they contend
bravely against the enemies of their salvation.

QUESTIONS.

1. After the death of Moses, what did the Lord command Josue
to do? What did He promise? When the people reached the banks
of the Jordan, what did Josue order the priests to do? 2. What
happened, when the priests, carrying the ark, touched the waters of the
river? What did the people celebrate on the following day? 3. What
was Jericho? What did the Lord, seeing their want of confidence, order
Josue to do? 4. What was to be done on the seventh day? This
being done, what happened? 5. What did Josue do when, after many
hard-fought battles, he at length made himself master of the land of
Chanaan? What did Josue experience during this especial time? What
happened while he waged war against the five kings? 6. Among whom
was Chanaan divided? What did the tribe of Levi receive? What
were thus fulfilled? 7. Of what was the promised land a figure? Why?

CHAPTER XLVI.

The Judges.—Gedeon.—Samson.

The weak things of the world hath God chosen, that He may confound
the strong.—*I. Cor., 1, 27.*

SO long as that generation of the Israelites lived who had
eaten of the manna in the desert, and who had seen
the wonders of the Lord wrought for them, both in the wilderness and in the taking of Chanaan, they did not depart
from the way of the Lord; but their children having inter-
married with the pagan nations around them, contrary to the
express command of God, began to adore the idols which
their wives worshiped. Then the Lord delivered them into
the hands of their enemies.

2. They afterwards repented, and turned again to the Lord,
their God. In this manner, falling into idolatry, and return-

ing again to the worship of the true God, they went on for several generations. Whenever they humbled themselves before God, and showed signs of true repentance, the Lord hastened to their relief. From time to time He raised up amongst them brave and pious men, who smote the enemy with a strong hand.

3. These men were called Judges. Amongst them were Barac, Jephte, Samson—who was famous for his great strength—and the pious Samuel. But the most renowned of all the judges was Gedeon, the son of a common Israelite, who lived at the time when God had delivered the children of Israel into the hands of the Madianites on account of their sins.

4. The Lord sent an angel to Gedeon, as he was threshing and winnowing wheat at his father's house. The angel said to him: "The Lord is with thee, O most valiant of men. Go in this thy strength, and thou shalt deliver Israel out of the hands of the Madianites." Gedeon asked how could he deliver Israel, seeing that his family was the lowest in the tribe of Manasses, and that he himself was the least in his father's house. The angel assured him that God would be with him, and that the Madianites should be cut off to a man.

5. Soon after this the Madianites crossed the Jordan with a large army, and encamped in the valley of Jezrael. But the spirit of the Lord came upon Gedeon, and he sounded the trumpet, and calling together the Israelites, formed an army of thirty-two thousand men, and put them in battle array. Before commencing the attack, Gedeon said to God: "If Thou wilt save Israel by my hand, I will put this fleece of wool on the floor; if there be dew in the fleece only, and it be dry on all the ground beside, I shall know that by my hand, as Thou hast said, Thou wilt deliver Israel." And it was so. The next day he asked God that the fleece might be dry and the ground wet with dew. And God did as Gedeon requested.

6. But the Lord spoke to Gedeon, and told him that his army was too great, and that the Madianites should not thus be delivered into his hands, lest the children of Israel should glory and say they conquered by their own strength.

7. And the Lord commanded Gedeon to speak to the people and proclaim in the hearing of all, that whosoever was fearful or timorous should return home. And the army hearing this, twenty-two thousand men retired from the field, leaving only ten thousand to meet the enemy. The Lord spoke again to Gedeon, telling him that there were still too many soldiers. "Bring them to the waters," he said, "and there I will try them."

8. He then told Gedeon to observe how the men would drink when they came to the water. "They that shall lap the water with their tongues, as dogs are wont to lap, thou shalt set apart by themselves; but they that shall drink bowing down their knees, shall be on the other side." The number of those who had lapped the water from the hollow of their hand, in order to save time, were three hundred men; all the rest of the multitude had knelt down to drink at their ease.

9. Gedeon kept with him only the three hundred who drank the water from the hollow of their hand; the rest he sent to their homes. He then divided the three hundred men into three companies, and gave them trumpets in their hands, and empty pitchers, and lamps within the pitchers. And he said to them: "What you shall see me do, do you the same; I will go into one part of the camp, and do you as I shall do."

10. Gedeon and the three hundred men that were with him approached the enemy's camp at the midnight watch, and entering in, began to sound their trumpets and to strike the pitchers one against the other, dazzling the bewildered enemy with the sudden light of the concealed lamps. At the same time the Israelites cried out with a loud voice: "The sword of the Lord and of Gedeon."

11. The sudden alarm, and the fierce attack of Gedeon's

men, threw the Madianites into such confusion that they turned their swords against each other, and fled in all directions. Then all the tribes of Israel, seeing that victory was on their side, rose up and pursued the Madianites, cutting off their retreat on every side, so that of the whole army of one hundred and thirty-five thousand men, only fifteen thousand returned alive to their own country. Israel had peace for forty years.

12. The Israelites fell again into idolatry, and were persecuted by the Philistines. But an angel appeared to the wife of Manue, of the tribe of Dan, and said: "Thou shalt bear a son; no razor shall touch his head, for he shall be a Nazarite of God from his infancy, and he shall begin to deliver Israel from the hands of the Philistines." When the child was born, he was called Samson.

13. Going to the city of the Philistines, he met a young lion; but the Spirit of the Lord came upon Samson, and he tore the lion to pieces. Being delivered into the hands of the Philistines, he tore the cords with which he was bound, and finding the jaw-bone of an ass, he slew with it a thousand men. Remaining over night in Gaza, the Philistines bolted the gates of the city to prevent his escape. But Samson arose at midnight, took the gates, with their posts and bolts and carried them to the top of a hill.

14. Dalila, a Philistine woman, after many pleadings extracted from him the secret of his strength. "The razor hath never come upon my head, for I am a Nazarite: that is to say, consecrated to God. If my head be shaven, my strength shall depart, and I shall be like other men." During his sleep Dalila cut off his hair, called the Philistines, who captured him, put out his eyes and cast him into prison. Some time after, a great feast was celebrated in honor of the idol Dagon, when more than three thousand Philistines were assembled in the house. Blind Samson, whose hair had grown again, was brought out, that he might amuse them by feats of his strength. He told the boy who led him to bring him to the

pillars upon which the whole house rested. Then he prayed: "O Lord God, remember me and restore to me my former strength." Then, grasping the pillars, he shook them so strongly that the whole house rocked and fell upon himself and all the people. In this manner he killed many more enemies of God at his death than he had killed during life.

QUESTIONS.

1. How long did the Israelites remain faithful to the Lord? What happened when their children began to intermarry with the pagan nations around them? What did the Lord then do? 2. What did the Israelites afterwards do? What did the Lord do whenever they humbled themselves and repented? Whom did He raise from time to time, amongst them? 3. What were these men called? Who were amongst them? Who was the most renowned of all the judges? 4. Whom did the Lord send to Gedeon? What did the angel say? What did Gedeon ask? What did the angel assure him? 5. What did the Madianites do soon after this? What did Gedeon do when the spirit of the Lord came upon him? What did the Lord tell Gedeon? Before going into battle, what did Gedeon say to God? What happened the next day? 6. What did the Lord say to Gedeon? 7. What did the Lord command Gedeon to tell the people? How many men went away? How many remained? What did the Lord tell Gedeon to do, as there were still too many men? 8. What did He tell Gedeon to observe? How many were there who lapped the water from their hand? 9. What did Gedeon do with the three hundred men? What did he say to them? 10. What did Gedeon and his men do at the midnight watch? What did they cry out when attacking the enemy? 11. What happened to the Madianites? What did the tribes of Israel do? How long had Israel peace? 12. Did the Israelites fall again into idolatry? What did the Lord say to Manue? What was the child called? 13. What did Samson meet on going to the city of the Philistines? What did he do when he was captured by them? 14. What was the secret of his strength? What did Dalila do when he was asleep? Some time after, what was celebrated? Who was brought to amuse the Philistines? What did he tell the boy to do? What did he do, after praying to the Lord?

CHAPTER XLVII.

Ruth's Affection for Her Mother-in-Law.

A faithful friend is a strong defence, and he that hath found him hath found a treasure.—*Ecclus. 6, 14.*

IN the days when the Judges ruled in Israel, there was a famine in the land. And a certain man of Bethlehem, with his wife and two sons, went to sojourn in the land of Moab. He was named Elimelech, and his wife Noemi. After having lived many years in Moab, Elimelech died, and his two sons, who had taken wives from amongst the daughters of Moab, also died, ten years after their father's death.

2. Noemi, being now left alone and full of sorrow for the loss of her husband and her sons, arose to return to her own country. Her two daughters-in-law, Orpha and Ruth, went forth with her. As they journeyed on towards the land of Juda, Noemi spoke to Orpha and Ruth: "Go ye home to your mothers. The Lord deal mercifully with you, as you have dealt with the dead and me." And she kissed them. But they lifted up their voice and wept, and said: "We will go with thee to thy people."

3. Noemi answered: "Do not so, my daughters; for I am grieved the more for your distress; and the hand of the Lord is gone out against me." Then Orpha kissed her mother-in-law and returned. Ruth, however, would not depart. Noemi spoke again: "Behold, thy kinswoman is returned to her people; go thou with her."

4. Thereupon Ruth replied: "Be not against me, for whithersoever thou shalt go, I will go: and where thou shalt dwell, I also will dwell. Thy people shall be my people, and thy God my God. The land that shall receive thee dying, in the same will I die, and there will I be buried." Then Noemi, seeing that Ruth was steadfast, would not urge her any more to return to her friends. So they journeyed on together, and

came to Bethlehem, where the report was quickly spread, and the women said, "This is that Noemi."

5. It was the beginning of the barley harvest, and Ruth asked Noemi: "If thou wilt, I will go into the field and glean the ears of corn that escape the hands of the reapers." And Noemi said: "Go, my daughter." Now, it so happened that the field in which Ruth went to glean belonged to a kinsman of Elimelech, named Booz, who was very rich. And behold, Booz came out to see the reapers, and said: "The Lord be with you." They answered: "The Lord bless thee."

6. And, having observed Ruth gleaning in the barley field, he asked the overseer: "Whose maid is this?" The overseer replied: "This is Ruth, who came with Noemi from the land of Moab; and she desires leave to glean the ears of corn that remain, following the steps of the reapers. She hath been in the field from morning till now, and hath not gone home for a moment."

7. Then Booz addressed Ruth very kindly, and said: "Hear me, daughter: Keep with my maids, and follow where they reap. I have charged my young men not to molest thee. And if thou art thirsty, go to the vessels and drink of the waters whereof the servants drink, and dip thy morsel in the vinegar." Full of gratitude for these kind words, Ruth bent down before Booz and asked how it came that she, a woman of another country, should find favor in his sight.

8. Booz told her that all she had done for her mother-in-law since the death of her husband, had been related to him. He prayed: "Mayest thou receive a full reward of the Lord, under whose wings thou art fled." He then privately told the reapers: "Let fall some of your handfuls of purpose, that she may gather them without shame." She gleaned, therefore, in the field till evening, and then beat out with a rod what she had gleaned, which was an ephi: that is, three bushels. Grateful for the kindness shown her, she returned to her mother-in-law, carrying with her the barley she had

threshed, and the leavings of the meal that had been given her. Noemi was astonished and asked: "Where hast thou gleaned to-day, and where hast thou wrought?   Blessed be he that has had pity on thee." Ruth told the man's name, that he was called Booz.

9. Next day she returned to the field of Booz, and continued to glean after the reapers, till all the barley was laid up in the barns. Some time after, Booz said to Ruth: "My daughter, all the people that dwell within the gates of my city know that thou art a virtuous woman." So he married her. Then the ancients came and said to Booz: "May this woman be an example of virtue in Ephrata, and may she have a famous name in Bethlehem." The Lord blessed their union, and gave them a son, whom they called Obed. Then Noemi, full of joy, taking the child, laid it in her bosom, and she carried it, and was a nurse to it. Now, Obed was the father of Isai, whose son was David, of whose race Christ was born.

QUESTIONS.

1. What man of Bethlehem went to sojourn in Moab with his wife and two sons?   2. What did Noemi, being left alone, resolve to do after the death of her husband and sons?   What did her daughters-in-law, Orpha and Ruth, agree to do?   What did Noemi, on the way to the land of Juda, advise her daughters-in-law to do?   What did they declare?   3. What did Noemi go on urging them to do?   Telling them what?   Who was persuaded to return home?   What did Ruth insist on doing?   4. What did Ruth exclaim?   5. Having arrived in Bethlehem, what did Ruth ask Noemi's permission to do?   To whom did the field, in which Ruth went to glean, belong?   6. Booz having inquired who Ruth was, what did the overseer reply?   7. What did Booz tell Ruth to do?   What did Ruth ask Booz?   8. What did Booz say to Ruth? What did he privately tell the reapers?   9. What did Booz, some time after, say to Ruth?   What did he then do?   What did the ancients say?   What did Booz and Ruth call the son whom God gave them?   Who nursed the child?   Whose father was Obed?   Who was the son of Isai?

CHAPTER XLVIII.

Samuel.—Impiety of the Sons of Heli.

He that spareth the rod hateth his son.—*Prov. 13, 24.*

IN the days when Heli, the high-priest, was judge in Israel, there lived at Mount Ephraim a virtuous man called Elcana, and the name of his wife was Anna. Now Anna had no children. She, therefore, multiplied her prayers before the Lord that he would deign to give her children. So one day she went to Silo to pray in the tabernacle of the Lord. There, before the door of the temple, she shed many tears and prayed, and made a vow, saying: "O Lord of Hosts, if Thou wilt be mindful of me, and wilt give me a man-child, I will give him to the Lord all the days of his life."

2. The Lord heard her prayer, and gave her a son, whom she called Samuel, which means God-given. Now, when three years were passed, and the child was yet very young, Anna took three calves, three bushels of flour and a bottle of wine, and carrying the boy with her, she went to the house of the Lord. There she offered her son to Heli, the high-priest, saying: "The Lord has granted my petition, therefore I also have lent my child to the Lord all the days of his life." But the child ministered in the sight of the Lord before the face of Heli. Now, the two sons of Heli, Ophni, and Phinees, were wicked, and had no fear of God; for, when the people came to offer sacrifices, Ophni and Phinees carried the flesh of the victims away by force. So their sin was very great, because they withdrew men from the sacrifice of the Lord.

3. Heli knew all this; he knew what wicked things his sons did in the sanctuary, and he mildly rebuked them, saying: "It is no good report that I hear, that you make the people of the Lord to transgress." But, being very old, he took no severe measures to punish them or prevent their evil

deeds. So it came to pass that one night, before the lamp of the Lord had gone out, Heli slept on a couch near the tabernacle, and Samuel hard by. The Lord called Samuel. He exclaimed: "Here am I," and went to Heli, and asked: "Why hast thou called me?" But Heli replied: "I did not call thee, my son; return and sleep."

4. So he returned and slept again. But the Lord called him a second time, and Samuel acted as before. Heli said: "I did not call thee, my son; return and sleep. Then the Lord called Samuel a third time. And Samuel, rising up, went again to Heli, saying: "Here am I, for thou didst call me." Heli now understood that the Lord had called the boy.

5. And he said to Samuel: "Go and sleep, and if He shall call thee any more, thou shalt say: 'Speak, Lord, for Thy servant heareth'." So Samuel went and slept in his place. Then the Lord came and stood, and called: "Samuel, Samuel." He answered: Speak, Lord, for thy servant heareth." The Lord spoke: "Behold, I will do a thing in Israel, and whosoever shall hear it, both his ears shall tingle. In that day I will raise up against Heli all the things that I have spoken. I will begin, and I will make an end, because he knew that his sons did wickedly, and he would not chastise them."

6. Next morning Heli asked the boy to tell him what the Lord had said. But Samuel was afraid. Heli, however, insisted, and Samuel at length told the vision. Thereupon Heli humbly replied: "It is the Lord; let Him do what is good in His sight."

7. Now, in those days it came to pass that the Philistines waged war against Israel, and when they joined battle, the Israelites were defeated, and lost about four thousand men. After the people had returned to the camp, the ancients of Israel said: "Let us fetch the ark of the covenant from Silo, that it may save us from the hands of our enemies." They sent, therefore, to Silo, and the two sons of Heli, Ophni and Phinees, accompanied the ark to the camp. The people, on

beholding the ark in their midst, set up a great shout, and the earth rang with their shouting.

8. The Philistines, however, made a new attack, and the Israelites were again defeated, with great slaughter—thirty thousand were slain, and the rest put to flight. And a messenger came to Heli, saying: "Thy two sons, Ophni and Phinees, are dead, and the ark of the Lord is taken." Now, Heli, who was far advanced in years, on hearing that the ark was taken, fell from his chair backwards by the door, and broke his neck and died. The Philistines took the ark of the Lord and placed it in the temple of Dagon, their false god.

9. Next morning, when they went to the temple, they found the idol lying prostrate on the ground before the ark. Besides, the Lord afflicted them with many evils on account of the ark. Many persons died, and from the fields there came forth a multitude of mice, and there was great confusion in the country.

10. Perceiving this, the Philistines resolved that the ark of God should no longer remain amongst them. Then they took the ark and laid it upon a cart, and taking two kine, or young cows, they yoked them to the cart. The cows took the way that led to Bethsames, and thus the ark was brought again into the country of the Israelites.

11. Meanwhile, after the death of Heli, Samuel had become judge in Israel. He assembled the people, reproached them for their evil doings, and then said: "If you turn to the Lord with all your heart, and put away the strange gods from among you, and prepare your hearts unto the Lord, and serve Him only, He will deliver you out of the hands of the Philistines."

12. So they humbled themselves before God in prayer and fasting. And the Lord took pity upon them, and gave them such a victory over the Philistines that for many years after they did not dare to approach the frontiers of Israel.

QUESTIONS.

1. Who lived at Mount Ephraim in the days when Heli was judge

in Israel? What was the cause of great grief to Anna? For what did she pray continually to the Lord? What did she promise to do if God gave her a son? 2. What did she call the son whom God gave her? What did Anna do when her son was three years old? Who were the sons of Heli? What did Ophni and Phinees do by their sins? 3. Heli, knowing all this, did he punish his sons as he ought to have done? What happened one night when Heli slept near the tabernacle and Samuel hard by? 4. How often did the Lord call Samuel in his sleep? 5. What did Heli, understanding that it was the Lord who had called Samuel, tell him to answer the third time? What did the Lord tell Samuel? 6. What did Heli humbly reply when Samuel told him what he had heard? 7. What happened when the Israelites went to war with the Philistines? What did the ancients of Israel then say? 8. How many of the Israelites were slain when the Philistines again attacked them? What did the messenger say to Heli? How did Heli die? 9. What happened when the Philistines brought the ark to the temple of Dagon? With what were the Philistines afflicted on account of the ark? 10. Seeing this, what did the Philistines do? 11. Meanwhile, who had become judge in Israel? What did he promise the Israelites after having reproached them for their evil doings? 12. What did the Israelites then do?

CHAPTER XLIX.

Saul Elected King. 1095 B. C.

Obedience is better than sacrifices.—*I. Kings, 15, 22.*

AFTER these days, it came to pass that when Samuel was old he appointed his two sons as judges over Israel. They, however, were not like their father, but they took bribes and perverted judgment. So the ancients came to Samuel and said: "Thy sons walk not in thy ways; therefore, give us a king to judge us, as all nations have." This word was displeasing to Samuel, for he knew that the Lord was their king and none other. Still, the Lord told him to hearken to the voice of the people, and to give them a king for their punishment. Moreover, he added, the king would rule over them with a heavy hand, and that they would cry out and lament, but the Lord would not hear them, because they had desired for themselves a king.

2. Now, there was a man of the tribe of Benjamin who lost his asses, and he said to Saul, his son: "Take one of the servants with thee and arise, go and seek the asses." So they both started out, and came to the land of Suph, and entered the city where Samuel dwelt. Now, the day before Saul's arrival the Lord had spoken to Samuel: "To-morrow, about this same hour, I will send to thee a man, whom thou shalt anoint king over My people Israel." It so happened that Samuel met Saul in the midst of the city. And Samuel said: "Go up before me, that you may eat with me to-day, and that I may let you go in the morning. As for the asses, be not solicitous, for they are found." Next morning, when the day began to dawn, Samuel took a little vial of oil and poured it upon the head of Saul, and kissed him and said: "Behold, the Lord has anointed thee to be prince over his inheritance."

3. Thereupon Samuel assembled the people, and Saul stood in their midst; and he was a choice man, being taller than any one else from the shoulders and upwards. Then Samuel said: "Behold him whom the Lord hath chosen." And the people cried out: "God save the king."

4. Now, the people of Amalec were very bad, and the measure of their iniquity was full. God, in His wrath, sent Samuel to Saul, saying: "Go and smite Amalec and all that he hath. Spare him not, nor covet anything that is his, but slay both man and woman and child, ox and sheep and camel."

5. Saul, therefore, waged war against Amalec, and defeated them along the line from Hevila till Sur. The common people he slew with the edge of the word; but, contrary to the command of God, he spared Agag, the king. The flocks and herds of little value he also destroyed, but spared the best flocks and the best herds. Moreover, filled with pride, and forgetting that success comes from God, he erected an arch of triumph in memory of his victory.

6. When Samuel had come to the camp of Israel, Saul s ᴀᴇ to him: "I have fulfilled the word of the Lord." Samuel

answered: "What meaneth, then, the bleating of the flocks, and the lowing of the herds which I hear?" Saul tried to excuse himself, saying that the people had spared the best flocks and herds, to sacrifice them to the Lord. Samuel, being angry, spoke to him in the name of the Lord: "Doth the Lord desire holocausts and victims, and not rather that the voice of the Lord should be obeyed? For obedience is better than sacrifices; and to hearken, better than to offer the fat of rams.

7. "Forasmuch, therefore, as thou hast rejected the word of the Lord, the Lord hath also rejected thee from being king over Israel. The Lord hath rent the kingdom from thee this day, and has given it to one who is better." Then Samuel departed, and beheld Saul no more till the day of his death. The rejection of Saul teaches us that disobedience to the voice of God is visited with severe chastisements.

QUESTIONS.

1. Whom did Samuel appoint as judges when he was grown old? What did the ancients ask Samuel to give them? Was their request pleasing to Samuel? What did the Lord tell Samuel to do? 2. Why did Saul come to the place where Samuel dwelt? What had God told Samuel the day before? What did Samuel tell Saul, on meeting him in the midst of the city? What did Samuel do next morning? 3. What happened when Samuel assembled the people? 4. What was Saul told to do to the people of Amalec? 5. How did Saul deal with common people, and with the flocks of little value? How with the king and the best flocks and herds? What did Saul erect in memory of his victory? 6. What did Saul say when Samuel came to the camp? What did Samuel answer? How did Saul excuse himself? What did Samuel say, being angry? 7. For what reason was Saul rejected? What does the rejection of Saul teach us?

CHAPTER L.

David, the Young Shepherd.

There is no peace to the wicked, saith the Lord.—*Is. 48, 22.*

SAMUEL loved Saul, and mourned for him because the Lord had rejected him. One day the Lord said to Samuel: "How long wilt thou mourn for Saul, whom I have rejected? Fill thy horn with oil, and come, that I may send thee to Isai, the Bethlehemite; for I have provided me a king among his sons."

2. So Samuel went to Bethlehem, and took with him a victim, and called Isai and his sons to partake of the sacrifice. Now, when Eliab, the eldest son, had come forward, who was of a high stature, the Lord said to Samuel: "Look not on his

SAMUEL ANOINTING DAVID.

countenance; for man seeth those things that appear, but the Lord seeth the heart."

3. Isai then called in his other sons, one by one, six in number. When Samuel had seen them all he said: "The Lord has not chosen any one of these. Are here all thy sons?" Isai replied: "There remaineth yet a young one, who keepeth the sheep." Samuel hastened to answer: "Send and fetch him; for we will not sit down till he come hither."

4. Now, when David came in he was beautiful to behold,

and of a comely face; and the Lord said: "Arise, and anoint him, for this is he." Then Samuel, taking the horn of oil, anointed him in the midst of his brethren. Immediately the spirit of the Lord came upon David, and remained with him.

5. But the spirit of the Lord departed from Saul, and an evil spirit troubled him. Wherefore the servants of Saul said to him: "Let our lord give orders, and we will seek out a man skillful in playing on the harp, that, when the evil spirit is upon thee, he may play with his hand, and thou mayest bear it more easily."

6. When the servants saw that this counsel was pleasing to the eyes of Saul, one of them added: "Behold, I have seen the son of Isai—a skillful player, and a man fit for war, and prudent in his words, and a comely person." Thereupon David was sent for. And whenever the evil spirit was upon Saul, David took his harp and played with his hand; and Saul was refreshed and better, for the evil spirit departed from him.

QUESTIONS.

1. What did the Lord say to Samuel, who mourned for Saul? What did Samuel do when he went to Bethlehem? 2. Which of Isai's sons came forward first? What did the Lord say to Samuel with regard to Eliab? 3. What did Isai then do? What did Samuel tell Isai? What did he ask him? What did Isai reply? 4. What did Samuel hasten to answer? What happened when David came? What came upon David? 5. From whom did the spirit of the Lord depart? What took possession of Saul? What did his servants tell him? 6. What did one of them add? Whenever the evil spirit troubled Saul, what did David do? What was the result?

CHAPTER LI.

David Fights With and Slays Goliath.

Humiliation followeth the proud, and glory shall uphold the humble of spirit.—*Prov. 29, 23.*

THE Philistines again took the field against the Israelites, and posted themselves on one mountain, and the Israelites were on another. And behold, there was in the camp of the Philistines a giant named Goliath. He was not only much taller than any other man, but his strength was in proportion to his size. He had a brazen helmet on his head, and was clothed in scaly armor of enormous weight.

2. He had greaves of brass on his legs, and a brazen shield on his shoulder, and the staff of his spear was like a weaver's beam. This giant, clad in armor from head to foot, came daily out, morning and evening, from the Philistine camp, and challenged any one of the Israelites to meet him in single combat, saying: "Give me a man, and let him fight with me hand to hand. If he be able to kill me, we will be servants to you; but if I prevail, and kill him, you shall serve us."

3. This went on for forty days, and there was no one found in all Israel to accept the challenge of Goliath. Hence Saul and the Israelites were in great terror and confusion because of Goliath and his proud boasting that he could find no man of Israel to fight him. Now David, after his three eldest brothers had gone out with Saul to battle, had returned to his father's house.

4. One day his father told him to take bread and go to the camp, and see how it fared with his brothers. Whilst David was conversing with the people, Goliath came out, as usual, from the Philistine camp, and repeated his insulting and contemptuous challenge. Full of surprise, David asked: "What shall be given to the man that slayeth this Philistine, who defieth the army of the living God?" Now, when Eliab, his eldest brother, heard that David was asking such questions of the soldiers, he grew angry, and said: "Why camest thou hither? Why didst thou leave those few sheep in the desert? I know thy pride, and that thou camest down to see the battle."

5. However, these words were reported to Saul, who sent for David and said to him: "Thou art not able to withstand this Philistine; for thou art but a boy, and he is a warrior." But David answered: "Let no man be dismayed. I, thy servant, will go and fight against the Philistine.

6. "For thy servant kept his father's sheep, and there came a lion and a bear and took a ram out of the midst of the flock. And I pursued after them and struck them; and they rose up against me, and I caught them by the throat, and I strangled and killed them. I will go now and take away the reproach of the people. The Lord, who delivered me out of the paws of the lion and the bear, will deliver me out of the hand of this Philistine."

7. At last Saul consented, and said: "Go, and the Lord be with thee." Saul then clothed David with his own armor, and put a helmet of brass on his head, and armed him with a coat of mail. But David, unused to wear armor, could not move freely under its weight, and, therefore, he laid it aside.

8. Then he took his staff, which he had always in his hands, and chose five smooth stones from the brook, and put them in the shepherd's scrip which he had with him; and taking a sling in his hand, he went forth to meet the Philistine.

9. When Goliath drew near and beheld David coming on, he despised him, and said: "Am I a dog, that thou comest to me with a staff?" Then, cursing David by his gods, he added: "Come to me, and I will give thy flesh to the birds of the air, and the beasts of the earth." David answered: "Thou comest to me with a sword, and with a spear, and with a shield; but I come to thee in the name of the Lord of Hosts whom thou hast defied. I will slay thee and take away thy head from thee, that all may know that there is a God in Israel."

10. Meanwhile, the Philistine arose, advanced and made ready for the fight; David, on his part, making haste, ran up to meet the giant. While running, he quickly took a stone from his scrip, laid it in his sling, and fetching it a few times about, he aimed and struck Goliath so violently in the forehead that he reeled and fell on his face upon the earth. Then David, rushing up, and taking Goliath's sword from its scabbard, cut off his head.

11. The Philistines, seeing that their champion was dead,

were seized with fear and fled. But the Israelites, following after, slew a great number of them, and took possession of their camp.

QUESTIONS.

1. Who again took the field against the Israelites? What remarkable person was in the camp of the Philistines? How was Goliath armed? 2. What did Goliath do every morning and evening? What did he propose? 3. How long did this go on? Was any one found in Israel to accept the challenge. How did Saul and the Israelites feel? Who was sent by his father to the camp to see his brothers? 4. What happened while David was conversing with the people? What did David ask, in surprise? What did Eliab say to David? 5. What did Saul do, hearing the words of David? What did Saul say to David? 6. After David had heard all this, what did he say? 7. What did Saul then say to David? With what did Saul then clothe David? What did David lay aside? 8. What did he do then? 9. What did Goliath do when David drew near? What did he say to him? What did David answer? 10. When Goliath was advancing towards David, what did the young man do? 11. What did the Philistines do, seeing that their champion was dead? What did the Israelites do?

CHAPTER LII.

Friendship of Jonathan and David.

Nothing can be compared to a faithful friend, and no weight of gold and silver is able to countervail the goodness of his fidelity.—*Ecclus. 6, 15.*

WHEN David returned from the slaying of the Philistine, Saul called for him and asked: "Young man, of what family art thou?" Then David related all about his family and about himself. Now, Jonathan, the eldest son of Saul, was standing by, and listened to the words of David; and when David had made an end of speaking, Jonathan began to love him as his own soul. Now, there was a custom for friends to exchange garments; so Jonathan took his coat and gave it to David. He took his sword, and his bow, and his girdle, and gave them to David.

2. Now, when David returned home with Saul, after hav-

ing slain Goliath, the women came out from all the cities of Israel, with flutes and cymbals, and they sang: "Saul slew his thousands, and David his ten thousands." Hearing this, Saul was angry, and ever after regarded David as a rival. Next day Saul was again troubled by the evil spirit, and, whilst David played the harp before him, he threw a spear at David, hoping to nail him to the wall.

3. David, however, stepped aside and avoided the blow. Some time after, David was appointed by Saul captain over a thousand men. He was, moreover, promised Michol, the king's daughter, in marriage, if he killed a hundred Philistines. By this proposal Saul hoped to get rid of David, thinking that he would never be able to fulfill the conditions, but that he would be slain by the Philistines.

4. Saul, however, was disappointed, for David slew two hundred of the enemy, and thereby gained the affection of the whole people. This unexpected success of David enraged Saul more than ever. Blinded by passion, he ordered Jonathan, his son, to kill David.

5. But Jonathan, knowing David's innocence and virtue, and loving him exceedingly, gave warning to him, and said: "My father seeketh to kill thee; wherefore look to thyself, and abide in a secret place, and thou shalt be hid." David listened to this advice, and remained in the fields.

6. One day, however, when Saul was in a better humor than usual, Jonathan said to him: "Sin not, O king, against thy servant David, because he hath not sinned against thee, and his works are very good towards thee. Why, therefore, wilt thou sin against innocent blood?"

7. Saul was appeased by these words of Jonathan, and swore that David should not be slain. And Jonathan brought David again into his father's presence, and Saul was gracious to him as he had been before. At this time, however, war was renewed against the Philistines, and David went out against them, and defeated them with great slaughter.

8. Then the evil spirit came back upon Saul, who tried to pierce David with his spear as he played upon the harp; but David warded off the blow, and fled. Jonathan, however, took occasion once again to speak to his father in behalf of David. But Saul was angry, and blamed his son for his affection for the son of Isai, who was supplanting him with the people.

9. He told Jonathan that so long as David lived he could have no hope of ascending the throne. "Therefore, now presently send and fetch him to me, for he is the son of death." Jonathan asked: "Why shall he die? What hath he done?" And Saul, being enraged at Jonathan, took his spear to strike him. But Jonathan escaped, and fled to David's hiding-place, in order to warn him against returning to the court. The two friends then embraced each other, wept together, and, before parting, renewed their vow of friendship, in the name of God.

QUESTIONS.

1. What did Saul ask David after he had slain the Philistines? What is said of Jonathan, who stood by listening to David? What did Jonathan give to David? 2. When David was returning home with Saul, what did the women do? What did they cry out? How did Saul ever after regard David? What did Saul do next day, when the evil spirit came upon him? 3. To what office was David, sometime after, appointed by Saul? What was he, moreover, promised? On what condition? What did Saul hope to do by this proposal? 4. Was Saul disappointed? What did Saul, blinded by passion, order his son Jonathan to do? 5. What had Jonathan to say to David? What did David then do? 6. What did Jonathan one day say to his father? 7. Was Saul appeased by these words? What did he swear? Against whom was war renewed? Who went out against them and defeated them with great slaughter? 8. When the evil spirit came again upon Saul, what did he try to do? Who took occasion to speak again to Saul in behalf of David? For what did Saul, being angry, blame his son? 9. What did he tell Jonathan? What did Jonathan ask? What did Saul do, being enraged? Whither did Jonathan fly? What did the two friends do?

CHAPTER LIII.

David's Noble Conduct towards Saul.

Rejoice not at the death of thy enemy.—*Ecclus. 8, 8.*

DAVID, seeing that he could no longer live in safety near Saul, fled to the mountains of Juda. Even there death threatened him on every side, but his courage never forsook him. He consoled himself with the thought that he who places himself under the protection of God is in safety everywhere, and has nothing to fear. His trust in God was rewarded.

2. Now, the men of Ziph came to Saul and said: "Behold, David is hid in the hill which is over against the wilderness." Immediately Saul arose, having with him three thousand chosen men, and encamped in the way of the wilderness. As soon as David heard that Saul had come after him into the desert, he sent out spies to see where the king had pitched his tents. David, on learning where Saul was, arose and came secretly to the camp of his enemy.

3. And David said to his followers: "Who will go down with me into the camp of Saul?" Abisai answered: "I will go with thee." So David and Abisai came upon the tents by night, and found Saul sleeping on his couch, and his spear fixed in the ground near his head. Moreover, all the soldiers were sleeping round about. And Abisai spoke to David: "Now, then, I will run thy enemy through with my spear, and there shall be no need of a second time." But David answered: "Kill him not; for who shall put forth his hand against the Lord's anointed, and remain guiltless? But now take the spear which is at his head, and the cup of water, and let us go."

4. So they took the spear and the cup of water, and went away. And no man saw it, or knew it, or awaked; for a deep sleep from the Lord was fallen upon them. They both

went on till they came to the other side, and stood on a hill afar off. There David called aloud to Abner, the captain of Saul's army, and said: "Wilt thou not answer, Abner? Art not thou a man? Why, then hast thou not kept the lord thy king? And now, where is the king's spear, and the cup of water which was at his head?"

5. At these words Saul awoke from his sleep, and cried out: "Is this thy voice, my son David?" And David answered: "It is my voice, my lord the king. Wherefore doth my lord persecute his servant? What have I done?" Saul, feeling his own injustice, exclaimed: "I have sinned. Return, my son David, for I will no more do thee harm, because my life has been precious in thy eyes this day. Blessed art thou, my son David." Then they parted in peace.

6. A short time after this there was a battle fought between the Israelites and the Philistines on Mount Gelboe. A great number of the Israelites were slain, and amongst them the three sons of Saul. At last the whole weight of the fight turned upon Saul; the archers overtook him and wounded him grievously.

7. Seeing himself surrounded by the enemy, who wished to take him alive, he drew his sword and fell upon it. David was thus delivered from his mortal enemy; yet, so far from rejoicing at his death, when he heard the sad news he wept, and forgetting all the injuries he had received, he remembered only the good qualities of the king.

8. Yea, filled with sorrow, he rent his garments and wept, and cursed the mountain of Gelboe, whereon the king and his three sons had met their death. Then he lamented and made a dirge over Saul and Jonathan: "How are the valiant fallen! Tell it not in Geth; publish it not in the streets of Ascalon. They were swifter than eagles, stronger than lions. I grieve for thee, my brother Jonathan, exceeding amiable. As the mother loveth her only son, so I did love thee." To forgive our enemies is a duty; and those that do not forgive cannot be saved. Yet we must admire the virtue

of David, who not only forgave, but loved his enemy tenderly.

QUESTIONS.

1. What did David do, seeing that he could no longer live in safety near Saul? With what thought did he console himself amid the dangers which even there threatened him? 2. What did the men of Ziph say to Saul? What did Saul then do? 3. What did David do, having heard of his coming? What did David do when he knew where Saul was? What did David say to his followers? What did Abisai say to David? In what condition did they find Saul and his people? What did Abisai propose to do? What did David answer? 4. How did David act? What did he command Abisai to do? What did David call out, having reached an opposite mountain? 5. What did Saul cry out on awaking from his sleep? What did David answer? What did Saul then say? 6. What happened a short time after this? Who fell amongst the great number of Israelites that were slain? What happened to Saul? 7. Was David glad to be thus delivered from his mortal enemy? 8. How did he show his sorrow? What did he say of Saul and Jonathan? How did he grieve for Jonathan? What virtue must we admire in David?

THE GREATNESS OF THE PEOPLE OF ISRAEL FROM THE BEGINNING OF THE REIGN OF DAVID TO THAT OF ROBOAM.

From the Year 1055 to 975 B. C.

CHAPTER LIV.

David's Piety.—His Zeal for God's Glory.

I will praise the name of God with a canticle; and I will magnify Him with praise.—*Ps. 68, 31.*

AFTER the death of Saul, David was chosen king. He established his court in Jerusalem, where he became renowned for his great valor. He defeated the Philistines and many other nations. His reign was glorious, because he governed his people with justice and clemency. As he feared God, he never imposed on his people any but just and righteous laws.

2. The counselors whom he chose to aid him in the government of his kingdom were not flatterers, but men of wisdom and virtue, whose advice was always founded on reason and justice. The promotion of God's glory was the primary object of all their plans and views. Near Jerusalem was Mount Sion, on which David erected a splendid tabernacle for the ark of the covenant.

DAVID PLAYING BEFORE THE ARK.

3. When the tabernacle was completed, he caused the ark to be carried in triumph to Mount Sion. The procession was very grand, comprising all the princes of Israel in purple robes, the priests in their rich garments, and thirty thousand armed men. The sound of all manner of musical instruments made the procession still more imposing. David himself went before the ark playing on the harp, and singing: "Lord, who shall dwell in Thy tabernacle, or who shall rest in Thy holy hill?"

4. At every few paces taken by the Levites who carried the ark, an ox and a ram were sacrificed to the Lord. And when the ark had been placed in its destined position, a great number of victims were offered. David then divided the priests into several classes, who were in turn to officiate in the divine worship. He established a like order amongst the Levites, four thousand of whom were chosen to sing the praises of the Most High.

QUESTIONS.

1. After the death of Saul, who was chosen king? Where did David establish his court? Whom did he defeat? Why was David's reign glorious? 2. What manner of men were his counselors? What was the primary object of all their plans? Where did David erect a splendid tabernacle for the ark of the covenant? 3. What did he cause to be done when the tabernacle was completed? What did the procession comprise? What made it still more imposing? Who went before the ark playing on the harp? What did he sing? At every few paces taken by the Levites who carried the ark, what was sacrificed? What was done when the ark had been placed in its destined position? What did David then do? How many Levites were chosen to sing the praises of the Most High?

CHAPTER LV.

The Prophecies of David.

Behold, the days come, saith the Lord; and I will raise up to David a just branch; and a king shall reign; and shall be wise; and shall execute judgment and justice in the earth.—*Jer. 23, 5.*

DAVID, as he had done when only a simple shepherd boy, composed psalms and canticles in honor of the Most High, and conducted himself, in all things, according to the holy will of God. Wherefore the Lord blessed him, and not only favored all his undertakings, but promised him that one of his descendants should rule the whole world, and sit upon a throne more lasting than the heavens.

2. He furthermore endowed him with the gift of proph-

ecy. He expresses in lofty and sublime language the eternal relation existing between the Father and the Son: "Thou art my son, this day have I begotten thee." He foreshows the boundless dominion which was to be the inheritance of the Redeemer, and the peaceful character of his reign. "I will give Thee the Gentiles for Thy inheritance, and the utmost parts of the earth for Thy possession. In His days shall justice spring up, and the abundance of peace."

3. He sees, in his prophetic visions, the Ethiopians falling down before the great Ruler, the Prince of Peace, and beholds His enemies prostrate at His feet. He sees the kings of Tharsis and of the Islands offering Him presents; the kings of the Arabians and of Saba bringing Him gifts. He foretells the future crucifixion, with all the sorrowful scenes and circumstances: "They have pierced my hands and my feet, they have numbered all my bones."

4. The gall and vinegar that were presented to the Divine victim suffering and dying on the cross; the lance that pierced His most sacred heart; the nails that held Him fastened to the cross; all these are mentioned by David in his psalms. Death overcome, the grave robbed of its prey, the earthquake that rent the rocks of Calvary, and the glory of the resurrection, were all and each familiar to the mind of the royal prophet.

5. He sees in the distant future the brightness of the ascension. He calls upon the eternal gates to be lifted up, that the triumphant Conqueror of sin and death may take possession of His everlasting throne in heaven. David, the progenitor, or forefather of Jesus Christ, who is Himself called the Son of David, was a figure of the Redeemer by the place of his birth, Bethlehem, by the obscurity and lowliness of his early years, by the victories he obtained over the enemies of the people of God, and also by his twofold character of king and prophet.

QUESTIONS.

1. What did David do in honor of the Most High? How did he conduct himself? What did the Lord, therefore, do? What did He promise David? 2. With what did He, furthermore, endow him? What does David express in lofty and sublime language? What does he fore-show? 3. What does he see in his prophetic visions? What is like-wise foreseen by David? 4. What are all mentioned by David in his psalms? What are all and each familiar to the mind of the royal prophet? What does he see in the distant future? Of whom was David the progenitor? Who is called the Son of David? Of whom was David a figure? Why was he a figure of Christ?

CHAPTER LVI.

Revolt and Punishment of Absalom.

Have mercy on me, O God, according to Thy great mercy, and according to the multitude of Thy tender mercies blot out my iniquity.—*Ps. 50, 1, 2.*

EVEN David was not sufficiently on his guard against temptations. He unhappily fell into two grievous sins. He took to himself Bethsabee, the wife of Urias, one of his captains, and in order to conceal his crime he caused Urias himself to be slain by exposing him for that purpose in the front of the battle. The Lord sent the prophet Nathan to reproach David with his double crime. David, filled with contrition, confessed his fault and asked pardon of the Lord. He then composed the seven penitential psalms, which ever since have been the consolation of all truly penitent sinners.

2. The Lord seeing the sorrow of David, ordered Nathan to tell him that his sin was forgiven, but that, nevertheless, he must undergo many temporal punishments, and that the child that was about to be born to him should die. David, humbling himself before God, willingly accepted this and many other punishments inflicted upon him, and added, on his own part, the most severe penance in expiation of his sins.

3. The most terrible chastisement inflicted on David was
the ingratitude of his son Absalom. Now Absalom was endowed with rare beauty of person, so that from the top of
his head to the sole of his foot there was no blemish in him.
His hair was long and very beautiful. And David gave
Absalom a princely retinue of chariots and horsemen, and a
guard of young men to accompany him everywhere.

4. Absalom was wont to rise early in the morning and
stand at the gate of the palace, and when any man presented
himself to ask justice of the king, he kindly inquired what
complaint he had to make, and on hearing it always replied:
"Thy words seem good and just to me; but there is no one
appointed by the king to hear thy cause." In this manner
he made friends for himself among the people, by wrongfully blaming his father.

5. Sometimes he would exclaim in the hearing of these
people: "Oh, that they would make me judge over the land,
that all who have business might come to me, that I might
do them justice." Moreover, when any man came to salute
him, he put forth his hand, and took him and kissed him.
Thus he enticed the hearts of the men of Israel.

6. When he thought he had gained over all the men of Israel
to his side, he asked his father to let him go to Hebron in ful-
fillment of a vow. David, suspecting no evil, allowed his son to
depart. And when Absalom had reached Hebron he sent
messengers to all the tribes of Israel, telling them that when
they heard the sound of a trumpet they should say: "Absalom
reigneth in Hebron." And it came to pass that many of the
people, not knowing his treachery, followed Absalom.

7. When David heard of Absalom's revolt he determined
to leave the city, lest the citizens should suffer on his account.
And having left the city with his attendants, he came to the
brook Cedron, his feet bare and his head veiled. And crossing the brook, he came to Mount Olivet, where he wept for
the guilt of his unnatural son, and for his own sins. And on

the side of Mount Olivet he was met by a man named Semei, of the family of Saul, who threw stones and earth at David, and cursed him: "Come out, come out, thou man of blood."

8. Abisai, full of wrath, cried out: "Why should this dead dog curse my lord, the king? I will go and cut off his head." But David answered: "Behold, my own son seeketh my life; how much more one of the house of Saul. Perhaps the Lord may look upon my affliction and render me good for the cursing of this day." He saw the hand of God in this new trial.

9. Absalom having resolved to destroy David and his army, went in pursuit of them. David, however, reviewed his men and placed brave captains in command, and said that he would himself march at their head. But this his men would not permit, saying that if ten thousand of them fell in battle they would not despair; but that if he perished, all was lost.

10. The king remained, therefore, in the city of Mahanaim, but he commanded Joab and his other officers, saying: "Spare me the boy Absalom." The battle was fought in the midst of a great wood, and Absalom's army was cut to pieces. He himself fled, but could not escape from divine justice, which pursues the wicked wherever they go. Having mounted a mule, he endeavored to escape through the forest, but his long hair having become entangled in a tree, he remained hanging from the branch, while his mule passed on.

11. And word was brought to Joab, general of the king's army. Joab, taking three javelins, went to the place where Absalom was hanging from the tree, and with his javelins pierced the ungrateful, unnatural heart of the king's son. Absalom still breathed and struggled for life, when some of Joab's soldiers, running up, slew him with their swords. They then took Absalom's body, and casting it into a deep pit in the forest, piled over it a large heap of stones.

12. A herald was sent to David with news of Absalom's defeat. David. with the anxiety of a loving father, asked:

"Is Absalom safe?" When told that Absalom was dead the king refused all comfort, and going up into a high chamber, mourned his ungrateful son for many days. "Absalom, my son!" he cried, "my son Absalom, who would grant me that I might die for thee, Absalom, my son, my son Absalom!"

13. The people of Jerusalem, hearing of David's victory, went out to meet him, and carried him in triumph into the city. David, in his crossing the brook Cedron in sorrow and tribulation, in his ascent of Mount Olivet, in his patient forbearance when outraged and insulted by Semei, and his triumphant entry into Jerusalem, presents a very striking figure of Christ.

QUESTIONS.

1. Into what did David unhappily fall? What were these sins? Whom did the Lord send to reproach him for his sins? What did David do? 2. What did the Lord, seeing David's sorrow for his sins, order Nathan to tell him? What did David do, humbling himself before God? What did he then compose? 3. What was the most terrible chastisement inflicted on David? With what was Absalom endowed? What did David give Absalom? 4. What was Absalom wont to do? 5. What would he sometimes exclaim in the hearing of these people? 6. When Absalom thought he had gained all the men of Israel, what did he ask his father to let him do? What did Absalom do when he reached Hebron? 7. When David heard of Absalom's revolt, what did he determine to do? What brook did he cross? Where did he come to? By whom was he met there? 8. What did Abisai ask permission to do? What did David tell Abisai? 9. What did Absalom do, having resolved to destroy David and his army? What did David say he would do? What did his men say? 10. What did the king command Joab and his officers to do? What happened to Absalom's army? What happened to himself? 11. What did Joab do when word was brought to him? What was done with Absalom's body? 12. What did David ask when he heard of Absalom's defeat? What did he do when told that Absalom was dead? 13. What did the people of Jerusalem do when they heard of David's victory? In what circumstances of his life does David present a striking figure of Christ?

CHAPTER LVII.

David's Last Words.—His Death.

Precious in the sight of the Lord is the death of His saints.—*Ps. 115, 15.*

DAVID was thirty years old when he ascended the throne of Israel, and he reigned forty years in honor and glory. When the time of his death drew near, he gathered together the princes of Israel, and told them that he had intended to build a house to the Lord, and had prepared all the materials for a new temple; but that the Lord had not allowed him to carry out his plan, because he had shed much blood in his many battles.

2. The building of the temple was reserved for Solomon, his son, whose kingdom should be great and powerful if he would be faithful to the commandments of God. David therefore, exhorted his son to serve God with a good will, because the Lord sounds the depths of hearts and penetrates the thoughts of men. "If thou seek Him," said David, "thou shalt find Him; but if thou forsake Him, He will cast thee off forever."

3. David then gave to his son gold and silver for the vessels of the sanctuary, together with the plan of the temple and its precincts, and said to him: "All these things came to me written by the hand of the Lord. Act like a man, take courage and fear not; for the Lord my God will be with thee, nor forsake thee till thou hast finished the house of the Lord." Then addressing the assembled princes, David said: "The work is great; for a house is prepared not for man, but for God. Now, if any man is willing to offer, let him fill his hand to-day, and offer what he pleaseth to the Lord." And the princes and the people joyfully brought their gifts for the temple of the Lord.

4. And David, rejoicing, exclaimed: "Blessed art Thou,

O Lord, the God of Israel, our Father from eternity to eternity. All things are Thine, and we have given Thee what we received of Thy hand. O Lord, keep forever this will of their heart, and let this mind remain always for the worship of Thee; and give to Solomon, my son, a perfect heart, that he may keep Thy commandments." Having thus spoken, David slept in peace. He was buried in Sion.

QUESTIONS.

1. How old was David when he ascended the throne of Israel? How long did he reign? What did he do when his death drew near? What did he tell the princes of Israel? 2. For whom was the building of the temple reserved? What did David exhort his son to do? Why so? 3. What did David then give to his son? What did he say to him? How did David address the assembly? 4. What did David, rejoicing, say? Having thus spoken, what followed?

CHAPTER LVIII.

Solomon's Prayer.—His Wisdom.

To fear God is the fullness of wisdom, and fullness is from the fruits thereof.—*Ecclus. 1, 20.*

AFTER the death of David, Solomon ascended the throne. He loved the Lord, and walked in the ways of David, his father. The Lord appeared to him in a dream by night, and told him to ask any favor he wished, and that it would be granted. Solomon answered: "O Lord God. Thou hast made Thy servant king instead of David, my father, and I am but a child. Give, therefore, to Thy servant an understanding heart to judge Thy people, and discern between good and evil."

2. The Lord was pleased with his petition, and He said to him: "Because thou hast asked this thing, and hast not asked for thyself long life, nor riches, nor the lives of thy enemies, but hast asked for thyself wisdom to discern judgment, behold! I have done for thee according to thy words,

and have given thee a wise and understanding heart, inso-much that there hath been no one like thee before thee, nor shall arise after thee.

3. "Yea, and the things, also, which thou didst not ask, I have given thee: riches and glory, so that no one hath been like thee among the kings in all days heretofore. And if thou wilt walk in My ways, and keep My precepts and My

SOLOMON'S JUDGMENT.

commandments, as thy father walked, I will lengthen thy days." And Solomon became renowned for wisdom and for power and glory.

4. On one occasion two women came to Solomon, asking him to decide their dispute. The first woman said: "We were living alone in a house, only we two. Now, I had a child and she had a child. And in the night, when she was asleep, she overlaid her child and it died.

5. "And, rising in the dead time of the night, she took my

child, while I, thy handmaid, was asleep, and laid her dead child in my bosom. When I arose in the morning, behold, my child was dead; but, considering him more diligently when it was clear day, I found that it was not mine." But the second woman answered: "It is not so as thou sayest, but thy child is dead and mine is alive."

6. But the first woman insisted that the living child was hers, and so they disputed before the king. Then Solomon ordered a sword to be brought to him, and when it was brought he said: "Divide the living child in two, and give half to the one and half to the other." Hearing this, the woman whose child was alive, being moved to pity, cried out in terror: "I beseech thee, my lord, give her the child alive, and do not kill it." But the other said: "Let it be neither mine nor thine, but divide it."

7. Then the king commanded the child to be given to her who would rather give it up to another than have it killed, knowing that she must be its mother. The report of this judgment having gone abroad, the people all feared the king, and knew that the wisdom of God was in him. How necessary it is that kings and rulers should examine all cases brought before them in a spirit of justice and of wisdom!

QUESTIONS.

1. After the death of David, who ascended the throne? Who appeared to him in a dream? What did the Lord tell him in that dream? What did Solomon answer? 2. Was the Lord pleased with his petition? What did the Lord say? 3. For what did Solomon become renowned? 4. Who came on one occasion to Solomon, asking him to decide a dispute? What did the first woman say? 5. What other circumstance did the first woman relate? What did the second woman answer? 6. What did the first woman still insist? What did Solomon order? What did the woman, whose child was alive, cry out in terror? What did the other say? 7. What did the king then command? When the report of this judgment went abroad, what was the result?

CHAPTER LIX.

The Building and Consecration of the Temple.

How lovely are Thy tabernacles, O Lord of Hosts.—*Ps. 83, 2.*

IN the fourth year of his reign Solomon began to build the temple of the Lord on Mount Moria, in Jerusalem. He had ten thousand men employed cutting cedars on Mount Lebanon. Seventy thousand were engaged in carrying the materials to the site of the temple. Eighty thousand were hewing stones, while three thousand three hundred were employed as overseers of the work.

2. The vast number of persons employed corresponded with the grandeur and magnificence of the house of God, the general plan of which was that of the tabernacle. In other respects, however, the tabernacle could not be compared with the temple, which was sixty cubits long, twenty cubits wide, and thirty cubits high. The house was built of stones, hewed and made ready, so that when it was in building, neither hammer nor any iron tool was heard. Then there were, besides, porches and galleries running all round it, and two large courts for the priests and the people.

3. The porch before the temple was twenty cubits in length and ten cubits in breadth. The inner walls were lined with planks of cedar, on which were carved cherubim and palm-trees and divers blooming flowers, all standing out, as it were, from the wall, so skillfully were they carved. All the furniture, including ten tables and ten candlesticks, was of the purest gold. The walls and floor of the Holy of Holies were covered with plates of fine gold, fastened by nails of gold.

4. When, after seven years, Solomon had finished the temple, he assembled all the ancients of Israel, with the princes of the tribes, to carry the Ark of the Covenant in triumph to the temple. And all the people marched before

the ark in an ecstasy of joy and religious fervor, making peace-offerings to the Lord at every step they took. The Levites played on the harp and cymbal and many other instruments of music, while a hundred and twenty priests sounded the trumpet.

5. And the multitude sang in one grand chorus: "Praise the Lord, for He is good, and His mercy endureth forever." Then the ark having arrived at the gates of the temple, only

SOLOMON PRAYING IN THE TEMPLE.

the priests who carried it entered in, and they brought it to the Holy of Holies, and the cherubim shaded it with their wings. And the majesty of God, in the form of a cloud, filled the temple, so that the priest could not stand to minister, because of the dazzling glory thereof.

6. Then Solomon, arrayed in his richest robes, fell on his knees before the altar of holocausts, and stretching out his hands, he said: "Lord God of Israel, there is no God like Thee in heaven or on earth. If heaven and the heaven of

heavens cannot contain Thee, how much less this house, which I have built! O Lord my God, hear the hymn and the prayer which Thy servant prayeth before Thee this day, that Thy eyes may be open upon this house night and day, that Thou mayest hearken to the prayer which Thy servant prayeth in this place to Thee. Mayest Thou hearken to Thy people when they pray in this place. Mayest Thou hear them and show them mercy."

7. Solomon's prayer being ended, fire fell from heaven and consumed the holocaust. Seeing this, the Israelites fell prostrate on the ground and adored the great God of heaven, who wrought such wonders before them, and they went away praising His awful name. The Lord appeared a second time to Solomon, and said: "I have heard thy prayer, and I have sanctified this house which thou hast built; and My eyes and My heart shall be always there."

8. With all its grandeur and magnificence, Solomon's temple was but a faint image of our temples in which Jesus Christ, true God and true man, dwells under the appearance of bread, pouring out upon us his most abundant graces.

QUESTIONS.

1. What did Solomon begin to do in the fourth year of his reign? Where did he build the temple? How many thousand men had he employed cutting on Mount Lebanon? How many were engaged in carrying the materials to the site of the temple? How many men were hewing stones? How many overseers were there? 2. What was the general plan of the temple? How long was the temple? How wide? How high? What were there besides? 3. With what were the inner walls lined? What were carved on them? With what were the walls and floor of the Holy of Holies covered? 4. What did Solomon do when, after seven years, he had finished the temple? What did the people do? What did the Levites do? and the priests? 5. What did the whole multitude sing in chorus? What was done when the ark arrived at the gates of the temple? Where did they place the ark? What then filled the temple? 6. What did Solomon then do? What did he say? 7. What happened when Solomon's prayer was ended? Seeing this, what did the Israelites do? What did the Lord say to Solomon when He appeared to him a second time? 8. Of what was Solomon's temple, with all its grandeur and magnificence, but a faint image?

CHAPTER LX.

Solomon's Magnificence.—His Sad End.

He that thinketh himself to stand, let him take heed lest he fall.—
I. Cor., 10, 12.

BESIDES the temple which he erected to the Lord, Solomon built for himself a palace of wonderful magnificence. His throne was of ivory, overlaid with the finest gold. It had six steps, and at the two ends of each step there stood a lion: six to the right and six to the left—in all, twelve lions. But the top of the throne was round, and had a large lion, well made, on either side. And Solomon made two hundred shields of the purest gold, and hung them in his palace.

2. All the vessels out of which the king drank were of gold, and all the furniture of his house was likewise of gold. In the days of Solomon there was no silver; no account was made of it, because the royal fleet brought from foreign countries riches of all kinds, and precious metals in abundance. Solomon built several new cities; he beautified and strengthened Jerusalem, so that, with few exceptions, it surpassed all the cities of that time in beauty and splendor.

3. And Solomon reigned from the Euphrates[1] to the confines of Egypt, and he was at peace with his neighbors on every side, and each man rested without fear under his own vine and fig-tree. Kings from far and near showed Solomon respect, and sent him presents. The queen of Saba came herself from her far-distant land to behold his magnificence and to hear the words of his wisdom. When she had seen and heard, her spirit failed, and she said to the king: "The report is true which I heard in my own country, but I would not believe. Blessed are thy servants who stand before thee and hear thy wisdom." Thus did

_____
[1] EUPHRATES (pr. U-fra'-tes), a great river of Asia.

King Solomon exceed all the kings of the earth in riches and in wisdom.

4. But glorious as was the beginning of Solomon's reign, its end was deplorable. Solomon was far advanced in life when his heart was corrupted by strange women; and that great king, hitherto so wise, became so blind and depraved that, in order to please these women, he offered incense to false gods, and built temples to them.

5. The Lord, being angry, said to Solomon: "Because thou hast done this, and hast not kept My covenant and My precepts, which I have commanded thee, I will divide and rend thy kingdom. Nevertheless, in thy days I will not do it for David, thy father's, sake; neither will I take away the whole kingdom, but I will give one tribe to thy son, for the sake of David, My servant, and for the sake of Jerusalem, which I have chosen."

6. Then secret revolt and sedition arose among the people, because Solomon, blinded as he was, had overtaxed and oppressed the people, to build palaces for the heathen women who had turned him away from God. Things were in this unhappy state when Solomon died, having reigned forty years; and he who had been a great and powerful king while he walked in the ways of David his father, died without honor, and, perhaps, without repentance. The sad end of Solomon teaches us that as long as we live we are liable to fall into sin, and that hence we should never lose sight of the fear of God, nor neglect to pray for perseverance. Solomon in his prosperity is a faint figure of Christ reigning gloriously in heaven.

QUESTIONS.

1. Besides the temple which he erected to the Lord, what did Solomon build? Of what was his throne? How many lions stood on each step of the throne? What did Solomon make of the purest gold? Of what were all the vessels and all the furniture of his house? 2. How was silver considered in the days of Solomon? Why so? What did Solomon build? What did he do to Jerusalem? 3. What was the extent of Solomon's kingdom? Was he at peace

with his neighbors? What did he receive from kings? Who came from her distant country to behold Solomon's magnificence and to hear his words of wisdom? What did the Queen of Saba say to Solomon? 4. Was the end of Solomon's reign as glorious as the beginning? How was Solomon's heart corrupted? What did he do to please these strange women? 5. What did the Lord tell Solomon that He would do? What did He promise to do for David's sake? 6. What then arose among the people? Why? How did Solomon die? What does the sad end of Solomon teach us? Of whom is Solomon in his prosperity a figure?

THIRD EPOCH.

Decline of the People of Israel. From the Time of Roboam to Jesus Christ.
(962 B. C.)

CHAPTER LXI.

Division of the Kingdom.

He that walketh with the wise, shall be wise; a friend of fools shall become like to them.—*Prov. 13, 20.*

AFTER the death of Solomon, all the people of Israel came to Roboam, his son, and said: "Thy father laid a grievous yoke upon us, do thou take off a little of his most heavy yoke, and we will serve thee." Roboam told them to come back on the third day and he would give them his answer. He then took counsel with the ancients of the people who had stood before Solomon, his father, as to what course he should pursue.

2. The ancients advised the king saying: "If thou wilt yield to this people and speak gentle words to them, they will be thy servants always." Roboam, not satisfied with this advice of the old men, betook himself to the young men who were his own companions, and asked what they would counsel him to do.

3. The young men who had been brought up with him said: "Thus shalt thou speak to this people: My father put a heavy yoke upon you, but I will add to your yoke; my father beat you with whips, but I will beat you with scorpions." When the people had returned on the third day, for an answer, Roboam spoke to them as the young men had advised.

4. Then the people, seeing that they had nothing to expect from their new king, began to say among themselves that Roboam was nothing to them. And ten of the tribes, throwing off his authority, chose for their king Jeroboam, who had been a servant of Solomon. Only the two tribes of Juda and Benjamin remained with Roboam. From that day forth the people of Israel were divided into two kingdoms, that of Juda and that of Israel.

5. Jerusalem continued to be the capital of Juda, and Samaria became afterwards the capital of Israel. But the effects of the separation went still farther; for Jeroboam, king of Israel, thought within himself that if the people continued to go up to Jerusalem to offer sacrifice to the Lord in the temple, their hearts would turn again to Roboam, and the kingdom of Israel would surely return to the house of David.

6. To avoid this danger he made two golden calves, which he placed at the two extremities of his kingdom—one at Dan, the other at Bethel—and told the people that they should not go up to Jerusalem to worship, for that these were the gods that had brought them out of Egypt. In this way he led the people into idolatry, for they repaired to the places pointed out to them by their king and worshiped the golden calves.

7. On the other hand, Roboam, king of Juda, who had seen with grief the defection of the ten tribes, was all his life making war on Jeroboam. This state of continued warfare was kept up by their successors on both sides, and more than once the aid of foreign nations was called in by one or the other. In this way did these wicked kings cause much sin and misery among their people.

8. Even the kings of Juda soon fell into idolatry, and the people, following their example, forgot the worship of the true God, and gave themselves up to all manner of wickedness. All this sin, misery, and ruin were partly the effects of Solomon's departure from the ways of justice: terrible

example of the ruin that sin brings on those who commit it, and even on their children after them.

QUESTIONS.

1. After the death of Solomon what did the people of Israel beseech Roboam, his son, to do? What did Roboam tell them? With whom did he then take counsel? 2. What did the ancients advise the king to do? Was Roboam satisfied with this advice? To whom did he betake himself? 3. What did the young men say? 4. What did the people, seeing that they had nothing to expect from their new king, begin to say among themselves? What did ten of the tribes do? What two tribes remained with Roboam? Into what two kingdoms were the people of Israel from that day divided? 5. What city continued to be the capital of Juda? What city was afterwards that of Israel? What other sad effect came of the separation? 6. To avoid this danger, what did Jeroboam do? Where did he place the two golden calves? What did he tell the people? 7. On the other hand, what did Roboam, king of Juda, grieved at the defection of the ten tribes, do all his life? What was kept up by their successors on both sides? Whose aid did they more than once call in? 8. Who fell into idolatry? What did their people do? To what did they give themselves up? What was partly the cause of all this sin and misery? Of what is it a terrible example?

DECLINE OF THE KINGDOM OF ISRAEL.

CHAPTER LXII.

God Raises up Prophets.—Mission of the Prophet Elias.

(907 B. C.)

The Lord is become a refuge for the poor: a helper in due time in tribulation.—*Ps. 9, 10.*

IN order to bring back the kings and the people to better sentiments, God raised up, at different times, holy persons, who are known as prophets. These prophets preached penance in a very impressive manner, and they proved the truth of their divine mission by working great miracles.

2. God revealed to them many future events. They predicted the principal circumstances of the birth, life, passion,

death and glory of the Messias. One of the most celebrated of the prophets was Elias. He lived in the reign of Achab, king of Israel. The king was very wicked. None of his predecessors had committed so many crimes as he.

3. He had married a Gentile woman named Jezabel; and he built a temple to Baal, and had consecrated to the service of that false god four hundred and fifty priests, whilst he had caused the priests of the Lord to be put to death. In a word, his intention seemed to be to destroy the true religion entirely among the ten tribes.

4. Elias, clad in a rough sheep-skin, and with a staff in his hand, presented himself before Achab and said: "As the Lord liveth, the God of Israel, in whose sight I stand, there shall not be dew nor rain these three years but according to the words of my mouth." Achab was very angry to hear these words of the prophet, and secretly resolved to put Elias to death.

5. Then the Lord, knowing the evil intention of the king, commanded Elias to go and conceal himself near the brook Carith, in the vicinity of the Jordan. The prophet obeyed, and behold, the ravens brought him bread or flesh every morning and every evening for many days; and he drank of the torrent.

6. Some time after, the brook ran dry, and the Lord commanded Elias to go to Sarepta, a city of the Sidonians. Elias went accordingly, and when he drew near the gate of the city he saw a woman gathering sticks, and he called her and said: "Give me a little water in a vessel that I may drink."

7. As the woman was going to fetch it, he called after her: "Bring me also a morsel of bread." She answered: "As the Lord thy God liveth, I have no bread, but only a handful of meal in a pot, and a little oil in a cruse; I am gathering two sticks that I may go in and dress it for me and my son, that we may eat and die."

8. The prophet assured her saying: "Fear not; but go and do as thou hast said; but first make for me of the same meal

a little hearth-cake. For thus said the Lord: 'The pot of meal shall not waste, nor the cruse of oil be diminished until the day wherein the Lord will give rain upon the earth'.''

9. The woman did as Elias told her and from that day forth she had meal in her pot and oil in her cruse, and knew no want, neither Elias, nor she, nor her son. Now, it happened some time after, that the son of the poor widow of Sarepta fell sick and died. She said to the prophet: "What have I done to thee, thou man of God? Hast thou come to me that my iniquities should be remembered?" Thereupon Elias took the child, and went into the upper chamber and laid it upon his own bed. Then he cried to the Lord: "O Lord, hast Thou also afflicted the widow with whom I am after a sort maintained?" Then he stretched himself and measured himself three times upon the child; and the soul of the boy returned and he revived.

10. Elias took the child and brought him down to his mother, and said: "Behold, thy son liveth." Full of joy and gratitude the woman exclaimed: "Now by this I know that thou art a man of God, and the word of the Lord in thy mouth is true." Elias, the grown man, stretching himself and measuring himself upon the small body of the dead child is a figure of the Incarnation, in which the Son of God so adapted himself to our human nature as to became man without ceasing to be God.

QUESTIONS.

1. Whom did God raise up at times, in order to bring back the kings and the people to better sentiments? What did these prophets preach? How did they prove the truth of their divine mission? 2. What did they predict? Who was one of the most celebrated of the prophets? In what reign did Elias live? 3. What great crimes had the king committed? 4. What did Elias say to Achab when he presented himself before him? What did Achab secretly resolve? 5. What did the Lord then command Elias to do? How was Elias fed in the wilderness? 6. Some time after, when the brook ran dry, whither did the Lord command Elias to go? Whom

did he see as he drew near the gate of the city? What did he ask the woman to do? 7. What did the prophet call after her when she was going to fetch the water? What did the woman answer? 8. What did the prophet tell her? What did he then command her to do? Telling her what? 9. Did the woman obey? What followed? Some time after this, who fell sick and died? What did the woman say to Elias? What did Elias do? What did he pray? Did the Lord hear his prayer? 10. What did the woman, full of joy and gratitude, say to Elias? How is the manner in which Elias raised the child to life a figure of the Incarnation?

CHAPTER LXIII.

The Sacrifice of Elias.

Thou shalt fear the Lord thy God, and shalt serve Him
only.—*Deut. 6, 13.*

AFTER the earth had remained three years and six months without rain or dew, the Lord spoke to Elias: "Go and show thyself to Achab, that I may give rain upon the face of the earth." The prophet obeyed. When Achab saw him he said: "Art thou he that troublest Israel?" The prophet answered: "I have not troubled Israel, but thou and thy father's house, who have forsaken the commandments of the Lord and have followed Baalim."

2. "Nevertheless, send now and gather unto me all Israel unto Mount Carmel, and the prophets of Baal, four hundred and fifty, and the prophets of the groves, four hundred." Achab obeyed, being afraid to do otherwise, on account of the famine that was everywhere, and he went himself to the mountain. Then Elias spoke to the people of Israel, saying: "How long do you halt between two sides? If the Lord be God, follow Him; but if Baal, then follow him.

3. The people feeling the justice of his reproach, made no answer. They were ashamed and afraid. Elias then added: "I only remain a prophet of the Lord, but the prophets of Baal are four hundred and fifty men. Let two bullocks be given us; and let them choose one bullock for themselves,

and cut it in pieces, but put no fire under; and I will dress the other bullock, and lay it on wood, and put no fire under it.

4. "Call ye on the names of your gods, and I will call on the name of my Lord, and the God that shall answer by fire, let Him be the God." All the people answered: "A very good proposal." Then the priests of Baal, clad in their richest garments and crowned with laurel, took an ox, and slew him.

5. Then they erected an altar, placed the dead ox upon it, and danced around it crying out: "Baal, hear us." This they did from morning until noon, but no fire came to consume their sacrifice. Then Elias, mocking them, called out: "Cry with a louder voice; for he is a god, and perhaps he is talking with some one, or on a journey, or is asleep and must be awaked."

6. Then they began to cry louder than ever, hacking their bodies with knives, as they were accustomed to do, until they were covered with blood. This they kept up till evening, but all in vain. Then Elias told the people to come to him. And he erected an altar to the Lord; took twelve stones, and laid the wood in order upon them, then placed the ox, which had been cut in pieces, upon the wood.

7. He then poured water upon the victim till it ran down on every side and filled the trench around the altar. This being done, he said: "O Lord God, show this day that Thou art the God of Israel, and I, Thy servant, and that according to Thy commandment, I have done all these things. Hear me, O Lord, hear me; that this people may learn that Thou art the Lord God, and that Thou hast turned their hearts again."

8. That instant fire came down from heaven and consumed the holocaust, the wood, the stones, and the water in the trench. The people having witnessed this prodigy, fell on their faces, exclaiming: "The Lord He is God! The Lord He is God!" And the prophet, retiring from the multi-

tude, went up alone to the top of the mountain, where he prostrated himself before the Lord in praise and thanksgiving.

9. Then he besought the Lord to refresh the earth with water. And behold a little cloud arose from the sea, no bigger than the foot of a man, and it spread itself gradually over the heavens, and rain fell in abundance. The land of Israel, suffering from the long drought, was a figure of the

ELIAS OFFERING SACRIFICE.

great spiritual drought from which the whole world suffered before the coming of Christ. Elias bidding the heavens to rain, was a figure of Christ opening the fountains of grace to a perishing world.

10. The rain itself, which gave a new life to the earth, is a type of the grace of God which renews the soul of the converted sinner.

QUESTIONS.

1. What did the Lord say to Elias after the earth had remained three years and six months without rain? What did Achab say

when he saw Elias? What did the prophet answer? 2. What did Achab do? What did Elias say to the people of Israel? What did Elias add? 3 and 4. Were the people satisfied with his proposal? 5. What did the priests of Baal then do? What did they cry out? Did fire come to consume their sacrifice? What did Elias, mocking them, call out? 6. What did the priests of Baal then do? What did Elias then do? 7. This being done, what did the prophet say, raising his hands and eyes to heaven? 8. What came down instantly from heaven? What did the people exclaim, falling on their faces? Whither did the prophet retire? What did he do there? 9. What did he beseech the Lord to do? What happened then? Of what was the land of Israel, suffering from the long drought, a figure? Of whom was Elias a figure? 10. Of what was the rain that gave new life to the earth a type?

CHAPTER LXIV.

Wickedness of Achab and Jezabel.—Their Punishment.

The Lord Thy God hateth all injustice.—*Deut. 25, 16.*

A CHAB had a palace at Jezrahel, and near it was a vineyard owned by a man named Naboth. Achab, coveting the vineyard, said one day to Naboth: "Give me thy vineyard, that I may make me a garden, and I will give thee a better vineyard, or I will give thee the worth of it in money." Naboth answered him: "The Lord be merciful to me, and not let me give thee the inheritance of my fathers." For the law of Moses forbade the son to sell the property which he had inherited from his forefathers.

2. The king was so troubled because he could not have the vineyard that he could neither eat nor sleep. Jezabel, his queen, perceiving this, inquired the cause of his sadness and his fretting. The king having explained the cause, Jezabel mockingly said: "Thou art of great authority, indeed, and governest well the kingdom of Israel! Arise, and eat bread, and be of good cheer: I will give thee the vineyard of Naboth the Jezrahelite."

3. She then wrote letters in the king's name to the chief men of the city, men whom she knew to be wicked like her-

self, requesting them to find some men who would wrongfully accuse Naboth. These men were easily found, and they bore false witness against Naboth, saying that he had blasphemed God and the king. And on their testimony Naboth was condemned, taken out of the city, and stoned to death.

4. Jezabel, being informed of Naboth's death, went and told her husband that he might now take the vineyard, as Naboth was dead. And Achab took the vineyard. Then the Lord commanded Elias to go to Achab, to reproach him with his crime, and tell him that the dogs would lick up his own blood on the very spot on which Naboth was slain, and that the queen would be devoured by dogs in the same field. This prediction was literally fulfilled.

5. Three years after, Achab was mortally wounded in a battle with the Syrians; and when the chariot in which he received the fatal wound was being washed, after his death, the dogs came and licked up the blood.

6. Some time after, when Jehu was king, he went to Jezrahel. And when Jezabel heard of his coming she dressed herself in her richest apparel. She painted her face and adorned her head, and stood at a window of her palace. Jehu, seeing her at the window, ordered her servants to cast her down. They did so, and the walls were sprinkled with her blood, and the hooves of the horses trod upon her, and the dogs came and ate her flesh. After Jehu had dined he ordered Jezabel to be buried, but only her head, feet, and hands remained.

QUESTIONS.

1. Who had a vineyard near Achab's palace at Jezrahel? What did Achab, coveting the vineyard, say one day to Naboth? What did Naboth answer him? 2. Why was the king so troubled that he could neither eat nor sleep? What did Jezabel, his queen, mockingly say? 3. What did she then do? What did these men say against Naboth? What was done to Naboth? 4. What did Jezabel, being informed of Naboth's death, tell her husband? What did the Lord then command Elias to do? What was he to tell the king? Was this prediction fulfilled? 5. How was it fulfilled? 6. Some time after, when Jehu was king, where did

he go? When Jezabel heard of his coming, what did she do? What did Jehu, seeing her at the window, order her servants to do? What followed?

CHAPTER LXV.

Elias Taken to Heaven.—The Prophet Eliseus Chosen to Succeed Him.

If any man minister to me, him will my Father honor.—*John 12, 26.*

A T one time Elias, being persecuted by Jezabel, fled into the desert. He was very sad, and desired to die, for he thought all the Israelites had fallen into idolatry. Being fatigued, he cast himself down and slept in the shadow of a juniper tree; and behold, an angel of the Lord touched him and said: "Arise, eat; for thou hast yet a great way to go." Elias looked, and saw at his head a hearth-cake and a vessel of water. He arose, ate and drank, and walked in the strength of that food forty days and forty nights, until he came to the mount of God, Horeb.

2. Then the Lord appeared to him amidst the whistling of a gentle wind, consoled him and said: "Return and anoint Eliseus to be prophet in thy room, and I will leave me seven thousand men whose knees have not bowed before Baal." Elias departed, and found Eliseus ploughing with oxen. He cast his mantle upon him, and Eliseus forthwith left the oxen and the plow, followed Elias and ministered to him.

3. But the time came when the Lord wished to take Elias from the earth. The spirit of God led him to the Jordan, and Eliseus accompanied him. Elias took his mantle, folded it together, and struck the water; the waters divided, and both passed over on dry ground. As they walked on, there appeared a fiery chariot, with horses. Elias was taken up alive to heaven. Eliseus saw him, and cried: "My father!

My father!" When he saw Elias no longer, he rent his garments in grief; then, taking the mantle which Elias had dropped, he went back and struck with it the waters of the Jordan. They were divided, and Eliseus passed over. The other disciples of Elias, seeing this, said: "The spirit of Elias hath rested upon Eliseus." And coming to meet him, they worshiped him, falling to the ground.

4. After Elias had been taken up into heaven, Eliseus

ELIAS GOING UP TO HEAVEN IN A FIERY CHARIOT.

arose and exhorted the Israelites to remain faithful to the Lord. God also favored him with the gift of miracles. When he came to Jericho, the men of the city said to him: "The situation of this city is very good, but the waters are very bad." Eliseus answered: "Bring me a new vessel, and put salt into it." When they had brought it he went out to the spring, cast the salt into it, and the waters were healed.

5. One day, when Eliseus was going up to Bethel, where

the golden calf was worshiped, some boys came out of
the city and mocked him, saying: "Go up, thou baldhead."
Eliseus, knowing that in dishonoring him they dishonored
God, turned back and cursed them in the name of the Lord.
Immediately two bears came out of the wood that was near
by, and killed forty-two of the boys.

6. Some time after, Eliseus cured of leprosy, in a miraculous
manner, Naaman, general of the Syrian army, a rich and valiant man. The wife of Naaman had in her service a young
Israelite girl who had been carried off into Syria by robbers.
This maiden then said one day to her mistress: "I wish my
master had been with the prophet that is in Samaria. He would
certainly have healed him of the leprosy." When Naaman
heard this he set out for Samaria with horses and chariots.

7. When Naaman reached the prophet's dwelling he sent
a messenger to let him know of his coming, and why he had
come. Eliseus sent him word to bathe seven times in the
Jordan, and he would be healed. Naaman was angry, and
went away, saying: "I thought he would have come out to
me, and standing, would have invoked the name of the Lord
his God, and touched with his hand the place of the leprosy,
and healed me. Are not the rivers of Damascus better than
all the waters of Israel?"

8. As he was thus turning angrily away, his servants
said to him: "Father, if the prophet had bidden thee to
do some great thing, surely thou shouldst have done it, how
much rather what he now hath said to thee, 'Wash, and thou
shalt be clean'." And Naaman, seeing that what they said
was just, alighted from his chariot, bathed seven times in the
Jordan, and was made clean.

9. He returned to the man of God, and told him that now
he knew for certain that there was no God but the God of
Israel; and he offered him presents, but Eliseus refused to
receive anything. Hardly had Naaman gone a little way,
when Giezi, the servant of Eliseus, went after him, and

said: "My master hath sent me to thee, saying: 'Just now there are come to me from Mount Ephraim two young men, sons of the prophets; give them a talent of silver and two changes of garments'."

10. Naaman gladly gave him two talents of silver and two changes of garments. Giezi returned with the presents, and having hidden them, he stood before Eliseus. The prophet asked him where he had been, and Giezi answered that he had been nowhere.

11. Eliseus being angry, said: "Was not my heart present when the man turned back from his chariot? Now thou hast money to buy olive-yards, and vineyards, and sheep and oxen, and men-servants and maid-servants; but the leprosy of Naaman shall stick to thee forever." And Giezi went out a leper, as white as snow.

12. One great miracle the prophet wrought, even after his death. It happened in this manner: On one occasion a number of men were carrying a corpse to the cemetery for burial. As they were making the grave, behold, robbers from Moab rushed in upon them. They, in their fright, cast the corpse into the sepulcher of Eliseus. No sooner had the dead man touched the bones of the prophet than he was instantly restored to life, and came forth from the tomb.

QUESTIONS.

1. Where did Elias go when he was persecuted by Jezabel? What did he think? Being fatigued, what did he do? What did the angel say to him? What did he see, on awakening? 2. Who appeared to Elias? What did the Lord say to him? 3. What did Elias do under the inspiration of God? What did Eliseus cry out? What did he do when he saw Elias no longer? What did the disciples of Elias say when they saw the waters divided by Eliseus? 4. What did Eliseus do after Elias was taken up into heaven? With what did God favor him? What did some of the men in the city say to him? What did Eliseus answer? 5. What happened when Eliseus was going up to Bethel? What did the boys, mocking him, say? What did Eliseus do? Why did he do so? What came out of the wood? How many of the boys did the bears kill? 6. Whom did Eliseus cure of leprosy, in a miraculous manner? What did the young Israelite say to Naaman's wife? When Naaman heard

this, what did he do? 7. What did Naaman do when he reached the prophet's dwelling? What did Eliseus send him word to do? What did Naaman say, going away angry? 8. As he was turning away, what did his servants say to him? What did Naaman do, seeing that what they said was just? 9. What did Naaman say, going to the man of God? When Naaman had gone a little way, what did Giezi, a servant of Eliseus do? What did he say to Naaman? 10. What did Naaman give him? What did Giezi do when he returned? What did the prophet ask him? What did Giezi answer? 11. What did Eliseus, being angry with his servant, tell him? 12. What great miracle took place after the death of Eliseus?

CHAPTER LXVI.

The Prophet Jonas.

Be converted to Me, and you shall be saved.—*Isaias 45, 22.*

AFTER the death of Eliseus, the Lord wishing to show mercy to the Gentiles, raised up the prophet Jonas, that he might go to Ninive, and preach penance to the inhabitants of that city. The wickedness of the pagan Ninivites had provoked the anger of God, and He had said to Jonas: "Arise, and go to Ninive, and preach in it, for the wickedness thereof is come up before me."

2. Jonas, however, knew that the Lord easily forgives; hence he was afraid that if he preached to the people of Ninive they would do penance, and that consequently the Lord would spare them, while he himself would be looked upon as a false prophet. So Jonas rose up to flee from the face of the Lord, and he embarked on board a ship which sailed for Tharsis. But the Lord sent a great storm, and the sea heaved and swelled, and the ship threatened to sink.

3. Then the sailors being frightened, threw into the sea all the merchandise that was on board in order to lighten the vessel. And each one began praying to his own god for help. But Jonas was below, fast asleep; and the shipmaster

went to him and said: "Why art thou asleep? Rise up, call upon thy God, if so be that God will think of us, that we may not perish!"

4. But the sailors, seeing that the violence of the storm continued to increase, proposed to cast lots that they might know why this evil had come upon them. And they cast lots, and the lot fell on Jonas. Then Jonas confessed his sin and said: "Take me up, and cast me into the sea, and the sea shall be calm to you."

5. The sailors, unwilling to throw Jonas overboard, rowed very hard to gain the shore, where they might leave him in safety. But they were not able; for the sea swelled and tossed higher than ever. At last they took Jonas and cast him into the sea, and immediately the storm ceased, and the sea was calm.

6. At the same moment the Lord sent a great fish, which opened its jaws and swallowed Jonas. And he remained three days and three nights in the belly of the whale, continually calling on God to save him, saying: "I am cast away, out of the sight of Thy eyes; but yet I shall see Thy holy temple again." His prayer was heard, and on the third day the fish threw Jonas out of its mouth on the dry land.

7. And the Lord spoke a second time to Jonas, and told him to go to Ninive, the great city, and preach penance. Jonas went without delay, and entering into the city he walked a whole day through its streets, calling out as he went: "Yet forty days, and Ninive shall be destroyed." The people of Ninive were struck with terror, knowing how guilty they were, and a general fast was proclaimed throughout the whole city, both for man and beast.

8. The king himself put on sackcloth and sat in ashes, and he and all his people, from the greatest to the least, fasted and did penance, in order to appease the anger of God. And because of their repentance, God had mercy on the people of Ninive, and spared the city. Meanwhile, Jonas had gone

out of the city, and sat down at some distance, towards the
east, to see what would happen. And finding that God had
spared Ninive, he was angry and much troubled lest he
should pass for a false prophet.

9. But God, wishing to show His prophet how unreasonable
was his anger, caused to spring up, during the night, a large
vine, which sheltered him next day from the scorching rays
of the sun. But on the following morning God sent a worm
which ate up the root of the plant, and it withered away.

10. Now, when the sun had risen, God sent a hot and
burning wind; besides, the sun struck full·on the head of
Jonas, so that he broiled with the heat to such a degree that
he desired to die. Then the Lord said to him: "Thou art
grieved for the ivy for which thou hast not labored, and shall
not I spare Ninive, in which there are more than a hundred
and twenty thousand persons that knew not how to distin-
guish between their right hand and their left?"· Jonas, lying three days in the whale's belly, was a figure of Jesus
lying three days in the tomb. So, also, Jonas coming forth
alive on the third day was a figure of our Lord's resurrection.

QUESTIONS.

1. After the death of Eliseus, whom did the Lord raise up? What
had provoked the anger of God? What did God say to Jonas? 2. Of
whom was Jonas afraid? What did he do in order not to preach in
Ninive? What happened then? 3. What did the sailors do in order to
lighten the vessel? Where was Jonas? What did the shipmaster say
to him? 4. What did the sailors then propose, seeing that the storm
continued to increase? When they cast lots, on whom did it fall? What
did Jonas then do? What did he tell the sailors to do? 5. What did
the sailors do, being unwilling to throw him overboard? What followed?
What did they at last do? What was the result? 6. What did the Lord
send at the same moment? What did it do? How long did Jonas remain in the whale's belly? How did Jonas pray? Did God hear the
prayer of Jonas? 7. What did the Lord tell Jonas a second time to
do? What did Jonas do? What did he cry out in the streets of Ninive?
What was then proclaimed? 8. What did the king do? What did
all the people do? Why had God mercy on the people of Ninive?
9. What did God do in order to show His prophet how unreasonable was his anger? 10. Of whom was Jonas, lying three days in

the whale's belly, a figure? Of what was his coming forth alive, on the
third day, a figure?

FINAL OVERTHROW OF THE KINGDOM OF ISRAEL (718 B. C.)

CHAPTER LXVII.

Tobias During the Captivity of Babylon.

Know that it is an evil and a bitter thing for thee, to have left
the Lord thy God.—*Jer. 2, 19.*

THE Lord ceased not to send to the Israelites holy prophets who preached penance to them, both by word and
example. But the Israelites would not be converted, and
their wickedness increased to such an extent that the Almighty resolved to punish them in His wrath, and utterly
to destroy them. He, therefore, caused Salmanazar, king
of Assyria, to come against them with a mighty army. He
laid siege to the strong city of Samaria, and after three years
took it, and carried off most of the inhabitants, and thus the
kingdom of Israel ceased to exist.

2. The Israelites having been slain or carried off into captivity, their land had become almost a wilderness, and the
Assyrian king, in order to people it again, sent thither thousands of his pagan subjects, who settling amongst the scattered remains of the ten tribes, were soon so mixed up with
them that they became, as it were, a new people, and scarcely
a trace remained of the people of Israel.

3. Those of this mixed race who settled in the northern
part of the country were called Galileans; those who lived
in the south were called Samaritans, from Samaria, the ancient capital of the kingdom; and those who dwelt beyond the
Jordan were called Pereans. The religion of these districts
was a mixture of Judaism and Paganism; hence they hated

the two tribes of Juda and Benjamin, who had remained true to the old religion.

4. Those who were taken captive to Assyria never returned to their own country. Still God did not fail to give numerous proofs of His watchful care over those unhappy exiles. One of the most remarkable of these instances is found in the history of the good Tobias. When he was in his own country, and in his earliest years, he never associated with the wicked; never went to adore the golden calf, but kept the law of God exactly.

5. Hence, God protected him in the land of captivity, and caused him to find favor in the sight of Salmanazar, who allowed him to go wherever he wished. He went, accordingly, to all his fellow-captives, consoling and encouraging them. He shared with them all he possessed, fed them when they were hungry, and clothed them when naked. His life was spent in such works of charity.

6. King Salmanazar being dead, Sennacherib, his son, who succeeded him on the throne, was not so favorable to Tobias, and put many of the Israelites to death. But Tobias, fearing God more than the king, hid the bodies of his brethren in his house, and buried them by night. The king, having heard this, sentenced Tobias to death, and took away all his property.

7. Tobias fled with his wife and son, and remained concealed in a place of safety, till the death of the wicked king, who forty days later was killed by his own sons. Then Tobias returned, and all his property was restored to him. But the persecution against the Israelites was still raging, so Tobias resumed his former works of charity, relieving the distressed and burying the dead. Coming home one day very much fatigued, he lay down near the wall and fell asleep.

8. While he was sleeping, the hot dung from a swallow's nest fell on his eyes and made him blind. This was a great affliction, but it did not prevent Tobias from fearing and

blessing God, and thanking Him for all His mercies—even for this new trial. Now Anna, his wife, was his only support. She went out every day to work, and by her hard earnings kept her blind husband from want. On one occasion, Anna received a young kid for the labor of her hands, and she brought it home.

9. Now Tobias, hearing it bleat, was afraid and said: "Take heed, lest perhaps it be stolen; restore it to its owner." He questioned Anna as to how she got the kid. Now Anna was a good and virtuous woman, but this suspicion of her husband roused her anger. She replied very sharply, and made use of words that were provoking to her husband. Tobias, however, only sighed and began to pray.

QUESTIONS.

1. Why did the Lord send prophets to the Israelites? Were they converted? What did the Almighty resolve to do? Whom did He cause to come against them with a mighty army? To what city did he lay siege? What did he do when he took it? 2. What did the Assyrian King do in order to repeople the land of Israel? What followed? 3. What were those called who settled in the northern part of the country? What were they who settled in the south called? And what were they who settled beyond the Jordan called? What was the religion of the Samaritans? How did they regard the people of Juda? 4. Did those who were taken as captives to Assyria ever return? What ceased to exist? Did God's care over these unhappy exiles continue? What was one of the most remarkable proofs of His watchful care? What was the life of Tobias in his own country? 5. What did God do for Tobias in the land of captivity? What use did he make of his liberty? How was his life spent? 6. Who succeeded Salmanazar? Was he as favorable to Tobias? What did he do to the Israelites? What did Tobias do? What did the king, hearing this, order to be done to Tobias? 7. What did Tobias do? When did he return home? Did the persecution of the Israelites, meanwhile, abate? What did Tobias resume? 8. What happened to him one day when he came home very much fatigued, and fell asleep near the wall? What effect had this new affliction on Tobias? Who was his only support? What did she do? 9. What did she receive, on one occasion, for the labor of her hands? What did Tobias fear? What did he ask his wife? How did she reply? What did Tobias do?

CHAPTER LXVIII.

*Parting Advice of Tobias to his Son.—Departure of
Young Tobias.*

The Angel of the Lord shall encamp round about them that fear
Him.—*Ps. 33, 8.*

TOBIAS, seeing himself surrounded by so many miseries, thought he could not live much longer. He, therefore, called his son, and said: "My son, when God shall take my soul, thou shalt bury my body; and thou shalt honor thy mother all the days of her life; for thou must be mindful what and how great perils she has suffered for thee. And when she also shall have ended the time of her life, bury her by me.

2. "And all the days of thy life have God in thy mind, and take heed thou never consent to sin, nor transgress the commandments of the Lord our God. Give alms out of thy substance, and turn not away thy face from any poor person. If thou hast much, give abundantly; if thou have little, take care even so to bestow willingly a little. For alms deliver from sin and death, and will not suffer the soul to go into darkness. Take heed to keep thyself, my son, from all fornication.

3. "Never suffer pride to reign in thy mind, nor in thy word, for from it all perdition took its beginning. If any man has done work for thee, pay him his hire. See thou never do to another what thou wouldst hate to have done to thee by another. Bless God at all times, and desire of Him to direct thy ways, and that all thy counsels may abide in Him."

4. Then the son answered saying: "I will do all these things, father, which thou hast commanded me." Tobias having thus advised his son, sent him to Rages, a distant city, to collect a debt of long standing. And the young Tobias not

knowing the road, went out to seek a guide who would show him the way.

5. He had not gone far when he met a beautiful young man, standing ready girt as for a journey. It was the Archangel Raphael. Tobias did not know who the young man was, but he addressed him, saying: "Good young man. knowest thou the way that leadeth to the country of the Medes?" The angel answered: "I know it." Then the young Tobias introduced him to his father, who asked him: "Canst thou conduct my son to Gabelus, at Rages?"

6. The young man replied: "I will conduct him thither, and bring him back to thee." Then Tobias blessed the two young men, praying: "May you have a good journey; may God be with you in your way, and may His angel accompany you." Then they both set out on their journey, and the dog followed them. But his mother wept and said to her husband: "Thou hast taken the staff of our old age, and hast sent him away." On the evening of the first day the travelers reached the banks of the river Tigris. Tobias, heated and warm, sat down on the bank and put his feet into the water.

7. Suddenly an enormous fish came up to devour him. Tobias cried out to the angel: "Sir, he cometh upon me!" The angel, seeing his terror, exclaimed: "Take him by the gill and draw him to thee." He did so, and when the fish lay panting before his feet, the angel said: "Take out his heart, his gall, and his liver; for these are useful medicines." Then, making a fire, Tobias broiled some of the fish, which furnished a repast; then he salted a portion of what remained to serve as provision for the journey.

8. When they came to a certain city, Tobias said to his guide: "Where wilt thou that we lodge?" The angel answered: "There is here a man named Raguel, a kinsman of thy tribe, who has a daughter named Sara: and thou must take her to wife." Tobias replied: "I hear that she hath

been given to seven husbands, and they all died, and a devil killed each of them on the night of his wedding."

9. Tobias added that, as he was the only son of his aged parents, and if such a misfortune should befall him, it would bring down their old age with sorrow to the grave. The angel answered that the devil had such power over those who in their marriage banish God from their heart, and

TOBIAS TAKING THE FISH.

think only of gratifying their evil passions. "But thou," he continued, "when thou shalt take her, give thyself for three days to nothing else but to prayer; then the devil shall be driven away and you shall obtain a blessing."

10. Having entered into the house of Raguel, Tobias made himself known, and was warmly received by Raguel, as the son of an old friend and of a most worthy man. At the same time Anna, the wife of Raguel, and Sara, his daughter, wept for joy. They then prepared a repast for the travel-

ers, and Raguel prayed them to sit down to eat. Tobias told him that he would neither eat nor drink till he promised to give him Sara, his daughter, in marriage.

11. Raguel seemed to hesitate, but the angel told him not to be afraid to give his daughter to the young man, for that he feared the Lord. Then Raguel consented, and taking his daughter's right hand, placed it in that of Tobias, saying: "The God of Abraham, the God of Isaac, and the God of Jacob be with you; may He join you together, and fulfill His blessing in you."

12. Then they sat down to eat. And Tobias and Sara spent three days in prayer, after which the devil had no power to harm them. Then, at the request of Tobias, the angel took the note of hand, went to the country of the Medes, collected the money from Gabelus, and returned with Gabelus to be present at the wedding.

13. Gabelus came with great joy, and when he saw the young husband he wept and embraced him, saying: "The God of Israel bless thee, because thou art the son of a very good and just man, and that feareth God, and doeth alms deeds. And may a blessing come upon thy wife."

QUESTIONS.

1, 2 and 3. What advice did the elder Tobias give to his son? 4. What did the son answer? What did Tobias send his son to Rages to do? Whom did Tobias go out to seek? 5. Whom did he meet on going out? Who was this young man? Did Tobias know who he was? What did he say to the angel? What did the angel answer? What did the father ask the angel? 6. What did he reply? What did Tobias do when the young men were setting out? What did his mother say? What river did they reach the first evening of their journey? 7. What came out of the water when Tobias put in his feet to cool them? What did the angel tell him to do? What did he do with the fish, by the angel's direction? 8. When they came to a certain city, what did Tobias say to his guide? What did the angel tell him? What did Tobias answer? 9. What did Tobias say? What did the angel answer? 10. How was Tobias received by Raguel? What did Anna, the wife of Raguel, and Sara, his daughter, do? What did Tobias tell Raguel when he invited the two travelers to sit down to eat. 11. What did the angel tell Raguel when he seemed to hesitate? What did Raguel say when he placed his daughter's hand in that of Tobias? 12. What did Tobias and Sara do? What followed? What did the angel do at the request of Tobias? 13. Whom did he invite to the wedding? What did Gabelus say when he saw the young husband?

CHAPTER LXIX.

Tobias Returns Home.

Praise the Lord, because He hath delivered the soul of the poor out of the hand of the wicked.—*Jer. 20, 13.*

FOURTEEN days had passed since the marriage of Tobias, and his parents at home began to be exceedingly sad, and they wept together because their son did not return. But his mother was quite disconsolate and she groaned and sighed: "Wo, wo is me, my son, why did we send thee to a strange country; the light of our eyes, the staff of our old age, the comfort of our life, the hope of our posterity!" Then Tobias said to her: "Hold thy peace, our son is safe." but she would not be comforted, but went out into all the ways that she might see him coming afar off.

2. Now Tobias the younger said to Raguel: "I know that my parents count the days, and their spirit is afflicted within them." However, Raguel pressed him to stay a little longer, but in vain. He then gave him Sara his wife, and the half of all he possessed, saying: "May the holy angel of the Lord be with you in your journey and bring you through safely, and that you may find all things well about your parents."

3. When the travelers had made half the journey homeward, the angel said to Tobias: "Let us go before and let the family softly follow after us." They did so and Raphael told Tobias to take with him the gall of the fish because it would be very useful.

4. Meanwhile Anna sat daily beside the way on the hilltop; and while she watched, she saw him coming far off.

When she was sure that it was her son coming, she ran to tell her husband. She had scarcely done so when the dog which had accompanied her son in his journey, running before, reached the house, wagging his tail and jumping for joy, as if he had brought the news. Thereupon, the elder Tobias, blind as he was, groped his way and went out to meet his son. And they all wept for joy.

5. Young Tobias then rubbed his father's eyes with the gall of the fish, and he saw, and the old man exclaimed: "I bless Thee, O Lord God of Israel, because Thou hast chastised me, and thou hast saved me, and behold I see Tobias my son!" Seven days after Sara and her retinue arrived and completed the joy of that favored and happy household. Then the son related to his parents all the benefits he had received from the young man, his guide. He said they could never repay him for all he had done for him, but asked his father's permission to give him one half of the money he had received from Gabelus.

6. The father willingly consented, and they pressed the young man to accept the money. But the heavenly messenger said to them: "Bless ye the God of heaven, and give glory to Him in the sight of all that live; because He hath shown His mercy to you. Prayer is good with fasting and alms, more than to lay up treasures of gold. When thou didst pray with tears, and didst bury the dead, I offered thy prayer to the Lord.

7. "And because thou wast acceptable to God, it was necessary that temptation should prove thee. The Lord hath sent me to heal thee, and to deliver Sara, thy son's wife, from the devil. For I am the angel Raphael, one of the seven who stand before the throne of God." Hearing this, they were seized with fear, and all fell prostrate on the ground. Still the angel told them not to fear, but to bless and thank the Lord, who had sent him to do His holy will in their regard.

8. Having spoken this, he vanished from their sight,

leaving the little family lost in wonder and full of gratitude
to God. The elder Tobias lived forty-two years after these
events to share in the happiness of his family, and died at
the age of one hundred and two years. Tobias, his son, lived
to be very old; he saw the children of his children, who remained faithful, were beloved by God and man.

QUESTIONS.

1. Fourteen days having passed since his marriage, what did the
parents of Tobias think and feel? What did his afflicted mother say?
What did his father say? 2. What did Tobias say to Raguel? What
did Raguel give him at his departure? 3. When the travelers had made
half the journey homewards, what did Raphael propose to Tobias?
What did the angel then tell Tobias to do when he got home? 4. What
was Anna, his mother, meanwhile doing? To whom did she tell the
news of his coming? What about the dog? What did the elder Tobias
do? 5. What did young Tobias do to his father? What did the old
man exclaim? Who arrived seven days after? What did the son relate
to his parents? What did he ask his father's permission to do? 6 and
7. What did the heavenly messenger say to them when they pressed
him to accept the money? What did the angel afterwards tell them?
8. How long did Tobias the elder live? What is said of Tobias the
younger?

DECLINE OF THE KINGDOM OF JUDA.

CHAPTER LXX.

The Prophets Joel and Micheas. (790 to 730 B. C.)

The Lord hath sent to you the prophets, and you have not hearkened,
nor inclined your ears to hear.—*Jer. 25, 4.*

GOD also sent to the inhabitants of the kingdom of Juda
a great number of prophets whose powerful voice was
heard throughout the land calling them to repentance. Many
times did their words produce the desired effect and bring the
people to repentance, and for awhile they served God with
fidelity and sincerity.

2. Unhappily, these returns to virtue and religion were of short duration. Then it was that the prophets, with sorrowful hearts, began to announce to the rebellious people the downfall of their country, and the only consolation left to the prophets was the thought of the Messias, whose coming they saw more clearly as time went on.

3. The prophet Joel spoke to the people in these terms: "Hear this, ye old men, and give ear all ye inhabitants of the land. Blow the trumpet in Sion, sound an alarm in My holy mountain; because the day of the Lord comes; because it is nigh at hand. A day of darkness and of gloom; a day of clouds and whirlwinds; a numerous people and a strong people, as the morning spread upon the mountains.

4. "Before the face thereof a devouring fire, and behind it a burning flame. Sacrifices and oblations have ceased to be offered in the house of the Lord. Rend your hearts and not your garments, and turn to the Lord your God. Between the portico and the altar the priests, the Lord's ministers, shall weep, and shall say: 'Spare, O Lord, spare Thy people'."

5. The prophet Micheas is not less terrible in his warnings. "Hear, all ye peoples," he cries out, "and let the earth give ear. I will make Samaria as a heap of stones! I will bring down the stones thereof into the valley, and will lay her foundations bare. Hear this, ye princes of the house of Jacob; you that abhor judgment and pervert all that is right; you who built up Sion with blood, and Jerusalem with iniquity."

6. "Therefore, on account of you Sion shall be plowed as a field, and Jerusalem shall be as a heap of stones, and the mountain of the temple as the high places of the forests. And thou, Bethlehem Ephrata, art a little one among the thousands of Juda; out of thee shall He come forth unto Me that is to be the Ruler in Israel; and His going forth is from

the beginning, from the days of eternity." These prophecies have been literally[1] fulfilled. The prophecy about Bethlehem refers to the Savior, so that the Jews might know that the Redeemer promised to Adam, to Abraham, Isaac and Jacob, to Juda, and to David would be born in Bethlehem.

QUESTIONS.

1. Whom did God also send to the inhabitants of Juda? Did their words ever produce the desired effect? 2. Were these returns to virtue and religion of long duration? What did the prophets, with sorrowful hearts, then begin to announce? 3 and 4. In what terms did the prophet Joel speak to the people? 5. What did the prophet Micheas cry out? 6. What remarkable prophecy did he make about the little city of Bethlehem? Have these prophecies been fulfilled? To whom does the prophecy about Bethlehem refer?

CHAPTER LXXI.

King Ozias, wishing to Usurp the Priestly Functions, is Stricken with Leprosy. (803 B. C.)

Neither doth any man take the honor to himself, but he that is called by God, as Aaron was.—*Heb. 5, 4.*

OZIAS was one of the few faithful kings who ruled in Juda. He reigned fifty-two years, and did that which was right in the sight of the Lord. And God directed him in all things. Unhappily, prosperity made him proud, and he carried his audacity so far as to usurp[2] the priestly office. One day, going into the temple, he went to burn incense upon the altar. Eighty priests, with Azarias the high-priest at their head, opposed the king, and prevented him from burning incense.

---

[1] Lit-e-ral-ly, to the letter.

[2] Usurp', to seize and hold in possession, by force or without right.

2. Ozias, being very angry, threatened to strike the priests with the censer which he held in his hand. No sooner had he raised his hand than he was stricken with leprosy, which appeared on his forehead before all the priests. And they, seized with horror at his sudden and awful punishment, took hold of the king and put him out of the temple.

3. He himself was terrified, feeling the leprosy all over his body, and he hastened away from the temple, to shut himself up in a palace apart from all others. He remained a leper till the day of his death. This was the fearful punishment which God sent to an otherwise faithful king, because of his sacrilegious[1] attempt to perform an office that belonged only to the priests.

QUESTIONS.

1. Who was Ozias? How long did he reign? How did he reign? What did prosperity make him? How far did he carry his audacity? What did he attempt to do one day when he went into the temple? Who opposed the king and prevented him from burning incense? 2. With what did Ozias threaten to strike the priests? With what was he stricken? What did the priests do? 3. What did he himself do, feeling the leprosy all over his body? How long did he remain a leper?

CHAPTER LXXII.

The Prophecies of Isaias. (*700 B. C.*)

I have declared Thy truth and Thy salvation.—*Ps. 39, 11.*

DURING the reign of the same Ozias, the people of Juda were guilty of many acts of idolatry. Wherefore, God sent them the great prophet Isaias. In sublime and terrific language he warned them of many fearful calamities that were to come upon their country.

2. The Lord also revealed to this prophet so many particu-

---

[1] SAC-RI-LE'-GIOUS, violating sacred things.

lars relating to the Savior of the world that, reading his prophecies, one would suppose Isaias had lived at the same time as our Divine Lord, instead of living seven hundred years before. A few of these prophecies will show how clearly this greatest of all the prophets foresaw the birth, passion and death of the Redeemer.

3. Speaking of the mother of the Messias, as well as of the Messias Himself, he said: "Behold, a virgin shall conceive and bear a son, and His name shall be called Emmanuel, that is God-with-us. And there shall come forth a rod out of the root of Jesse, and a flower shall rise up out of his root. And the Spirit of the Lord shall rest upon Him, the spirit of wisdom and of understanding, the spirit of counsel and of fortitude, the spirit of knowledge and of godliness. And He shall be filled with the spirit of the fear of the Lord.

4. "A Child is born to us, a Son is given to us, and the government is upon His shoulder. His name shall be called Wonderful, Counselor, the Father of the world to come, the Prince of Peace. God himself will come and save you, then shall the eyes of the blind be opened and the ears of the deaf shall be unstopped." Concerning the passion of our Lord, he prophesied: "There is no beauty in Him, nor comeliness. Despised, and the most abject of men, a man of sorrows. He has borne our infirmities; He was wounded for our iniquities; He was bruised for our sins, and by His bruises we are healed. The Lord hath laid on Him the iniquity of us all. He was offered because it was His own will and He opened not his mouth. He shall be led as a sheep to the slaughter, and shall be dumb as a lamb before his shearer." Regarding His future glory, the prophet says: "The Gentiles shall beseech Him, and His sepulchre shall be glorious." Isaias prophesied about fifty years. It is said that he, while yet alive, was sawed in two by order of the impious king Manasses.

QUESTIONS.

1. Of what were the people of Juda guilty during the reign of the same Ozias? Whom did God, therefore, send them? Of what did Isaias warn the people? 2. What did the Lord also reveal to this prophet? What would one suppose reading his prophecies? 3 and 4. What did Isaias foretell concerning the mother of the Savior? What did Isaias prophesy concerning the birth of the Redeemer? What, concerning His passion? What, regarding His future glory? How long did Isaias prophesy? What is said about the death of this great prophet?

CHAPTER LXXIII.

The Pious King Ezechias. (723-694 B. C.)

He that is good, shall draw grace from the Lord.—*Prov. 12, 2.*

DURING the reign of Achaz the people of Juda were visited with a terrible calamity. That unhappy king had sacrificed his own children to the idol Moloch,[1] one of the chief gods of the Gentiles. He had broken the sacred vessels, and closed the gates of the temple. The Lord, therefore. delivered him into the hands of the king of Syria, who slew in one day a hundred and twenty thousand men of Juda, while two hundred thousand women and children were carried into captivity.

2. Achaz having died a short time after, his son Ezechias ascended the throne. This pious prince immediately cast down the altars which his unhappy father had everywhere raised to the pagan gods; he threw open again the gates of the temple, and exhorted the Levites to purify it from the profanations that had taken place there; saying that it was because of the sins of the people, and, above all, because of their idolatry, that so many misfortunes had come upon them.

3. And God blessed Ezechias, and was with him in all he

---

[1] MOLOCH (pr. Mo'-lok).

did; so that, in his days, the kingdom of Juda regained all its former prosperity. Nevertheless, it came to pass that, after some years, Sennacherib, king of Assyria, came with a mighty army and besieged Jerusalem.

4. Then Ezechias went to the temple and prayed. He also sent priests clothed in sackcloth, to the prophet Isaias, to ask him to intercede with God in behalf of him and his people. The prophet sent word to Ezechias not to fear, for that God had heard his prayer, and would destroy the Assyrians, and that their king, returning to his own country, should perish by the sword.

5. That same night the angel of the Lord went to the camp of the Assyrians and killed one hundred and eighty-five thousand warriors. Thus Sennacherib was obliged to return with disgrace to his own country. There he went to the temple of his god, and his own sons slew him with the sword. Thus was fulfilled the prophecy of Isaias. Ezechias some time after, fell sick and lay at the point of death. The prophet Isaias was sent to tell him to put his house in order, for that he must die.

6. The king, terrified at the thought of death, turned his face towards the temple, and prayed with tears that God might prolong his life. God heard his prayer, and set the prophet again to tell him that fifteen years should be added to his life. And so it came to pass; and at the end of the fifteen years he died, after a happy and a prosperous reign, the reward of his fidelity to God.

QUESTIONS.

1. With what were the people of Juda visited during the reign of Achaz? What had the unhappy king done? Into whose hands did the Lord deliver him? How many of the men of Juda were slain in one day? How many women and children were carried into captivity? 2. Who ascended the throne when Achaz died? What did this pious prince immediately do? Saying what? 3. How did God reward Ezechias? Who came soon after with a mighty army to besiege Jerusalem? 4. What did Ezechias then do? What did he also do? What word did Isaias send to the king? 5. What

happened that same night? What was Sennacherib obliged to do? What
happened to him on his return home? Who was taken sick some time
after? What was Isaias sent to tell him? 6. What did the king do,
terrified at the thought of death? What was the prophet sent again to
tell him? What sort of reign had Ezechias? In reward of what?

CHAPTER LXXIV.

Judith.

The Lord is my strength and my praise.—*Exod. 15, 2.*

AFTER a brief season of repentance and of penance, the
people of Juda again forgot the Lord. Then God, in
His anger, sent them a new and terrible punishment, which
would have ended in the total destruction of their nation,
were it not for the heroic courage of a certain holy woman.
At that time Holofernes, general-in-chief of the Assyrian
forces, came at the head of a mighty army to overthrow the
kingdom of Juda, as he had overthrown many other kingdoms.

2. Having taken all the cities and strongholds of the country, and treated their inhabitants with savage cruelty, he came
to lay siege to Bethulia. He cut off the aqueducts which
supplied the city with water, and thereby reduced the citizens
to such an extremity that the elders resolved to give up the
city in five days unless they were relieved before that time.
Meanwhile, they prayed fervently to God, humbled themselves before Him, and strewed ashes on their heads.

3. Now there was in the city a woman named Judith, of
rare beauty and of great wealth, who, being a widow, lived
retired in her own house, and spent her days in prayer and
good works. Being touched with compassion for the sad condition of her people, she presented herself before the ancients
of the city and said: "What is this word by which you have
consented to give up the city within five days? You have

set a time for the mercy of the Lord according to your pleasure. This is not a word that may draw down mercy, but rather indignation. Let us therefore be penitent for this same thing, and remember that all the saints were tempted and remained faithful; but that those who rejected the trials of the Lord were destroyed. And let us believe that these scourges have happened for our amendment and not for our destruction."

4. The ancients, inspired by these noble words, begged her to pray for the people. She consented, and retiring to her oratory, clothed herself in haircloth, put ashes on her head, and falling prostrate before the Lord, she besought Him to humble the enemies of her nation. While she thus prayed, Almighty God inspired her with the thought that she should go into the camp of the enemy and cut off the head of the Assyrian general Holofernes.

5. Then putting off the hair-cloth, she immediately arrayed herself in the richest garments, perfumed herself with the best ointments, plaited her hair, and adorned herself with bracelets, earlets and rings. And the Lord increased her beauty, because all her dressing up did not proceed from vanity. Then she took a servant maid with her and set out for the camp of Holofernes.

6. Being brought before Holofernes, the tyrant was charmed by her majestic beauty, and, supposing that she had fled from her own people, ordered her to receive every attention, and to be allowed to go and come as she pleased. On the fourth day Holofernes gave a grand banquet to the officers of his army. He and they overcharged themselves with wine, and when they lay down on their couches they fell into a death-like sleep. Then Judith resolved to strike the decisive blow that was to save her country and her people.

7. She besought God, saying: "Strengthen me, O Lord God of Israel, and in this hour look upon the works of my hands, that I may bring to pass that which I have purposed, having a belief that it might be done by Thee." Then she

moved softly towards the tent of Holofernes. And taking his sword, which hung from a pillar near by, she drew it from its scabbard, raised it aloft, and at the second stroke cut off the head of the sleeping tyrant. She then gave the head to her maid, who waited without, and bade her put it into her wallet.

8. Departing from the camp, she returned with her servant to Bethulia, and having assembled the people, showed them the head of Holofernes, saying: "Praise ye the Lord our God, who hath killed the enemy of His people by my hand. His angel hath been my keeper and hath brought me back to you." Then Ozias, the prince of the people of Israel, said to her: "Blessed art thou, O daughter of the Lord, the most high God, above all women upon the earth." Then the people, praising God, rushed towards the camp of the Assyrians. The guards, terrified and confused, made a great noise at the door of their general's tent in order to awaken him.

9. But finding their efforts useless, they at length ventured to enter the tent, and seeing the headless body of their mighty general weltering in blood, they were seized with fear, and fled in haste, crying out that Holofernes was slain. A great confusion ensued, and the people of Bethulia had only to complete the work commenced by Judith, and take possession of the Assyrian camp with all its rich spoils.

10. Then the Jewish people, turning to Judith, sang with one accord: "Thou art the glory of Jerusalem; thou art the joy of Israel; thou art the honor of our people." The rejoicings following on this splendid victory were kept up for three months. And Judith became great throughout all Israel. She died at an advanced age, and was mourned by all the people.

11. Judith is, in some degree, a figure of Mary the Immaculate Virgin. Mary is the true heroine of Israel, and of mankind. Judith was praised by the people of one city as

the pride and ornament of Jerusalem.   Mary is praised
throughout the whole earth as the glory of her people, the co-
operatrix in the redemption of the whole human race, the
woman whose seed conquered death and hell, as the Almighty Himself foretold to Adam and Eve after their fall.

QUESTIONS.

1. Did the people of Juda again forget God? What did God send
them in His anger? Who saved them from destruction? Who came at
the head of a mighty army to overthrow the kingdom of Juda? 2. To
what city did he lay siege, after taking all the other cities? What had
the citizens at length resolved to do if relief did not come? Meanwhile,
what did they do? 3. What particular person was in the city? Before
whom did she present herself? What did she tell the ancients? 4. What
did the ancients beg Judith to do? Having consented, what did she do?
While she thus prayed, with what did God inspire her? 5. What did she
then do? For what place did she set out? 6. What happened when
she was brought before Holofernes? What did Holofernes do on the
fourth day? What followed? What did Judith then resolve to do?
How did she pray? 7. What did she do? 8. What did Judith do
on returning to Bethulia? What did she call upon the people to do?
What did the people do, praising God? What did the Assyrian guards
do? 9. What did they do when, going into the tent, they saw the dead
body of their general? What had the people of Bethulia only to do?
10. What did the Jewish people, turning to Judith, sing with one accord? 11. Of whom is Judith, in some degree, a figure? Who is the
true heroine of Israel and mankind?

CHAPTER LXXV.

The Babylonian Captivity.—Fall of the Kingdom of Juda.
(*588 B. C.*)

The wicked shall be destroyed from the earth.—*Prov. 2, 22.*

A T last the people of Juda became so hardened in sin that
the divine chastisements had no longer any effect
upon their hearts. They gave themselves wholly up to the

vile practices of idolatry, and persecuted the prophets of God, several of whom they put to death. In vain did the great prophet Jeremias, who lived at that time, endeavor to recall them to repentance. Finally the patience of the merciful God was exhausted, and the ruin so often foretold by the prophet Isaias fell heavily on the people.

2. In the year 606 before Christ, Nabuchodonosor, king of Babylon, placed himself at the head of an immense army,

JEREMIAS LAMENTING THE FALL OF JERUSALEM.

marched against Jerusalem, and, having taken it, carried away the king and the principal inhabitants as captives. Sixteen years later, those who were left in Jerusalem, revolted against Nabuchodonosor, and the latter returned with a still greater army, and, after a siege of eighteen months, he took Jerusalem by storm.

3. Then the whole city was given up to fire and pillage.

The temple itself was consumed by fire, and the sacred vessels were carried off. All the people that escaped the sword were led into captivity in Babylon, and the splendid city of Jerusalem was reduced to a heap of ruins.

4. Jeremias remained in Jerusalem, and sitting on the ruins of the desolate city he lamented in the most pathetic manner the miseries of his people and the destruction of Jerusalem. "How doth the city sit solitary that was full of people; how is the mistress of nations become as a widow; the princess of provinces made tributary? The ways of Sion mourn because there are none that come to the solemn feast. O all ye that pass by the way, attend, and see if there be any sorrow like to my sorrow. To what shall I compare thee, or to what shall I liken thee? Great as the sea is thy destruction. Who shall heal thee? Convert us, O Lord, to Thee, and we shall be converted; renew our days, as from the beginning."

5. Jeremias, however, was not without consolation. He knew that Israel would be restored and that God would make a new covenant with His people. "The days shall come, saith the Lord, and I will make a new covenant with the house of Israel and with the house of Juda. Not according to the covenants which I made with their fathers, which they made void. But this shall be the covenant that I will make with the house of Israel after those days. I will give my law and write it on their hearts, and I will be their God, and they shall be my people. I will forgive their iniquity and I will remember their sin no more."

6. The captive Jews were treated with kindness by the king of Babylon, but they longed for the land of their fathers and for the city of Jerusalem. This longing of their hearts is beautifully expressed in one of the psalms: "Upon the rivers of Babylon, then we sat and wept, when we remembered Sion. On the willows in the midst thereof we hung up our instruments, for there they that led us into captivity re-

quired of us the words of songs. How shall we sing the song of the Lord in a strange land? If I forget thee, O Jerusalem, let my right hand be forgotten. Let my tongue cleave to my jaws if I do not remember thee, if I make not Jerusalem the beginning of my joys."

7. During the captivity, God did not abandon his people but sent the prophet Ezechiel, who admonished and instructed them. He also consoled them by telling them of a vision which foreshadowed the deliverance of the people from their captivity. The spirit of the Lord brought Ezechiel to a plain filled with bones. Being told by God, he commanded the bones to come together, which was done, and they were covered with flesh and skin, but there was no spirit in them. And the Lord told Ezechiel to say to the spirit: "Come spirit, and let them live again." The spirit entered into them, and they lived; they stood upon their feet, an exceeding great army. Then the Lord said: "These bones are the house of Israel; they say that our bones are dried up and our hope is lost, but say to them: 'Thus saith the Lord God: Behold I will open your graves and bring you into the land of Israel, and you shall know that I am the Lord, O my people."

8. Amongst the captives were several young men of high rank, belonging to the first families. The king ordered the most distinguished of these to be brought to his own palace, clothed in kingly apparel, and fed with meats from his own table. Amongst these young men were Daniel, Ananias, Misael, and Azarias.

9. They resolved not to eat of the meats from the king's table, because the Jewish law forbade the use of certain meats, and they begged the chief steward to allow them to eat only vegetables, and to drink only water. The steward was disposed to comply with their request, but he told them that

if they lived on such diet they would become so lean that the
king would blame him, and perhaps punish him severely.

10. Daniel besought the steward to try them for ten days
with the food and drink they desired to have. The steward
consented, and at the end of ten days the faces of these young
men were fresher and more comely than those of the other
young men of the court.

11. After this, the steward gave them only vegetables and
water; but God gave them wisdom and science. When the
time came that they were presented to the king, he was so
charmed with their beauty and wisdom that he retained them
in his service. The new covenant which Jeremias foretells is
the Christian religion, in which the greater grace is given to
men; for this reason it is called the law of grace, while
the old testament was called the law of fear.

QUESTIONS.

1. What did the people of Juda at last become? To what did they
give themselves wholly up? What more did they do? What was the
result? 2. Who marched against Jerusalem, in the year 606 before
Christ? What did Nabuchodonosor do when he took the city? What
happened sixteen years after? 3. Where were all the people taken that
escaped the sword? To what was the splendid city of Jerusalem reduced? 4. What prophet bewailed the destruction of Jerusalem? Repeat his lamentation. 5. Was Jeremias left without consolation? What
did he know? How was he consoled by the Lord? How were the captive
Jews treated by the king? How is the longing of their hearts expressed?
Repeat the lamentation. 7. Did God abandon His people? Whom did
He send to them? How did Ezechiel console them? Where did the
spirit of God lead Ezechiel? What did God command him to do? Did
the spirit obey him? 8. Who were amongst the captives? What did the
king order with regard to these young men? Give the names of three
of them? 9. What did they resolve not to do? Why? What did they
beg the chief steward to give them? Why did the steward fear to grant
their request? 10. What did Daniel beseech the steward to do? What
happened at the end of ten days? 11. After this, what did the steward
give them? What did God give them? How did the king receive them?
What is the new covenant or law which the prophet Jeremias foretells?

CHAPTER LXXVI.

Daniel Saves Susanna.

O how beautiful is the chaste generation with glory.—*Wis. 4, 1.*

A MONG the captive Jews in Babylon there was a man named Joakim, whose wife, Susanna, was very beautiful, and feared God. Now Joakim being very rich and influential, it happened that many of his countrymen resorted to his house. Among these were two of the ancients who had been appointed judges for that year. The two old men were considered by the people as wise and virtuous, but in reality they were very wicked.

2. Now the visitors that came to Joakim generally left at noon, and then Susanna would walk forth into the orchard near by to refresh herself in the shade. The two old men knew this, and one day they went into the orchard and hid themselves behind the trees. A little later Susanna came in and fastened the gate, believing herself alone. Then the wicked old men came forth from their hiding-place and tried to make her commit sin.

3. Susanna was horrified at their proposal; but they said that if she did not consent to their wishes, they would publicly accuse her of a great crime. Then Susanna raised her beautiful eyes to heaven, sighed and said: "I am straitened on every side, for if I do this thing, it is death to me, and if I do it not, I shall not escape your hands. But it is better for me to fall into your hands, without doing it, than to sin in the sight of the Lord."

4. She then cried out with a loud voice; but the elders cried out against her. One of them ran to the orchard-gate and opened it, that the people might enter. Then he and his companion accused Susanna of a most wicked act. Next day, accompanied by her parents and children, and other relatives, Susanna was brought before the tribunal of justice,

where she was condemned and sentenced to death. But she weeping, looked up to heaven, for her heart had confidence in God.

5. And the Lord heard her prayer. As she was led out to death, Daniel, inspired from above, exclaimed: "I am clear from the blood of this woman." Then all the people began to ask him: "What meaneth this word that thou hast spoken?" He told them to return to judgment, because the elders had borne false witness against Susanna. Then the people went back in haste. But Daniel ordered the two accusers to be brought in separately.

6. This being done, he said to the first that came: "O thou that art grown old in evil days, now are thy sins come out. Tell me under what tree thou sawest them conversing together?" He said: "Under a mastic-tree." Daniel replied: "Thou hast lied against thy own head." Then he sent him away, and had the other brought in, whom he asked: "Tell me, under what tree didst thou take them conversing together?" He answered: "Under a holm-tree." Daniel replied: "Thou hast lied against thy own head."

7. The people saw by the contrary statements of the old men that their testimony was false, and rising up against them, they put them both to death. Susanna was restored to her joyful husband and children, and they and all the people blessed God, who always saves and protects those who place their hopes in Him. Whereupon Daniel became great in the sight of the people.

QUESTIONS.

1. Who was among the captive Jews in Babylon? Who was his wife? What sort of a woman was she? Who were among the Jews that frequented the house of Joakim? What sort of men were these judges? 2. What was Susanna accustomed to do about noon when the visitors retired? What did the two old men, knowing this, do? How did they act when Susanna came in and fastened the door, believing herself alone? 3. Susanna being horrified at their proposal, what did they tell her? What did Susanna then

say, raising her eyes to heaven? 4. What did she then do? What did the elders do? What did one of them do? Of what did he and his companion then accuse Susanna? What happened to Susanna when she was brought next day before the tribunal of justice? In whom had Susanna confidence? 5. Did the Lord hear her prayer? As she was led out to death, what did Daniel, inspired from above, exclaim? What did the people then begin to ask him? What did he tell them? When the people went back in haste, what did Daniel order to be done? 6. What did he say to the first that came in? What did the old man say? What did Daniel say? What did Daniel ask the other old man? What did he answer? What did Daniel reply? 7. What did the people see by the contrary statements of the old men? What did they do to them? What was done to Susanna? What did all the people do? What did Daniel become?

CHAPTER LXXVII.

The Prophet Daniel.—The Three Young Men in the Fiery Furnace.

Call upon Me in the day of trouble; I will deliver thee, and thou shalt glorify Me.—*Ps. 49, 15.*

NABUCHODONOSOR had a dream which terrified him greatly. He saw a large statue, the head was of gold, the breast and arms of silver, the belly and thighs of brass, the legs of iron, and the feet, part iron and part clay. Then he noticed a stone rolling from the mountain, which struck the statue on the feet and shattered it; and behold, the stone became a great mountain and filled the whole earth. None of the wise men could interpret the dream. Then the king called for Daniel to whom God had revealed the meaning of the dream.

2. The whole statue signified the great empires of the world that would succeed each other. The head of gold betokened the reign of Nabuchodonosor himself, most glorious among kings; the breast and the arms of silver represented the next empire, that of the Medes and Persians; the belly

and the thighs of brass prefigured the dominion of Alexander the Great; the legs and feet of iron signified the great Roman empire which conquered all the others. The stone that fell from the mountain, typified a new kingdom that God himself would found on earth, and which, from a small beginning, would gradually grow strong and overcome all other kingdoms, and would last forever. The king, hearing the interpretation, said to Daniel: "Verily your God is the God of gods, and Lord of kings, and a revealer of hidden things." He raised Daniel to a high station and bestowed on him many gifts.

3. About this time king Nabuchodonosor made a great statue of gold which he placed on a pillar in the plain of Babylon. All the princes and nobles of his kingdom were invited to assist at the dedication of this statue. Heralds were sent out everywhere to announce to all the people that when they heard the sound of the trumpets and flutes and other instruments of music, they should fall down and adore the golden statue. And it came to pass that no one disobeyed this order except Ananias, Misael, and Azarias.

4. It was announced to the king that the three young men had refused to worship the golden statue. Then Nabuchodonosor, full of rage, said to them: "Who is the god that shall deliver you out of my hand?" They answered: "Our God whom we worship is able to save us from the furnace of burning fire; but if He will not, we will not worship thy god, nor adore the golden statue." The king then ordered that a furnace should be heated seven times more than ordinarily, and that three of the strongest soldiers of his army should bind the young men and cast them clothed as they were, into the furnace.

5. The order was instantly executed. But the angel of the Lord went down with the three holy youths into the furnace and behold, inside, the flames were extinguished, but outside, the fires burned and flashed and destroyed the men who

had executed the king's cruel order. They were instantly consumed by the raging fire.

6. Within the furnace the air was cool and fresh, like to the breeze when the dew is falling. And the three young men, seeing themselves so wonderfully preserved, sang a glorious canticle of praise and thanksgiving, which the Church of God still sings in her divine service.

THE THREE YOUNG MEN IN THE FURNACE.

7. The king, astonished to hear voices in the furnace singing, rose up and said to his nobles: "Did we not cast three men bound into the midst of the fire? I see four men loose, and walking in the midst of the fire, and the form of the fourth is like the son of God."

8. Then going to the door of the furnace, he cried: "Ye servants of the Most High God, go ye forth and come." Thereupon the young men came forth safe and sound, not so much as a hair of their heads was burned, nor was the smell

of fire on their garments. Seeing this prodigy,[1] Nabuchodo-
nosor blessed God, saying: "Blessed be the God of Ananias,
Misael, and Azarias, who has sent His angel, and delivered
His servants that believed in Him."

9. He then decreed that whosoever, in all his kingdom,
blasphemed the God whom these young men adored should
be put to death, for there was no other God who had power
to save. The three young men were raised to high dignities
in the kingdom of Babylon. The last kingdom, or the stone
falling from the mountain, mentioned by Daniel, signifies
the Catholic Church which Jesus Christ established upon
earth. At first it was small, but it kept on increasing and
still increases and will endure to the end of the world.

QUESTIONS.

1. Relate Nabuchodonosor's dream. 2. Explain the dream. What
did the king say to Daniel? To what did the king raise him? 3. What
did King Nabuchodonosor make? Who were invited to assist at the
dedication of this statue? What were heralds sent out to announce to
all the people? Who alone disobeyed this order? 4. What did the
king order to be done to the young men? 5. Who went down into the
furnace with the young men? Who were consumed by the raging fire?
6. What was there within the furnace? What did the three young
men sing? 7. What did the king say to his nobles? 8. What did the
king cry out, going to the door of the furnace? How did the young
men come forth from the furnace? Seeing this prodigy, what did
Nabuchodonosor do and say? 9. What did he then decree? What
was done for the three young men? Of what is the stone falling from
the mountain a figure?

[1] PROD'IGY, something which surpasses the power of nature.

CHAPTER LXXVIII.

King Baltassar—The God Bel.

I will call upon the name of the Lord.—*Ps. 115, 13.*

AFTER the death of Nabuchodonosor, Baltassar, his grandson, ascended the throne. One day Baltassar gave a great banquet to the nobles of his kingdom, and ordered the golden cups, which his grandfather had taken from the temple of Jerusalem, to be brought forth and to be used at the banquet.

2. The sacred vessels were brought, and the king and his wives and his officers drank from them, and they praised their gods of gold and of silver and of stone. At that moment a hand appeared and fingers were seen writing three words upon the wall over against the king. Baltassar grew pale and trembled, for the points of that hand were moving and wrote: Mane, Thecel, Phares. He called for his wise men, that they might interpret the writing. But none of them could do so. Then Daniel, who had received from God the gift of prophecy, together with that of explaining hidden things, came forth, and spoke to the king:

3. "Thou hast lifted up thyself against the Lord of heaven. Thou hast praised thy gods of gold and silver; but the Lord of heaven who hath thy breath in his hand, thou hast not glorified. Thou knowest that thy grandfather was punished for his pride; that he was driven away from the sons of men, and that he ate grass in the field with the ox and the ass, and yet thou hast not humbled thy heart.

4. "Wherefore God hath sent the fingers of the hand to write, and this is the writing, and this is the interpretation thereof: Mane: God hath numbered thy kingdom, and hath finished it. Thecel: thou art weighed in the balance, and art found wanting. Phares: thy kingdom is divided, and is

given to the Medes and Persians." That very night Baltassar was slain and the prophecy of Daniel was thus fulfilled. Some time after the army of the Medes and Persians, under Darius, their great leader, took the city of Babylon, and divided the kingdom.

5. Cyrus, king of Persia, and successor of Darius, soon took possession of all the Assyrian empire, of which Babylon was the capital. He treated Daniel with marked respect and made him sit down at his own table. At this time the god Bel was worshiped in Babylon as the supreme deity. There were spent upon him every day twelve large measures of flour, forty sheep, and sixty vessels of wine.

6. The king went every day to adore this god Bel. But Daniel adored the true God. Then the king asked him why he did not adore Bel. Daniel replied that he adored the true and living God, who created earth and heaven, and whose power extends over all things. The king, much surprised, asked Daniel, if he did not believe that Bel was a living god, seeing how much he consumed every day.

7. Daniel smiled and said: "O king, be not deceived; for this Bel is clay within and brass without, neither has he eaten at any time." The king, being angry, called for the priests of the god, and said to them: "If ye tell me not who it is that eats up these provisions, ye shall die. But if ye can show that Bel eateth these things, Daniel shall die, because he has blasphemed against Bel." Daniel agreed to the king's proposal.

8. Then the king, accompanied by Daniel, went to the temple of Bel. And the priests of Bel said to the king: "Behold, we go out, and do thou, O king, set on the meats, and make ready the wine, and shut the door fast, and seal it with thy own ring; and when thou comest in the morning, if thou find not that Bel has eaten up all, we will suffer death, or, else Daniel who has lied against us."

9. They were not afraid, because they had a secret door under the altar, whereby they entered and consumed the

meats. The priests having gone out, the king caused the meats and the wine to be placed before Bel. This being done, the servants of Daniel brought ashes, and he sifted them all over the temple in the presence of the king. Then they all left the temple, the door of which was sealed with the royal seal.

10. But the priests went in by night with their wives and children, as they were accustomed to do, and they ate and drank all that had been placed before the idol. The king arose early in the morning and went to the temple with Daniel. They found the seal unbroken, and opening the door, went in. The king looked at the table, and seeing that all the provisions had disappeared, cried out: "Great art thou, O Bel, and there is not any deceit with thee."

11. Daniel laughed, and pointing to the floor, said: "Mark, whose footsteps these are!" The king, much amazed, said: "I see the footsteps of men, women and children." Then examining more closely, he found the secret door by which the priests were wont to go in and out. Thereupon the king, being enraged against the priests of Bel, ordered them all to be put to death. And he gave Bel up to Daniel, who destroyed him and his temple.

QUESTIONS.

1. Who ascended the throne after Nabuchodonosor? One day when Baltassar gave a great banquet, what did he order to be brought and used? 2. What did the king, his wives, and his officers do with the sacred vessels? What was seen at that moment? Whom did Baltassar order to be sent for to interpret the writing? Could they do so? Who then came forth? 3. What did Daniel say to the king? Of what did he tell him? 4. What did he say was the meaning of the writing on the wall? When was this prophecy of Daniel fulfilled? How was it fulfilled? Who took the city some time after? 5. Who soon took possession of the whole Assyrian empire? What city was the capital of that empire? How did Cyrus treat Daniel? What was worshipped at this time in Babylon as the supreme divinity. What provisions were given to Bel every day? 6. What did the king do every day? What did he ask Daniel? What did Daniel reply? What did the king, much surprised, ask Daniel? 7. What did Daniel say, smiling? What did the

king, being angry, say to the priests of Bel? 8. When the king and Daniel went to the temple of Bel, what did the priests say? 9. Why were they not afraid? The priests having gone out, what did the king cause to be done? This being done, what did Daniel command the servants to do? What was then done to the door? 10. What did the priests, with their wives and children, do during the night? What did the king and Daniel find on going to the temple next morning? What did the king cry out, seeing that all the provisions had disappeared? 11. What did Daniel say, pointing to the floor? What did the king say? On examining closely, what did they find? What did the king then order to be done to the priests of Bel? What did he give up to Daniel? What did Daniel do with the idol?

CHAPTER LXXIX.

Daniel in the Lions' Den.

Thou hast remembered me, O God, and Thou hast not forsaken them that love Thee.—*Dan. 14, 37.*

THE people of Babylon worshiped also a great dragon. One day the king said to Daniel: "Behold, thou canst not say now that this is not a living god; adore him, therefore." Daniel replied: "Give me leave, O king, and I will kill this dragon without sword or club." The king returned: "I give thee leave." Then Daniel took pitch, fat and hair, and boiling them together, he made lumps and put them into the dragon's mouth.

2. The monster, swallowing the lumps, very soon burst asunder, and Daniel said to the king: "Behold him whom you worshiped!" The Babylonians hearing this, assembled in crowds, and said that the king had become a Jew; had destroyed Bel, killed the dragon, and put the priests to death. They came, therefore, to the king threatening and saying: "Deliver Daniel to us, or else we will destroy thee and thy house."

3. Although the king loved Daniel, he was forced through the violence of the people to give him up to their fury. Immediately they cast him into a den of lions. There were seven lions in the den to whom they gave two carcasses

every day and two sheep; but now, nothing was given them, that they might devour Daniel. Yet Daniel remained unhurt.

DANIEL IN THE LIONS' DEN.

4. Daniel, having been for some time in the lions' den, needed food. Now there was at that time in Judea a prophet named Habacuc, who carried food to the field for the reapers. The angel of the Lord appeared to him and said: "Carry thy dinner to Daniel, who is in the lions' den at Babylon."

5. Habacuc replied: "Lord, I never saw Babylon, nor do I know the den." Then the angel took him by the hair of his head,—carried him in an instant to Babylon, and placed him over the den of the lions. And Habacuc called to Daniel: "Thou servant of God, take the dinner that God has sent thee!" Daniel exclaimed: "Thou hast

remembered me, O God, and Thou hast not forsaken them that love Thee." Then he arose and ate.

6. But the angel of the Lord carried Habacuc back to his own place. On the seventh day the king came to bewail Daniel. And standing near the den he looked in and saw Daniel sitting amongst the lions, and he cried with a loud voice: "Great art Thou, O Lord, the God of Daniel!"

7. Immediately he drew Daniel out of the den, but those who had desired the prophet's death he threw in, and they were devoured by the lions in a moment. Then the king said: "Let all the inhabitants of the whole earth fear the God of Daniel, for He is the Savior, working signs and wonders."

QUESTIONS.

1. What did the people of Babylon and their king worship? What did the king say one day to Daniel? What did Daniel tell the king? What did Daniel do when the king gave permission? 2. What happened to the monster? What did Daniel then say to the king? What did the Babylonians do on hearing this? What did they say? What did they threaten to do? 3. What was the king forced to do through the violence of the people? What did they do with Daniel? Did the lions harm Daniel? 4. How long had Daniel been in the lions' den? Who was at that time in Judea? What did the angel of the Lord tell him when he was carrying food to the reapers? 5. What did Habacuc tell the angel? What did the angel then do? What did Habacuc call to Daniel? What did Daniel exclaim? 6. What did the angel then do with Habacuc? Why did the king come to the lions' den on the seventh day? When he saw Daniel sitting among the lions, what did he cry with a loud voice? 7. What did he do with Daniel? What did he do to those who had desired the prophet's death? What was the result? What did the king then say?

CHAPTER LXXX.

Return of the Jews from Babylon. (536 B. C.)

Thou who art a forgiving God, long-suffering and full of compassion
didst not forsake them.—*II. Esd. 9, 17.*

THE prophet Jeremias had foretold that the captivity of
Babylon would not last longer than seventy years, and
that the Jews should then return to their own country.
Daniel had renewed this consoling promise, and had added
another prophecy of greater importance; namely, that from
the day on which the order should be given to rebuild Jerusalem till the death of the Messias, there would remain only
seventy weeks of years; that is, four hundred and ninety
years. So that the Jews knew not only the family from
which the Savior would spring, but also the city where He
would be born, and the year in which He would die.

2. The severe sufferings of the captivity of Babylon,
together with the exhortations of the prophets, particularly
those of Daniel and Ezechiel, had brought the Jewish people
to a sense of their duty. Wherefore, it happened that in the
seventieth year of their sad captivity, Cyrus, king of Persia,
by a divine inspiration, issued an edict that all the Jews who
were in his kingdom should go back to Jerusalem and rebuild
the temple of the Lord.

3. He also restored to them the sacred vessels which Nabuchodonosor had carried away. Thereupon, more than forty
thousand Israelites, under the leadership of Prince Zorobabel,
and of the high priest Josue, returned to Judea, the name
thenceforward given to the ancient kingdom of Judea, together with the remnants of the other ten tribes which had
joined themselves to Juda and Benjamin before the downfall of Israel. They immediately built an altar, and offered
sacrifice every morning and evening.

4. One year after the return from captivity, the founda-

tions of the new temple were laid in Jerusalem. The priests and the Levites were there with their trumpets and cymbals, as of old, singing to the Lord canticles of praise and thanksgiving, while the people all rejoiced with exceeding great joy. And when, after many years, the temple was completed, it was consecrated and dedicated with great solemnity.

5. Many of the old people who remembered the former temple wept to see that the new one did not equal the old in magnificence. But the prophet Aggeus consoled them with the assurance that the second temple should be more glorious than the first, because the Messias, the Desired of all nations, would be seen in it, and would honor it with his presence. The same prediction was made by the prophet Zachary.

6. About eighty years after their return from captivity, the Jews, by command of the king of Persia, commenced to rebuild the walls of Jerusalem. The Samaritans opposed them and tried even by violence to prevent the people from rebuilding their city. But the Jews prayed to God to assist them, and in order to prevent surprise from the Samaritans, divided themselves into two great bodies.

7. Those who were most brave and courageous they placed on the outposts of the city, well armed, in order to keep off the enemy, while those who were skilled in masonry and other mechanical arts, carried on the work. At the end of fifty-two days all the walls and ramparts were completed. The Samaritans, seeing that the hand of God was there, ceased to trouble their neighbors.

8. The Jews, understanding that they had been successful in rebuilding the temple and the walls of Jerusalem in spite of so many obstacles, returned sincere thanks to God. And Esdras, the high-priest, having publicly read the law of the Lord, they all promised with tears, to be faithful to it. For they had received a new and strong proof that God had forgiven their own sins, and the ingratitude of their fathers.

QUESTIONS.

1. What had the prophet Jeremias foretold? Who had renewed this promise? Adding what? 2. What had brought the Jewish people to a sense of their duty? What edict did Cyrus, king of Persia, issue, by divine inspiration? 3. What did he also restore to the Jews? Under whose leadership did the Jews return from captivity? What remnants had long before joined themselves to the tribes of Juda and Benjamin? How long was it after the return from captivity that the foundations of the new temple were laid in Jerusalem? 5. What did many of the old people do who remembered the former temple? Who consoled them? With what assurance? By what other prophet was the same prediction made? 6. How long was it after their return from captivity that the Jews commenced to rebuild the walls of Jerusalem? By whose command did they commence? Who opposed them? But what did the Jews do? 7. What did the Samaritans do, seeing that the hand of God was there? 8. What did the Jews do when the work was finished? Who read the law publicly? What did the Jews promise to do?

CHAPTER LXXXI.

Esther.

Pride goeth before destruction; and the spirit is lifted up before a fall.—*Prov. 16, 18.*

A S the government of the kings of Persia was exceedingly mild, many of the Jews remained in the kingdom of Babylon. God permitted this for the spiritual good of the Gentiles, so that the latter, being brought into daily contact with the Jews, might more easily arrive at the knowledge of the true God, and be instructed in the promises made concerning a Savior to come.

2. It happened, by a special dispensation of God, that many of the Jews, like Daniel and his companions in former years, were in high favor with the kings of Persia, and made use of their influence to protect their countrymen and to propagate the true faith. At a certain time it pleased Divine Providence to employ in this way a pious Jewess, named Esther.

3. She lived in the reign of Assuerus, in the house of Mar-

dochai, her uncle, who had brought her up from her infancy. Assuerus having seen her was pleased with her beauty and virtue, placed the crown upon her head, and made her his queen. But she, by Mardochai's advice, left the king in ignorance regarding her nation. And Mardochai, who loved Esther as his own child, came every day and sat at the gate of the palace.

4. Now it came to pass that two of the officials of the palace had conspired together to kill the king. Mardochai, having discovered the plot, revealed it to Esther, who immediately told the king. The affair being examined, Mardochai's statement was found to be true. The two conspirators[1] were hanged, and the facts were recorded in the annals of the kingdom.

5. Some time after, Assuerus raised a certain Aman to the highest dignity in the empire. All the king's servants bent the knee before Aman and worshiped him. Mardochai alone did not bend the knee before Aman, as he would not give to man the honor due to God alone. Aman perceiving this, and learning that Mardochai was a Jew, became very angry.

6. To be revenged on Mardochai he told Assuerus that the Jews were planning a revolt, and prevailed upon the king to publish an edict commanding all the Jews in his empire to be put to death, and their property to be taken away. The Jews were terrified, and began to weep and lament. But Mardochai told Esther of the edict, so that she might intercede with the king for her own people.

7. Then Esther said: "All the provinces know, that whosoever cometh into the king's inner court, who is not called for, is immediately put to death. How then can I go in to the king, not being called." To these words Mardochai replied: "Who knoweth whether thou art not therefore come

---

[1] Conspirators, persons who plot against any one.

to the kingdom that thou mightest be ready for such a time as this?" Esther, therefore, praying fervently, and abstaining from food and drink for three days, resolved to go in to the king, not being called, against the law, and to expose herself to death and to danger.

8. On the third day she put on her glorious apparel and wore her glittering robes, and passed through the door with a smiling countenance which hid a mind full of anguish and exceeding great fear. But when the king had lifted up his face, and with burning eyes had shown the wrath of his heart, Esther sank down and rested her head upon her handmaid. Then the king was seized with pity. He leaped from his throne, and upheld her in his arms, and said: "What is the matter, Esther? I am thy brother, fear not! Thou shalt not die, for this law is not made for thee, but for all others. What wilt thou, Queen Esther?" She, recovering herself, answered: "If it please the king, I beseech thee to come to me this day, and Aman with thee, to the banquet which I have prepared."

9. The king acceded to her wish; and, during the repast, he desired to know her request. She answered: "If it please the king to give me what I ask, and to fulfill my petition, let the king and Aman come again to the banquet which I have prepared them, and to-morrow I will open my mind to the king." The king promised to do so, and Aman left the palace with a joyful heart. But in going out he saw Mardochai sitting at the door of the palace.

10. And because Mardochai would not bow down before him like the others, he was filled with rage; and going home to his house, ordered a gallows fifty cubits high to be erected to hang Mardochai on the following morning. Now it so happened that the king could not sleep that night, and to divert his mind, he ordered the annals of his reign to be read to him.

11. When the reader came to the place which related how Mardochai had discovered the plot against the king's life,

Assuerus suddenly asked what reward Mardochai had received for this important service. He was told that the man had never received any reward. Then the king called for Aman, whom he asked what ought to be done to honor the man whom the king desired to honor.

12. Aman, supposing that there was question of himself, said that the man whom the king desired to honor, ought to be clothed with the king's apparel, and be set upon the king's horse, and have the royal crown put upon his head, and that the first of the king's princes and nobles should hold his horse, and going through the streets of the city they should proclaim before him: "Thus shall he be honored whom the king hath a mind to honor!"

13. Then the king said to him: "Make haste and take the robe and the horse, and do as thou hast spoken to Mardochai, the Jew, who sitteth before the gate of the palace." Aman was surprised and enraged to hear these words, but he dared not disobey the word of the king. He went, therefore, and did as he was ordered. Meanwhile the hour came for the queen's banquet, and Aman went thither in all haste.

14. While they sat at the table the king said again to the queen: "What is thy petition, Esther, that it may be granted thee? Although thou ask the half of my kingdom, thou shalt have it." Esther replied: "If I have found favor in thy sight, O king, give me my life, for which I ask, and my people, for which I request. For we are given up, I and my people, to be destroyed, to be slain, and to perish."

15. The king, in surprise, asked: "Who is this and of what power that he should dare to do these things?" Esther answered: "It is Aman that is our most wicked enemy." But Aman, hearing what the Queen said, was seized with terror. The king arose from the table in great wrath. Being told by one of the attendants that Aman had prepared a gibbet fifty cubits high whereon to hang Mardochai, he ordered Aman himself to be hanged upon it.

16. The same day King Assuerus raised Mardochai to the

high dignity which Aman had held, and the edict against the Jews was immediately revoked. The Jews rejoiced beyond measure at their unexpected deliverance, and many of the Gentiles, seeing how wonderfully God protected them, embraced their religion. Queen Esther is a striking figure of Mary, the immaculate Queen of Heaven. For as Esther alone was exempted from the law of death, so Mary alone was preserved from original sin, in which the rest of mankind are born into this world. Again, Esther saved her people from slaughter, and Mary by her intercession, saves all her faithful clients from the flames of hell.

QUESTIONS.

1. Why did many of the Jews remain in Babylon? Why did God permit this? 2. What happened by a special dispensation of God? Who was, at a certain time, employed in this way by Divine Providence? 3. In what reign did Esther live? Who was her uncle? What did the king do when he had seen Esther and was charmed with her beauty? What did she do by Mardochai's advice? What did Mardochai do every day? 4. What had two officials of the palace conspired to do? Who discovered the plot? To whom did he reveal it? What did Esther do? 5. Whom did Assuerus, some time after, raise to the highest dignity in the empire? What did all the king's servants do to Aman? Who alone did not bend the knee to Aman? Why so? How did Aman feel, hearing that Mardochai was a Jew? 6. What did Aman tell Assuerus in order to be revenged on Mardochai? What did he prevail upon the king to do? How did the Jews feel? But what did Mardochai do? 7. What did Esther say about the law not to appear before the king without being invited? What did Mardochai answer? But what did Esther resolve to do? 8. What did she do on the third day? How did the king look when he saw Esther approach unbidden? What did the king do, being seized with pity? What did he say? What did Esther answer? 9. What did the king, next day, during the repast, desire to know? What did Esther answer? Whom did Aman see, as he went out with a joyful heart? 10. Why was Aman filled with rage? What did he order? What happened that night? What did he order to be read to him? 11. What did the king ask when the reader came to the place which related how Mardochai had discovered the plot against the king's life? What was he told? For whom did the king call? What did he ask when Aman came? 12. What did Aman say, supposing that there was question of himself? 13. What did the king then say to him? Did Aman obey this order? 14. While they sat at table, what did the king say again to the queen? What did Esther reply? 15. What did the king ask, in surprise? What did Esther tell

him? What did the king do? What was he told by one of the attendants? What did he order? 16. What did King Assuerus do the
same day? How did the Jews feel? What effect had all this on the
Gentiles? Of whom is Queen Esther a striking figure?

CHAPTER LXXXII.

Translation of the Old Testament into Greek.   (285 B.C.)
Wise Sayings of Jesus, the Son of Sirach.

The Lord giveth wisdom; and out of His mouth cometh prudence and
knowledge.—*Prov. 2, 6.*

THE Jews, who had returned to their country, lived in
peace for two hundred years under the dominion of the
successors of Cyrus. This peace was not disturbed even
when Alexander the Great, king of Macedon, destroyed the
Persian Empire. Whilst Alexander lived, he treated the
Jews with great kindness; but when, at his death, the Mace-
donian empire was divided, evil times came upon Judea.

2. That province became the object of dispute between the
kings of Syria and those of Egypt, who made it the battle-
ground for their contending armies, so that it was turned
almost into a desert. As a natural consequence of these protracted wars, ignorance, corruption and vice struck daily
deeper root among the Jewish people. This was one of the
darkest periods of their history.

3. It was about this time that the king of Egypt wished to
have a Greek translation of the sacred books of the Jews.
He therefore, expressed his desire to the High Priest at Jerusalem, who granted the request and sent to Alexandria, the
capital of Egypt, seventy-two wise men who were versed
both in Greek and Hebrew. These men were well received by the king, and they made for him a correct translation.
At that time the educated among the heathen nations knew

and spoke the Greek language. So this translation of the
scriptures began to be read by the pagans, who thereby came
to the knowledge of the true God and to the belief in the
Messias. In all this we see the hand of divine providence, who
wished to prepare the Gentiles for the coming of the Savior.

4. Almighty God also inspired a pious Jew, Jesus the son
of Sirach, to write a book of religious and moral instruction.
It is one of the books of the Catholic Bible, and is called
Ecclesiasticus. Here are a few of the beautiful maxims contained in it: "The fear of the Lord is the beginning and a
crown of wisdom. The word of God is the fountain of wisdom, and her ways are everlasting commandments. The
fear of the Lord shall delight the heart, and shall give joy,
and gladness, and length of days. It shall go well with him
that feareth the Lord, and in the days of his end he shall be
blessed. My son, from thy youth up receive instruction, and
even to thy gray hairs thou shalt find wisdom.

5. "Come to her as one that plougheth and soweth, and
wait for her good fruits. For in working about her thou shalt
labor a little, and shalt quickly eat of her fruits. Take all
that shall be brought upon thee, and keep patience, for gold
and silver are tried in the fire, but acceptable men in the
furnace of humiliation. Hear the judgment of your father,
and grieve him not in his life. The father's blessing establisheth the houses of the children, but the mother's curse
rooteth up the foundation.

6. "Despise not a man in his old age, for we also shall become old. Despise not the discourse of them that are ancient and wise; but acquaint thyself with their proverbs.
Praise not a man for his beauty, neither despise a man for
his look. The bee is small among flying things, but her
fruit hath the chiefest sweetness. Be in peace with many,
but let one of a thousand be thy counselor.

7. "Nothing can be compared to a faithful friend, and no

weight of gold and silver is able to countervail the goodness of his fidelity. If thou wouldst get a friend, try him before thou takest him, and do not credit him easily. For there is a friend for his own occasion, and he will not abide in the day of thy trouble. A lie is a foul blot in a man. In nowise speak against the truth, but be ashamed of the lie in thy ignorance.

8. "Let not the naming of God be usual in thy mouth, and meddle not with the names of saints. A man that sweareth much shall be filled with iniquity, and a scourge shall not depart from his house. Before thou hear, answer not a word, and interrupt not others in the midst of their discourse. Hast thou heard a word against thy neighbor, let it die within thee, trusting that it will not burst thee. Hedge in thy ears with thorns; hear not a wicked tongue; and make doors and bars to thy mouth.

9. "Melt down thy gold and silver, and make a balance for thy words. Flee from sin as from the face of a serpent. All iniquity is like a two-edged sword; there is no remedy from the wound thereof. Observe the time, and fly from evil. He that loveth danger shall perish therein, and he that toucheth pitch shall be defiled with it. In every work of thine regard thy soul in faith, for this is the keeping of the commandments. In all thy works remember thy last end, and thou shalt never sin."

QUESTIONS.

1. Under whom did the Jews, having returned from Babylon, live in peace for two hundred years? Was this peace disturbed when Alexander the Great destroyed the Persian empire? How did Alexander, while he lived, treat the Jews? But what came for the Jews at his death? 2. Between what kings did the province of Judea become the object of dispute? What was the natural consequence of these protracted wars? 3. What did the king of Egypt wish to have about this time? Whom did the High Priest send to him? How were the seventy-two wise men received by the king? What language did the educated heathens speak at this time? What was the good done by this translation? Was the hand of God in all this? 4. What did Almighty God inspire Jesus the son of Sirach to do? Which of the books of the Catholic Bible is this? What

is the fear of the Lord? What is the word of God? 5. What does the father's blessing establish? 6. Whom are we not to despise? What are we not to despise? 7. What is here said of a faithful friend? What is a lie? 8. What is not to be usual in our mouth? With what are we not to meddle? What is said of a man that swears much? 9. From what are we here told to flee as from the face of a serpent? What are we to remember in all our works?

CHAPTER LXXXIII.

The Martyrdom of Eleazar. (168 B. C.)

Many are the afflictions of the just.—*Ps. 33, 20.*

THE most terrible trial which the Jews had to undergo was that which came upon them at the time when they were made subject to the proud and cruel Antiochus, king of Syria. That king ordered the Holy Books to be torn and burned; he profaned the temple, and forbade the observance of the divine laws, under the penalty of death.

2. Unhappily, many of the Jews, yielding to a guilty fear, obeyed the king's order; but many more refused to comply with the impious mandate, and chose to die rather than violate the holy precept of God. Among these was an old man named Eleazar, ninety years of age, who was renowned as a doctor of the law.

3. When Eleazar refused to eat swine's flesh, the use of which was forbidden by the law of Moses, they opened his mouth by force in order to compel him to eat. But he still refused, and declared he would undergo any torment that might be inflicted upon him rather than stain his soul with sin by a violation of the commandment of God. But some of those who stood by, pitying the good old man, advised him to eat of some other meat which was not forbidden, so as to feign compliance with the king's command.

4. Eleazar replied: "It does not become our age to dissemble." He then explained to these false friends that even

if he made a mere show of complying with the king's orders in this matter, the young men of his nation might be tempted to follow his example, saying: The aged Eleazar has become a pagan, why may not we do the same? Moreover, he exclaimed: "Though for the present time, I should be delivered from the punishment of men; yet should I not escape the hand of the Almighty, neither alive nor dead."

5. Having thus spoken, the holy old man was dragged to the place of execution, where he suffered a glorious death. In the midst of his torments he cried out: "Lord, Thou knowest I suffer grievous pains, but I am well content to suffer these things, because I fear Thee." Eleazar, by his steadfast adherence to the law of God, and the fortitude wherewith he suffered a most cruel martyrdom has left a fine example of fidelity and heroic virtue.

QUESTIONS.

1. What was the most terrible trial which the Jews had to undergo? What did Antiochus order? 2. Did many of the Jews obey the king's order? What did many more choose, rather than comply with the impious mandate? Who was among these? 3. What was done to Eleazar when he refused to eat swine's flesh? What did he declare, still refusing? What did some of those who stood by, advise Eleazar to do? 4. What did Eleazar reply? What did he then explain to these false friends? What did he, moreover, exclaim? 5. What happened when the holy old man had thus spoken? In the midst of his torments, what did he cry out? What has Eleazar left by his steadfast adherence to the law of God?

CHAPTER LXXXIV.

The Martyrdom of the Seven Machabees.

The sufferings of this time are not worthy to be compared with the glory to come.—*Rom. 8, 18.*

ANTIOCHUS commanded that a certain widow, with her seven sons, should be brought into his presence, and should be forced to eat the forbidden flesh. They all told him that, as their law did not allow them the use of that meat, they could not obey his command. He immediately had them scourged with whips.

2. The eldest of the brothers told the king that they were ready to die rather than transgress the law of their God. Then the king, enraged at the young man's boldness, ordered his tongue to be plucked out, the skin of his head to be torn off, his hands and feet to be cut off, and finally that he

THE MARTYRDOM OF THE SEVEN MACHABEES.

should be burned alive before his mother and brothers. While he was suffering these cruel torments his mother and his brothers exhorted him to die courageously.

3. The first brother being dead, they seized the second, and, having torn the skin from off his head, they asked him if he would eat rather than undergo the rest of the torment. But he, refusing no less firmly and courageously than his elder brother, was tortured in the same way till he expired. When he was about to die, he exclamed: "Thou, O most

wicked man, destroyest us out of this present life, but the King of the world will raise us up who die for His laws, in the resurrection of eternal life."

4. The third brother offered his hands and feet to be cut off, saying: "These I have from heaven, but for the law of God I now despise them, because I hope to receive them again from Him." Some minutes before his death he declared aloud his willingness to die for God, as his brothers had already done. When he was dead, the fourth brother, the fifth, and the sixth—these three were subjected to the same torments as their elder brothers, but they all died in the same manner, having the same spirit. They made no account of pain and death, because they suffered all for God.

5. The king and his courtiers were amazed at the constancy of these young men, so that when the seventh, a mere youth, was brought forward, the king told him, with an oath, that he would make him rich and happy if he would obey his command. Seeing that his words had no effect on the courageous boy, Antiochus called on the mother to advise her son for his own good.

6. The mother agreed to do so. Then addressing her son, she said with all a mother's tender affection: "My son, look upon heaven and earth, and all that is in them; and consider that God made them out of nothing, and mankind also; so thou shalt not fear this tormentor, but, being made a worthy partner with thy brethren, receive death, that in that mercy I may receive thee again with thy brethren."

7. While she was yet speaking, the boy said: "For whom do ye stay? I will not obey the commandment of the king, but the commandment of the law which was given us by Moses." Then, turning to the king: "Thou," said he, "that hast been the author of all mischief against the Hebrews, shâlt not escape the hand of God." But the king, inflamed with rage, tortured him most cruelly till he yielded up his soul. Last of all, the mother herself was put to death.

1. Whom did Antiochus command to be brought into his presence? What did he order them to do? What did they all tell him? What did he order to be done to them? 2. What did the eldest of the brothers tell the king? What did the king, enraged at the young man's boldness, order to be done? 3. The first brother being dead, what did they do to the second? What was done to him when he answered, like his elder brother, that he would not eat? What did he exclaim when at the point of death? 4. What did the third brother do? Saying what? What did he declare aloud some minutes before his death? When he was dead, what was done to the fourth, fifth, and sixth of the brothers? How did they all die? 5. What did the king, amazed at the constancy of the brothers, tell the seventh, with an oath, when he was brought forward? Seeing that his words had no effect on the courageous boy, what did Antiochus do? 6. What did the mother do? What did she say to her son? 7. While she was yet speaking, what did the boy say? What did he say, turning to the king? What did the king do, being inflamed with rage? Who was, last of all, put to death?

CHAPTER LXXXV.

Valiant Exploits of Judas Machabeus. (*160 B. C.*)

It is easy for the Lord to save either by many or by few.
—*I. Kings 14, 6.*

AT the time when Antiochus was thus cruelly persecuting the Jews, there was in Judea a priest named Mathathias, who had five sons. This zealous priest, having learned that Antiochus had profaned the temple and nearly destroyed the worship of the true God, was filled with the deepest sorrow. He knew that the wicked king would soon succeed in his impious design if the Jews did not offer a vigorous resistance.

2. He, therefore, called upon all who had any zeal for the laws of God to rise up, with him, in the defence of their sacred rights. Then he and his sons fled to the mountains, where they were joined by the valiant men of Israel, and soon they became a powerful army. They destroyed the altars of the

false gods, bravely defended the law of the Lord, and compelled the apostate Jews to leave the country.

3. After the death of Mathathias, Judas, surnamed Machabeus, or the Hammerer, on account of his invincible courage and great valor, assumed the command of the Jewish army. In battle he showed himself brave as a lion—had several engagements with the Syrian generals, and recovered Jerusalem and the temple. With a sorrowful heart he saw the temple in its desecrated and desolate state, the altar profaned and the grass growing in the deserted courts.

4. He then purified the temple, celebrated his victory by a grand festival, and dedicated the altar anew, with the sound of harps, and lutes, and cymbals, and hymns of joy in the sight of the wondering multitude. Antiochus, hearing of the splendid victories of Judas Machabeus, was roused to fury, and putting himself at the head of his army, set out at once for Jerusalem.

5. But, riding at full speed in his war-chariot, he was thrown to the ground and grievously wounded. Soon worms came forth from the body of that impious king, the flesh rotted on his bones, and he became an object of horror and disgust, so that no one could approach him. He who so lately thought that the very stars of heaven should obey him, was deserted even by his slaves.

6. Then, seeing the folly and wickedness of his pride, he began to humble himself before the Lord, promising to repair all the evil he had done, and to proclaim throughout the whole earth that there was no god but the great God whom the Jews adored. But, inasmuch as his repentance proceeded only from the fear of death, and the dread of temporal punishment, it was of no avail before God. His sufferings continued unabated, and at last the wicked king, the blasphemer of God, the oppressor of His people, died in torment, the death of a reprobate.

7. The son and successor of Antiochus sent his ablest generals, with mighty armies, to take Judea and Jerusalem again. Judas Machabeus and his small army, seeing the hosts that were marching against them, had recourse to God in humble prayer. Then they took up their arms and advanced to meet the enemy, trusting in God alone.

8. In the midst of the combat five horsemen, in shining armor, were seen by the enemy in the air above, fighting for the Jews. Two of these heavenly warriors were with Judas Machabeus, as it were shielding him from danger, while the other three cast darts from on high against the Syrian host. Seeing this strange sight the enemy were seized with terror, and fled in confusion, leaving thirty thousand of their number dead on the field.

9. Thus favored by divine assistance, Judas Machabeus defeated the Syrians in many other bloody engagements. But it happened in one of these that some of the Jews were slain, and on the following day, when Judas and his soldiers came to bury them, they found under their tunics certain heathen charms, or amulets, which it was not allowable even to touch.

10. It became manifest to all that it was because of the amulets that these men had been killed: and praising the justice of God, they besought Him to pardon the sins of the unhappy dead. But Judas collected a sum of twelve thousand drachms[1] of silver and sent it to Jerusalem to have sacrifices offered for his soldiers who had thus fallen in battle. "It is therefore," says the scripture, "a holy and wholesome thought to pray for the dead, that they may be loosed from their sins."

11. Before one of the many battles which Judas fought, he had a vision. He saw the deceased high priest, Onias, holding up his hands and praying for the Jewish people. After this another man appeared, surrounded with great glory.

---

[1] DRACHMS (pr. drams)

Onias said: "This is he that prayeth much for the people, and for all the holy city, Jeremias, the prophet of God." Then Jeremias gave Judas a sword of gold, saying: "Take this holy sword, a gift from God, wherewith thou shalt overthrow the adversaries of My people Israel."

12. Judas, encouraged by these heavenly favors, gained many battles. At last it happened that he engaged the enemy with very unequal numbers. In this battle he was vanquished and slain. Then all the people mourned him for many days, saying: "How is the mighty man fallen that saved the people of Israel!" That Judas sent money to Jerusalem, wherewith sacrifices might be offered for the repose of the dead, is a sign that the Jews also believed in purgatory. For, if the prayers of the living brought no relief to the dead, neither would Judas have collected money for sacrifices, nor would the priests have accepted it for that purpose. Besides we learn from this chapter of the Bible that the saints pray for their friends on earth, and that their prayer is heard.

QUESTIONS.

1. At the time when Antiochus was persecuting the Jews, who was there in Judea? What did he know? 2. What did he, therefore, do? Whither did he and his sons flee? By whom were they joined there? What did they do? 3. After the death of Mathathias, who assumed the command of the Jewish army? Why was Judas surnamed Machabeus? How did he show himself in battle? What did he recover? What did he see? 4. What did he then do? What did Antiochus, roused to fury, do when he heard of the splendid victories of Judas Machabeus? 5. What happened to him on the way to Jerusalem? Describe the state to which he was reduced? By whom was he deserted? 6. Seeing the folly and wickedness of his pride, what did he then do? What did he promise? Why was his repentance of no avail before God? How did he die? 7. What did the son and successor of Antiochus do? What did Judas Machabeus and his small army do, seeing the hosts that were marching against them? 8. What was seen by the enemy in the midst of the combat? How many of their number did the enemy leave dead on the field? 9. What was found on the dead bodies of some of the Jewish soldiers who fell in battle on one occasion? 10 What was manifest to all? What did Judas do? What does scripture say of praying for the dead? 11. Before one of the battles, what did Judas see? What did Onias say? What did

Judas receive from Jeremias? 12. What happened at last to Judas Machabeus? What did the people say when they mourned him for many days? What is a sign that the Jews believed in purgatory? What do we learn besides from this chapter of the Bible History?

CHAPTER LXXXVI.

The Last Times Before Christ.

Let the clouds rain the Just; let the earth be opened and bud forth a Savior.—*Is. 45, 8.*

AFTER the death of Judas Machabeus, his brothers Jonathan and Simon successively placed themselves at the head of the Jewish people, and performed wonderful exploits. Their successors, however, fell away from God, and brought the people, always unsteady and prone to evil, into a multitude of sins and vices. They, indeed, still worshiped the true God, but it was only with their lips, and their hearts were far from him.

2. Their chief care consisted in the outward observance of the law; the inward disposition and purity of heart they neglected. Whatever good there might be among the Jews was stifled by the sect of the hypocritical Pharisees, or of the unbelieving Sadducees, and those two sects, although mortal enemies one of the other, exercised a great power over the people.

3. Throughout all the rest of the world idolatry reigned supreme, and all the nations of the earth were sunk in misery and corruption. The few just men who were scattered here and there among the different races of men, sighed for the coming of the promised Redeemer, the only hope of fallen man. They prayed that the clouds might rain down the Just One, and that the earth might bud forth the Savior.

4. All was in readiness for the coming of the Savior, which event, according to signs and prophecies, must be near at hand. Four hundred years before the birth of Christ, Mal-

achias, the last of the prophets, could not restrain his joy at
the near approach of the Messias. He told the Jewish
priests that their temple should soon be closed forever, and
the fires on their altars extinguished, for their offerings
had ceased to be pleasing to the Lord of Hosts. He said: "I
have no pleasure in you, saith the Lord of Hosts, and I will
not receive a gift of your hand. For from the rising of the
sun even to the going down, My name is great among the
Gentiles, and in every place there is sacrifice, and there is
offered to my name a clean oblation. For My name is great
among the Gentiles, saith the Lord of Hosts." The clean
oblation, of which the prophet Malachias speaks, is the Holy
Sacrifice of the Mass, which is offered every day, and in many
places from the rising of the sun to the going down thereof
Nothing remained to be accomplished, save the prophecy of
Jacob to his son Juda. This last sign was not delayed.

5. The Jewish people, torn and weakened by continual
dissensions among themselves, called in the Romans to decide their quarrels, and the Romans, a great and powerful
nation, settled the dispute by taking possession of all Judea,
and placing on its throne Herod, a stranger, a satellite of the
Roman emperor. Thus was the scepter of Juda broken, and
that event ushered in the Redeemer of the world. Herod
reigned in Judea when the Messias, so long promised, appeared on earth in human form, Christ the Lord, to Whom
be honor and glory for ever and ever.

QUESTIONS.

1. After the death of Judas Machabeus, who successively placed themselves at the head of the Jewish people? What did they perform? What
did their successors do? Did the people still worship the true God? 2.
In what did their chief care consist? What hypocritical or unbelieving
sects stifled whatever good might be among the Jews? What did these two
sects exercise over them? 3. What reigned supreme throughout all the
rest of the world? In what were all the nations of the earth sunk? For
what did the few just men sigh? For what did they pray? 4. For what
was all in readiness? What had Malachias, the last of the prophets, told
the Jewish priests four hundred years before the birth of Christ?

What did Malachias further predict? What was the only sign that was yet to be accomplished? Was that last sign long delayed? 5. What people did the Jews call to decide their quarrels? How did the Romans settle the dispute? Whom did they place on the throne? What event ushered in the Redeemer of the world? Who reigned in Judea when the Messias, so long promised, appeared on earth in human form?

History of the New Testament

HISTORY OF JESUS CHRIST.

His Birth and Infancy.

CHAPTER I.

Annunciation of the Birth of John the Baptist.

Behold, I send My Angel, and he shall prepare the way before My
face.—*Mal. 3, 1.*

AT the time when Herod was king in Judea, there lived
in a small city in the hill country, a priest named
Zachary, whose wife was called Elizabeth. They were both
just before God, and walked blamelessly in all the commandments of the Lord. They had no children, which was the
cause of great affliction to them.

2. They often prayed that God would give them a son; but
their prayer seemed to remain unanswered, as they were now
both advanced in years. It so happened that Zachary went
to Jerusalem, when his turn came to perform the priestly office. He entered into the sanctuary to offer incense on the
altar while the people prayed without; and, behold, an angel
of the Lord appeared to him, standing at the right hand of
the altar of incense.

3. Zachary was troubled at the sight of the angel; but the
angel said to him: "Fear not, Zachary, for thy prayer is
heard. Thy wife Elizabeth shall bear thee a son, and thou
shalt call his name John. Thou shalt have joy and gladness,
and many shall rejoice at his birth; for he shall be great before
the Lord, and shall drink no wine nor strong drink, and he

shall be filled with the Holy Ghost even from his mother's
womb.

4. "He shall convert many of the children of Israel to the
Lord their God. He shall go before Him in the spirit and
power of Elias to prepare for the Lord a perfect people."

ZACHARY AND THE ANGEL.

Zachary said to the angel: "Whereby shall I know this?
For I am an old man, and my wife is advanced in years."
The angel replied: "I am Gabriel, who stand before God,
and am sent to speak to thee, and to bring thee these good
tidings.

5. "Behold, thou shalt be dumb, and shalt not be able to
speak until the day in which these things shall come to pass,
because thou hast not believed my words." Having spoken
thus he disappeared. Meanwhile, the people without in the
temple were expecting Zachary, and wondered at his long
delay. When he at length appeared, he could not speak to
them, except by signs; and the people knew that he had seen

a vision[1] in the temple. After the days of his ministry were accomplished, Zachary departed to his own house.

QUESTIONS.

1. At the time when Herod was king in Judea, who lived in a small city in the hill country? What was his wife called? How did they both walk before the Lord? What was the cause of great affliction to them? 2. What did they often pray? Why did their prayer seem to remain unanswered? Who appeared to Zachary in the temple? 3. What did the angel say to Zachary? 4. What did Zachary say to the angel? What did the angel reply? 5. At what did the people without wonder? What did they know when Zachary could not speak to them except by signs?

CHAPTER II.

Annunciation of the Birth of Christ.

Behold, a virgin shall conceive, and bear a son, and His name shall be called Emmanuel, God-with-us.—*Is. 7, 14.*

SIX months later, the angel Gabriel was sent from God to a virgin living in a city of Galilee called Nazareth. The virgin's name was Mary, and she was espoused to a man called Joseph and they both belonged to the house of David.

2. The angel being come in said to her: "Hail, full of grace, the Lord is with thee; blessed art thou among women." Mary, hearing these words, was disturbed and troubled, thinking what this strange salutation[2] meant. But the angel spoke again: "Fear not, Mary, for thou hast found grace with God. Behold thou shalt conceive in thy womb, and bring forth a son, and thou shalt call his name Jesus.

3. "He shall be great, and shall be called the Son of the Most High, and the Lord God shall give Him the throne of David, His father; and He shall reign in the house of Jacob forever, and of His kingdom there shall be no end." Mary asked how this could be, seeing that she was a virgin. The angel answered: "The Holy Ghost shall come upon thee,

---

[1] A supernatural sight.   [2] Greeting.

and the power of the Most High shall overshadow thee.
And therefore, also, the Holy which shall be born of thee
shall be called the Son of God.

4. "And behold, thy cousin Elizabeth, she also hath conceived a son in her old age, because no word shall be impos-
sible with God." Then Mary said: "Behold the handmaid
of the Lord; be it done to me according to thy word." The

THE ANNUNCIATION.

angel, having thus delivered his message, and having obtained the consent of Mary, departed from her. Joseph knew
not as yet that Mary was the chosen mother of the Savior;
but an angel of the Lord appeared also to him in his sleep,
and said: "Joseph, son of David, fear not to take unto thee
Mary, thy wife; for that which is conceived in her is of the
Holy Ghost. And thou shalt call his name Jesus, for He
shall save His people from their sins."

QUESTIONS.

1. Who was sent from God to a virgin living in a city of Galilee, called Nazareth? What was the virgin's name? To whom was she espoused? To what house did they both belong? 2. What did the angel say to Mary? Why was Mary troubled? What did the angel, speaking again, say? 3. What did Mary ask the angel? What did the angel answer? 4. What did Mary say? Who appeared to Joseph in his sleep? What did the angel tell him?

CHAPTER III.

The Visitation.

All generations shall call me blessed.—*Luke 1, 48.*

MARY, rising up in those days, went in haste in to the hill country to visit and congratulate her cousin Elizabeth. No sooner did Mary enter into the house than Elizabeth, filled with the Holy Ghost, cried out: "Blessed art thou among women, and blessed is the fruit of thy womb. And whence is this to me, that the mother of my Lord should come to me? Blessed art thou that hast believed, because those things shall be accomplished[1] that were spoken to thee by the Lord."

2. Whereupon Mary exclaimed: "My soul doth magnify[2] the Lord, and my spirit hath rejoiced in God my Savior. Because He hath regarded the humility of His handmaid: for, behold, from henceforth all generations shall call me blessed. For He that is mighty hath done great things to me; and holy is His name. And His mercy is from generation to generation, to them that fear Him. He hath shown might in His arm: He hath scattered the proud in the conceit[3] of their heart. He hath put down the mighty from their seat and hath exalted[4] the humble. He hath filled the hungry with good things; and the rich He hath sent empty

---

[1] Fulfilled; done.   [2] Extol; praise; to sound the praises of.

[3] Over-estimation of one's self.   [4] Raised high; lifted up.

away. He hath received Israel His servant, being mindful of His mercy. As he spoke to our fathers, to Abraham and to his seed forever." Mary abode[1] with her cousin about three months; then she returned to Nazareth.

3. St. Elizabeth praises the Blessed Virgin for her faith, because what was lost to us by the unbelief of Eve, the same was gained back for us by the faith of Mary.

THE VISITATION OF ST. ELIZABETH.

QUESTIONS.

1. Whither did Mary go in those days? What did Elizabeth, filled with the Holy Ghost, cry out when Mary entered the house? 2. What did Mary, transported with joy, exclaim? How long did Mary remain with her cousin? 3. Why did Elizabeth praise the faith of Mary?

[1] Remained, dwelt.

CHAPTER IV.

Birth of John the Baptist.

Thou shalt have joy and gladness, and many shall rejoice in his nativity.—*Luke 1, 14.*

THE time of her delivery being come, Elizabeth brought forth a son. All her neighbors and her kinsfolk rejoiced with her. Eight days after his birth the child was circumcised. The relatives and friends thought the child should be called Zachary like his father. But Elizabeth answered: "Not so, he shall be called John." But they reminded her that there was no one in the family who bore that name.

2. Then they made signs to his father, how he would have him called. But he, being still dumb, made signs and demanded a tablet,[1] and wrote: "John is his name." At the same moment his tongue was loosened and he spoke. And all those who were present were amazed,[2] saying one to another: "What think ye shall this child be? for the hand of the Lord was with him."

3. Zachary, in an ecstasy[3] of joy and gratitude, began to bless God in a canticle[4] which still bears his name:

"Blessed be the Lord God of Israel; because he hath visited and wrought the redemption of His people,

And hath raised up a horn of salvation to us, in the house of David His servant.

As he spoke by the mouth of His holy prophets, who are from the beginning:

Salvation from our enemies, and from the hand of all that hate us,

To perform mercy to our fathers, and to remember His holy testament:

[1] A small, flat piece of anything on which to write. [2] Astonished.
[3] Rapture; enthusiastic delight. [4] A song of praise.

The oath which He swore to Abraham our father, that He
    would grant to us,

That, being delivered from the hand of our enemies, we may
    serve Him without fear,

In holiness and justice before Him, all our days.

And thou child, shalt be called the prophet of the highest:
    for thou shalt go before the face of the Lord to prepare
    His ways;

To give knowledge of salvation to His people, unto the re-
    mission of their sins.

Through the bowels of the mercy of our God: in which the
    Orient, from on high, hath visited us,

To enlighten them that sit in darkness, and in the shadow
    of death; to direct our feet into the way of peace."

And the child grew, and strengthened in spirit; and was in
the deserts until the day of his manifestation to Israel.

QUESTIONS.

1. The time for her delivery being come, what did Elizabeth bring
forth? What was done to the child eight days after his birth? What
did the relatives and friends who were present, think? What did
Elizabeth answer? Of what did they then remind her? 2. What was
the father then asked? For what did he make signs? What did he
write on the tablet? What happened at the same moment? What did
all those who were present say one to the other? 3. What did Zachary,
in an ecstasy of joy and gratitude, begin to do? When the child was
grown, where did he take up his abode?

CHAPTER V.

The Birth of Jesus Christ.

A CHILD IS BORN TO US, and a son is given to us, and the government is
upon His shoulder.—*Is. 9, 6.*

IN those days a decree[1] went forth from the Roman emperor, Cæsar[2] Augustus, commanding that all the people
of his empire should be enrolled.[3] Each one had to give in

[1] Decree, an order from one having authority. [2] Cæsar (pr. Se′-zer).
[3] Enrolled, to have one's name written in a roll or register.

his name in the tribe and city to which he belonged. So Joseph and Mary went to Bethlehem, the city of David, because they were of the family of that king.

2. But the city being crowded with strangers who had come for the enrollment, they could not obtain lodging in any of the inns, and were forced to seek shelter in a stable outside the city. And it came to pass that when they were there, Mary brought forth her first-born son, and wrapped Him up in swaddling clothes, and laid Him in a manger, because there was no room for them in the inn.

QUESTIONS.

1. What decree did the emperor, Augustus, send forth? Whither did Joseph and Mary go to be enrolled? 2. Why were they forced to seek shelter in a stable? What happened while they were there? Wherein did the virgin mother lay her divine Son?

CHAPTER VI.

The Shepherds at the Manger.

In the name of Jesus every knee should bow of those that are in heaven, on earth, and under the earth.—*Phil. 2, 10.*

THERE were, in the neighborhood of Bethlehem, shepherds watching and keeping the night watches over their flock. Suddenly an angel of the Lord appeared before them, and the brightness of God shone round about them, and they were seized with a great fear. But the angel said: "Fear not, for behold, I bring you good tidings of great joy, that shall be to all the people; for this day is born to you a Savior, who is Christ the Lord, in the city of David. And this shall be a sign unto you: You shall find the infant wrapped in swaddling clothes and laid in a manger."

2. Then there was with the angel a multitude[1] of the heavenly host, praising God and singing: "Glory to God in the highest, and on earth peace to men of good-will." When

[1] MULTITUDE; a great number.

the angels had disappeared, the shepherds said one to another: "Let us go over to Bethlehem and see the word that has come to pass, which the Lord has shown us." Going in haste, they found Mary and Joseph in the stable, and the new-born babe lying in the manger.

3. The shepherds adored Him, and went back to their

THE ADORATION OF THE SHEPHERDS.

flocks, praising and glorifying God for the wonders they had seen and heard. All the people that heard these things from the shepherds were astonished. But Mary kept all these words, pondering them in her heart. And after eight days the child was circumcised, and his name was called Jesus, that is Savior, as the angel had commanded.

QUESTIONS.

1. What were some shepherds doing by night in the neighborhood of Bethlehem? Who appeared suddenly before them? With what were they seized? What did the angel tell them? 2. Who accompanied the angel? What were the angels singing? When they had disappeared.

what did the shepherds say one to the other? What did they find in the stable? 3. What did they then do? What was done after eight days? What name did the child receive?

CHAPTER VII.

The Presentation in the Temple.

The Desired of all nations shall come; and I will fill this house with glory.—*Agg. 2, 8.*

FORTY days after His birth, Mary and Joseph brought Jesus to the temple of Jerusalem to present Him to the Lord, as the law of Moses prescribed.[1] They carried with

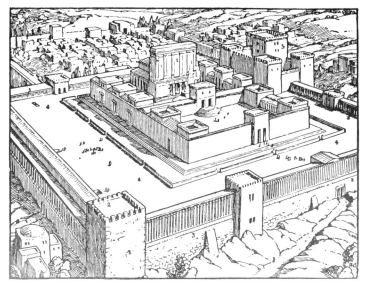

THE TEMPLE.

them the usual offering of the poor—a pair of turtle-doves. There was at that time in Jerusalem a just and God-fearing

[1] PRESCRIBED, directed; laid down as a rule.

man named Simeon. He was looking anxiously for the coming of the Messias, the Holy Spirit having revealed[1] to him that he should not die till he had seen the Christ of the Lord.

2. Led by the spirit, he came that day to the temple, and seeing the child brought in by Mary and Joseph, he took Him in his arms, and blessed God, saying: "Now Thou dost dismiss Thy servant, O Lord, according to Thy word in

THE PRESENTATION.

peace: Because my eyes have seen Thy salvation, which Thou hast prepared before the face of all peoples; a light to the revelation of the Gentiles, and the Glory of Thy people, Israel."

3. He then blessed Joseph and Mary, and to Mary he said: "Behold, this child is set for the fall and for the resurrection of many in Israel, and for a sign which shall be contradicted. And thy own soul a sword shall pierce, that out of

1 REVEALED, made known.

many hearts thoughts may be revealed." There was also in Jerusalem a prophetess[1] named Anna—a woman far advanced in years, who departed not from the temple—by fasting and prayer, serving the Lord night and day.

4. She also coming in, and seeing the child, gave praise to the Lord, and spoke of Him to all who were looking for the redemption of Israel. And when these things were accomplished in obedience to the law of God, Mary and Joseph, with the Divine Babe, returned to Galilee, to their own city of Nazareth, and dwelt there in peace.

QUESTIONS.

1. Where did Mary and Joseph bring Jesus forty days after His birth? What did they carry with Him? Who was there at that time in Jerusalem? For what was he looking anxiously? What had the Holy Spirit revealed to him? 2. Who led him to the temple that day? What did he do, seeing the child brought in by Mary and Joseph? Saying what? 3. What did he then do? What did he say to Mary? Who was there also in Jerusalem? 4. What did Anna do, coming in and seeing the child? When these things were accomplished, what did Mary and Joseph do?

CHAPTER VIII.

Adoration of the Magi.

All they from Saba shall come, bringing gold and frankincense.
—*Is. 60, 6.*

NOW when Jesus was born in Bethlehem in the days of King Herod, behold there came three wise men, or kings, from the East to Jerusalem, saying: "Where is He that is born King of the Jews? for we have seen His star in the East, and we are come to adore Him." Herod, hearing this, was troubled, and all Jerusalem with him. And having assembled[2] all the chief priests and scribes and the ancients of the people, he inquired of them where the promised Messias should be born.

2. They said to him: "In Bethlehem, of Juda, for so it is

---

[1] PROPHETESS, a female prophet.   [2] ASSEMBLED, brought together.

written by the prophet." Then Herod privately questioned the three Magi as to the exact time when the star appeared to them. When they had told him, he said: "Go, and search after the child, and when you have found him, bring me word again, that I also may come and adore him."

3. The Magi set out for Bethlehem, and no sooner had they left the palace of Herod than the star, which they had not seen since their entrance into Jerusalem, again appeared

THE ADORATION OF THE MAGI.

in the heavens; and, following its guidance, they came to the place where the divine infant was, with Mary its mother, and St. Joseph. And entering in they adored the child, and opening their treasures they offered him gifts—gold, frankincense[1] and myrrh.[2]

4. That night God appeared to the kings in a dream and commanded them not to return to Herod. So they went back

[1] FRANKINCENSE, a sweet smelling resinous substance.

[2] MYRRH (pr. *mer*), a costly eastern drug, used in embalming the dead.

by another way to their own country. Thus was the wicked king disappointed in his expectation of finding out, by means of these royal strangers, where he could find the child.

QUESTIONS.

1. When Jesus had returned with Mary and Joseph to Bethlehem, who came from the East? Saying what? Hearing this, how did Herod feel? What did he do? 2. What did they tell him? What did Herod then do? When they had told him, what did he request them to do? 3. What appeared to them again when they left the king's palace? Following the guidance of the star, whither did they come? Entering in, what did they do? What did they offer to the child? 4. What did God tell them in a dream? How did they return to their country? Who was thus disappointed?

CHAPTER IX.

The Flight into Egypt.

A voice in Rama was heard, lamentation and great mourning: Rachel bewailing her children, and would not be comforted because they are not.—Matt. 2, 18.

HEROD awaited, with anxiety, the return of the Magi. At last, perceiving that he waited in vain, he became furious,[1] and gave orders that all the male children in Bethlehem, and in all the confines thereof, of two years old and under that age, should be slain. He thought that, in this way, the child Jesus would certainly perish.

2. But the angel of the Lord appeared by night to Joseph and said: "Arise, and take the child and His mother, and fly into Egypt, and be there until I shall tell thee; for Herod seeks the child, to destroy Him." Then Joseph arose, took the child and his mother by night, and retired into Egypt.

3. Hardly had the Holy Family departed from Bethlehem, when the men of blood whom Herod had chosen to execute his cruel order, suddenly rushed into the city, dragged the infants from the arms of their mothers, and massacred[2] them

---

[1] FURIOUS, very angry.   [2] MASSACRED (pr. mass'-a-kerd).

all. Then was heard throughout the city of David the pite-
ous cry of the bereaved mothers mourning and bewailing the
innocent babes that were so cruelly put to death by the tyrant.

4. The punishment of this dreadful crime was not long delayed. A few years after the bloody deed Herod was strick-
en with a most loathsome disease, and died in fearful torments. Then the angel of the Lord appeared again to Joseph
in Egypt during his sleep, and said: "Rise, take the child

THE HOLY FAMILY IN NAZARETH.

and his mother, and go into the land of Israel; for they are
dead that sought the life of the child."

5. Then Joseph, taking Mary and the child, went back to
the land of Israel, and retired into the parts of Galilee. And
he dwelt in Nazareth, that the word of the prophet might be
fulfilled: "He shall be called a Nazarene." In the peaceful
retirement of that quiet town the child Jesus grew in wisdom
and in grace, before God and men. What a heaven on earth

was that thrice-hallowed,[1] though humble home in Nazareth!

QUESTIONS.

1. What did Herod await with anxiety? What happened when he perceived that he waited in vain? What orders did he give? What did he think? 2. Who appeared by night to Joseph? Commanding him to do what? What did Joseph then do? 3. When the Holy Family had departed from Bethlehem, who rushed into the city? What did they do? What was then heard throughout the city of David? 4. What was the punishment of this dreadful crime? Who then appeared to Joseph in his sleep? What did the angel of the Lord tell him to do? 5. In what town of Galilee did the Holy Family again take up their abode? What was thus fulfilled?

CHAPTER X.

Jesus at the Age of Twelve Years goes to the Temple.

I rejoiced at the things that were said to me; we shall go into the House of the Lord.—*Ps. 121, 1.*

NOW Mary and Joseph went every year to Jerusalem to celebrate the Pasch.[2] But it happened that when Jesus was twelve years old He accompanied His parents on their way to the holy city.

2. The festival days being over, Mary and Joseph set out for their distant home; but the child Jesus remained in Jerusalem, and His parents knew it not. They thought, at first, that He was in company of some of their relatives, and so they journeyed a whole day without noticing His absence. But when evening came, they sought Him, and not finding Him, they were overwhelmed with grief.

3. They returned immediately to Jerusalem, and, for three days, sought Him through the city, but in vain; no one had seen the child. At length, on the third day, they went to the temple, and there they found Him, sitting in the midst of the doctors of the law, hearing them and asking them

---

[1] HALLOWED, consecrated, holy.

[2] Easter or Passover.

questions. All the doctors were astonished at His wisdom and His answers.

4. Mary and Joseph were filled with joy on seeing Him again, and His mother said to Him: "Son, why hast Thou done so to us? Behold Thy father and I have sought Thee sorrowing." But He answered: "How is it that you sought me? Did you not know that I must be about My Father's

JESUS AMONGST THE DOCTORS.

business?" But rising, He went with His mother and His foster-father to Nazareth, and was subject to them.

5. Although Jesus, even in His human nature, was full of wisdom, from the very first moment of his incarnation, yet it was His will to manifest, only by degrees, the knowledge that was in Him. Hence it is said that He increased in wisdom, and age, and grace with God and men.

QUESTIONS.

1. Whither did Mary and Joseph go every year? What happened when Jesus was twelve years old? 2. The festival days being over, what

did Mary and Joseph do? What did Jesus do? What did His parents think at first? How long did they journey without noticing His absence? 3. What did they do when they missed Him? How long did they seek Him? Where did they find Him on the third day? Whom was He asking questions? 4. What did His blessed mother say to Him? What did Jesus reply? What did He then do? 5. Although Jesus knew all things, what was it His will to do? Hence what is said of Him?

CHAPTER XI.

John the Baptist, the Precursor of Christ.

I am the voice of one crying in the wilderness.—*John 1, 23.*

THE time was approaching when Jesus would show Himself publicly as the Redeemer of the world. Wherefore the Lord spoke to John, son of Zachary, in the desert. Obedient to the divine will, John came to the country about the Jordan. He was clothed in camel's hair, with a leathern girdle around his loins, and his food was wild honey and locusts.

2. He cried aloud to all the people: "Do penance, for the kingdom of heaven is at hand!" In order to excite his hearers more efficaciously[1] to repentance, as also to prepare them for Christian baptism, he baptized those that were sorry for their sins in the waters of the Jordan. Then the multitudes came to him from Jerusalem and Judea to listen to his preaching, and many people of all conditions, who, after hearing him, confessed their sins, and were baptized.

3. Some of the Sadducees and Pharisees being present among the crowd, John addressed them sternly, saying: "Ye brood of vipers, who hath shown you to flee from the wrath to come? Bring forth, therefore, fruit worthy of penance, and think not to say: 'We have Abraham for our father,' for I tell you that God is able, of these stones, to raise up children to Abraham."

[1] EFFICACIOUSLY, in a way to produce the effect intended.

4. "For now the axe is laid to the root of the trees. Every tree, therefore, that yieldeth not good fruit shall be cut down and cast into the fire." And the people asked him: "What then shall we do?" He answered: "He that hath two coats, let him give to him that hath none; and he that hath meat, let him do in like manner." The soldiers also asked what they should do, and John said to them: "Do violence to no man, neither calumniate[1] any man; and be content with your pay." Now, the austere[2] appearance of the Baptist, and his startling exhortation, led the people to believe that he was the Messias. John, perceiving this, told them that he was not the Messias, but that there was One coming, mightier than he, the latchet of whose shoes he was not worthy to loose.

5. He told them, moreover, that he, indeed, baptized with water, but that the Savior who was to come after him would baptize with the Holy Ghost and with fire. "Whose fan is in His hand, and He will thoroughly cleanse His floor, and gather the wheat into His barn, but the chaff He will burn with unquenchable[3] fire."

6. Then the High Priest and the Council sent priests and Levites from Jerusalem to ask John: "Who art thou?" He answered: "I am not the Christ." They continued: "Art thou Elias?" He replied: "I am not." They spoke again: "Art thou the great prophet?" He said "No." At last they exclaimed: "Why, then, dost thou baptize, if thou be not Christ, nor Elias, nor the prophet?" John answered that the Messias would soon appear in their midst, preaching penance and announcing the good tidings of salvation.

QUESTIONS.

1. What time was approaching? To whom, therefore, did the Lord speak in the desert? Whither did John come, obedient to the divine will? How was he clad? 2. What did he cry aloud to all the people? In order to excite his hearers to repentance and to prepare them for Christian baptism, what did John do? 3. What did John say to the

---

[1] CALUMNIATE, to accuse falsely.　　[2] AUSTERE, stern, severe, harsh.
[3] UNQUENCHABLE, that which cannot be extinguished.

Sadducees and Pharisees?   4.   What did the austere appearance and the startling exhortations of John the Baptist lead the people to believe? What did John tell them?   5.   What did he say that the Messias would do?   6.   What did John answer, when the priests and Levites asked him whether he was Christ, or Elias, or the prophet?

CHAPTER XII.

Jesus is Baptized by John and Tempted by the Devil.

Your adversary, the devil, as a roaring lion, goeth about, seeking whom he may devour.—*I. Peter 5, 8.*

IN those days when Jesus was about thirty years of age, He went from Nazareth to the Jordan to be baptized by John. But John stayed him, saying: "I ought to be bap-

THE BAPTISM OF CHRIST.

tized by Thee, and comest Thou to me?" Jesus answering, said: "Suffer it now, for so it becometh us to fulfill all justice." John obeyed, the command, and Jesus was baptized.

2. Then the heavens were opened, the Holy Ghost descended upon Him in the form of a dove, and a voice from heaven exclaimed: "This is My beloved Son, in whom I am well pleased." Thus did the Eternal Father and the Holy Ghost give testimony that Jesus was the Son of God and the Redeemer of the world.

3. Before commencing His great work, Jesus was led by the spirit into the desert, where He fasted and prayed forty days and forty nights. Then He was hungry, and Satan, coming to tempt Him, said: "If Thou be the Son of God, command that these stones be made bread." But Jesus answered: "It is written: Man liveth not by bread alone, but by every word that proceedeth[1] out of the mouth of God."

4. Then Satan took Him up into the holy city, and set Him on the pinnacle[2] of the temple, and said: "If Thou be the Son of God, cast Thyself down; for it is written: 'That He hath given His angels charge of Thee, and in their hands shall they bear Thee up, lest, perhaps, Thou hurt Thy foot against a stone'." Jesus said to him: "It is written: 'Thou shalt not tempt the Lord thy God'."

5. But Satan made another attempt. He took our Lord to a very high mountain, and showed Him all the kingdoms of the world, and the glory thereof, and said: "All these will I give Thee, if falling down, Thou wilt adore me." Jesus answered: "Begone, Satan; for it is written: 'The Lord Thy God, thou shalt adore, and Him only shalt thou serve'." Then the devil left Him; and, behold angels came and ministered[3] to Jesus.

QUESTIONS.

1. What did Jesus do in those days when He was about thirty years of age? What did John do and say? What did Jesus answer? 2. What descended then upon Jesus? What did a voice from heaven exclaim?

[1] PROCEEDETH, comes forth.   [2] PINNACLE, a high, spiring point, summit.

[3] MINISTERED, served.

What did the Eternal Father and the Holy Ghost thus confirm? 3. Before commencing His great work, whither was Jesus led by the spirit? What did He do in the desert? Who came to Him when He was hungry? What did Satan say? What did Jesus answer? 4. Whither did Satan take Jesus? Where did he place Him? What did he then say to Him? What did Jesus answer? 5. Where did Satan then take our Lord? What did he show Him? What did he say to Him? What did Jesus then say? Who then came and ministered to Jesus?

CHAPTER XIII.

The First Disciples of Jesus Christ.

Walk worthy of God who hath called you into His kingdom.—
I. Thess. 2, 12.

JESUS left the desert, and returned to the country about the Jordan. As soon as John saw Him, he said to the multitude that surrounded him: "Behold the Lamb of God! Behold, He who taketh away the sins of the world! This is He, of whom I said: 'After me cometh a man who is preferred before me, because He was before me.' I gave testimony[1] that this is the Son of God."

2. On the following day, when John was on the banks of the Jordan, with two of his disciples, he beheld Jesus coming again towards him, and he again said: "Behold the Lamb of God." The two disciples, hearing this, left John and followed Jesus. And Jesus, turning, spoke to them: "What seek you?" They asked Him: "Master, where dwellest Thou?" He said: "Come and see." They came and saw where He abode, and they remained with Him all that day.

3. These two disciples were John and Andrew. The latter had a brother named Simon, who was wishing to see the Messias. Andrew went to seek Simon and said: "We have found the Messias." And he conducted him to Jesus. When Jesus saw Simon, he looked upon him and said: "Thou art Simon, the son of Jona; thou shalt be called Cephas, that is to say, Peter, a rock.

[1] TESTIMONY, proof, evidence.

4. The next day Jesus went forth into Galilee, and on the road He met a man named Philip, who also longed for the coming of the Messias. Jesus said to him: "Follow me." Now Philip had a friend named Nathanael, an upright, God-fearing man. Philip hastened to him and told him: "We have found Him of whom Moses, in the law and the prophets, did write, Jesus of Nazareth." But Nathanael said to him: "Can anything good come from Nazareth?" Philip answered: "Come and see."

5. When Jesus saw Nathanael coming, He said: "Behold an Israelite indeed, in whom there is no guile." Nathanael asked in surprise: "Whence knowest Thou me?" Jesus answered and said to him: "Before that Philip called thee, when thou wast under the fig-tree, I saw thee."

6. Then Nathanael, filled with wonder and respect, cried out: "Rabbi,[1] Thou art the Son of God; Thou art the King of Israel." Jesus spoke to him: "Because I said unto thee: 'I saw thee under the fig-tree,' thou believest; greater things than these shalt thou see. Amen, Amen, I say unto you, you shall see the heaven opened, and the angels of God ascending and descending upon the Son of Man."

QUESTIONS.

1. Whither did Jesus return after leaving the desert? As soon as John saw Him, what did he say to the multitude that surrounded him? 2. The next day, when John saw Jesus coming towards him, what did he again say? Hearing this, what did the disciples do? What did Jesus, turning round, say to them? What did they ask Him? What did He reply? What did they do? 3. Who were these two disciples? What relative had Andrew? What was Simon wishing to see? What did Andrew tell him when he found him? What did Jesus do and say when He saw Simon? What does Peter mean? 4. Whom did Jesus meet on the following day when going to Galilee? What did He say to him? What friend had Philip? What did Philip, hastening to him, tell him? What did he invite him to do? 5. When Jesus saw Nathanael coming, what did He say? What did Nathanael ask in surprise? What did Jesus answer and say to him? 6. What did Nathanael, penetrated with reverence and respect, then say? What did Jesus say to him?

[1] RABBI, master, lord.

CHAPTER XIV.

First Miracle of Jesus.—He Changes Water into Wine.

No man can do these signs which Thou doest, unless God be with him.—*John 3, 2.*

THREE days after these events there was a wedding in Cana of Galilee, and the mother of Jesus was there. Jesus also, together with His disciples, was among the guests.

CHANGING WATER INTO WINE.

Whilst they were at table, the wine failed; and Mary said to Jesus: "They have no wine." He answered: "My hour is not yet come. But Mary, knowing the goodness of her divine Son, and convinced that He would not refuse her request, spoke to the waiters: "Whatever He shall say to you, do ye."

2. Now there were in the room six water-jars of stone, con-

taining two or three measures apiece. Jesus gave orders to
the waiters: "Fill the water-pots with water." They immediately filled them to the brim. He then said to them:
"Draw out now, and carry to the chief steward of the feast."

3. They did so; and the steward, not knowing whence the
wine was, said to the bridegroom: "Every man at first sets
forth good wine, and later on that which is worse; but thou
hast kept the good wine until now." This first miracle
Jesus wrought in Cana of Galilee, at the request of His
blessed mother; and His disciples, seeing His divine power,
believed in Him.

QUESTIONS.

1. Where was there a wedding three days after these events? Who
was among the guests? What happened whilst they were at table? What
did the mother of Jesus say to her Son? What did He answer? What
did Mary tell the waiters? 2. What were there in the room? What did
Jesus order the waiters to do? What did He say to the waiters? 3.
What did the master of the feast say to the bridegroom? At whose
request did Jesus work His first miracle? Who, seeing His divine power,
believed in Him?

CHAPTER XV.

*Jesus Drives the Sellers out of the Temple.—His Discourse
with Nicodemus.*

Thou, O Lord, hast chosen this house that it might be a house of
prayer.—*I. Mach.* 7, 37.

THE passover of the Jews being now at hand, Jesus went
up to Jerusalem. Finding in the court of the temple
men that sold oxen, sheep, and doves, for sacrifice, together
with money-changers, He made a whip of small cords and
drove them out of the temple. He overthrew the money-
tables and said: "Take these things hence, and make not
the house of My Father a house of traffic."

2. Then the disciples remembered that it was written:
"The zeal of Thy house hath eaten me up." Now some of

the Jews who had remained in the temple, being angry, asked Him: "What sign dost Thou show us, seeing Thou doest these things?" Jesus, referring to His own sacred body, said: "Destroy this temple, and in three days I will raise it up."

3. The Jews, supposing that He spoke of the material temple in which they stood, said to Him: "Six and forty years was this temple in building, and wilt Thou raise it up in three

DRIVING THE MONEY-CHANGERS FROM THE TEMPLE.

days?" But Jesus spoke of the temple of His body. Many other signs and wonders did He work in presence of the Jews, many of whom were converted. But many others would not be convinced of His divinity. Like their fathers of old, they wilfully closed their eyes to the light of truth.

4. Among those who believed was Nicodemus, a ruler in Israel. He had a great desire to become a disciple of Jesus, and coming to Him by night, for fear of the Jews, he said to Him: "Rabbi, we know that Thou art come a teacher from

God, for no man can do these miracles which Thou does.,
unless God was with him." Then Jesus explained to him
how he was to become a member of His mystic body on
earth, which is the church, and told him: "Amen, amen, I
say to thee, unless a man be born again of water and the
Holy Ghost, he cannot enter into the kingdom of God."

5. These words referred to the sacrament of baptism. He
next instructed Nicodemus in the mystery of the redemption.
"As Moses," said He, "lifted up the serpent in the desert,
so must the Son of man be lifted up, that whosoever believeth in Him may not perish, but may have life everlasting. For God sent not His Son into the world to judge the
world, but that the world may be saved by Him. He that
believeth in Him, is not judged, but he that doth not believe
is already judged." In these words the Savior taught Nicodemus that He would redeem the world by His passion and
death upon the cross.

QUESTIONS.

1. The passover of the Jews being at hand, whither did Jesus go?
Whom did He find in the court of the temple? What did He do?
What did He say? 2. What did the disciples then remember? What
did the Jews, being angry, ask Him? What did Jesus, referring to His
own sacred body, say? 3. What did the Jews say to Him, supposing
that He spoke of the material temple in which they stood? What did
He work in presence of the Jews? Were any of them converted? Were
they all converted? 4. Who was among those who believed? What
great desire had he? Coming to Jesus by night, what did he say to
Him? What did Jesus then explain to him? What did He tell him?
5. To what did these words refer? In what did He next instruct
Nicodemus? What did He say? What did the Savior teach Nicodemus
by these last words?

CHAPTER XVI.

Jesus at the Well of Jacob.

Let us search our ways, and return to the Lord.—*Lament. 3, 40.*

NOW it came to pass that Herod cast John the Baptist
into prison; whereupon the Pharisees, taking courage,
began to persecute the Savior. He, therefore, left Judea and

returned again to Galilee. On His way He came to a town called Sichar, where there was a well which had been dug by the patriarch Jacob.

2. Jesus, being weary from the journey, sat down by the well, whilst His disciples went into the city to buy provisions. But, behold, a Samaritan woman came to the well to draw water. Jesus said to her: "Give me to drink." The woman, surprised, asked Him: "How dost Thou, being a Jew, ask me to drink; I being a Samaritan woman."

3. Jesus said to her: "If thou didst know the gift of God, and who it is that saith to thee: 'Give me to drink,' thou, perhaps, wouldst have asked of Him, and He would have given thee living water." The woman replied: "Sir, Thou hast nothing wherein to draw, and the well is deep; whence, then, hast Thou living water? Art Thou greater than our father Jacob, who gave us the well?"

4. Jesus answered: "Whosoever drinketh of this water shall thirst again; but he that shall drink of the water that I shall give him, shall not thirst forever. The water that I shall give him shall become in him a fountain of water, springing up into everlasting life." Then the woman spoke again: "Sir, give me this water, that I may not thirst, nor come hither to draw." Thereupon Jesus said: "Go call thy husband." She answered: "I have no husband." Jesus replied: "Thou hast said well; for now thou hast no husband, although thou hast had several husbands." The woman exclaimed: "Sir, I perceive that Thou art a prophet.

5. "Our fathers adored on this mountain, Garizim, and you say that at Jerusalem is the place where men must adore." Jesus said to her: "Woman, believe me, the hour cometh when you shall neither on this mountain nor in Jerusalem adore the Father. The hour cometh, and now is, when the true adorers shall adore the Father in spirit and in truth. God is a spirit, and they that adore Him, must adore Him in spirit and in truth."

6. The woman answered Him: "I know that the Messias, when He is come, will tell us all things." Jesus replied: "I am He, who am speaking with thee." Rejoiced at this news, the woman left her pitcher, and going into the city in all haste, she said to the people: "Come out and see a man who has told me all my sins. Is not He the Christ?" Meanwhile, the disciples returning with the food they had purchased, pressed Jesus to eat. But He said to them: "I have food to eat which you know not of. My food is to do the will of Him that sent Me."

7. While He was speaking to His apostles, the Samaritans coming out of the city desired that He would stay there. He remained two days, teaching and instructing them. Many of that city believed; and they said to the woman: "We now believe, not for thy saying, for we ourselves have heard Him, and we know that this is indeed the Savior of the world."

QUESTIONS.

1. Who cast John the Baptist into prison? Who began to persecute the Savior? To what town did Jesus come on leaving Judea? What well was there? 2. Weary from the journey, what did Jesus do? Whilst He sat there, who came to the well? What did Jesus say to her? What did the woman ask Him? 3. What did Jesus say to her? What did the woman say to Him? 4. What did Jesus answer? What did the woman say to Him? What did Jesus tell her about her husband? 5. What did she then say? What did Jesus say to her? 6. What did the woman say about the Messias? What did Jesus reply? What did the woman, rejoiced at this news, do? What did she tell the people? What did Jesus say to His apostles when they pressed Him to eat? 7. Who came out of the city? What did they desire Him to do? How long did He remain there? What did many of that city, who believed, say to the woman?

CHAPTER· XVII.

Jesus Preaches at Nazareth.

They repaid Me evil for good.—*Ps. 34, 12.*

FROM Sichar, Jesus returned to Nazareth, His own city, and preached the word of life, as He went. Now in Nazareth He entered the synagogue[1] on the Sabbath day, and stood up to read. They gave Him the book of Isaias the prophet. He unfolded the book, and found the place where it was written:

2. "The spirit of the Lord is upon me; wherefore He hath anointed me to preach the gospel to the poor. He hath sent me to heal the contrite of heart, to preach deliverance to the captives, and sight to the blind, to set at liberty them that are bruised, to preach the acceptable year of the Lord, and the day of reward."

3. When He had closed the book, He returned it to the minister and sat down. But the eyes of all the synagogue were fixed upon Him. He then told them: "This day is fulfilled this scripture in your ears." As He thus continued His discourse, all wondered at the words of grace that fell from His lips. Still they did not believe in Him; for they said to one another: "Is not this the son of Joseph?" As if they wished to say that He was of poor parents, and that He had not received a learned education.

4. But He, answering them, said: "Amen, I say to you, that no prophet is accepted in his own country. There were many widows in the days of Elias, in Israel, when heaven was shut three years and six months, when there was a great famine throughout all the land. Yet to none of them was Elias sent but to a widow at Sarepta of Sidon. There were also many lepers in Israel in the time of Eliseus the prophet;

[1] SYNAGOGUE (pr. sin'a-gog), a local temple or chapel of the Jews.

yet none of them was cleansed but Naaman the Syrian."

5. Now all those who heard these things in the synagogue were filled with anger. And rising up, they drove Him out of the city, and took Him to the brow of a mountain to cast Him down headlong. But He, striking them with a sudden terror, passed through their midst, and went His way.

QUESTIONS.

1. Whither did Jesus go from Sichar? Where did He go on the Sabbath day? What book was given Him when He stood up to read? 2. What place did He find on opening the book? 3. What did He do when He had finished reading this passage? What did He then tell them? At what did all wonder? Did they believe in Him? What did they say, one to another? 4. What did Jesus, answering, say to them? 5. Hearing these things, with what were all who were in the synagogue filled? Rising up, what did they do? But what did Jesus do?

CHAPTER XVIII.

The Miracles of Jesus at Capharnaum.

The Son of God appeared that He might destroy the works of the devil.—*I. John 3, 8.*

FROM Nazareth, Jesus went to Capharnaum, and there He taught in the synagogue. The people were astonished at His doctrine, and at the wonderful force and unction[1] of His preaching. There was, in the synagogue, a man who had an unclean spirit, and he cried aloud, saying: "Let us alone; what have we to do with Thee, Jesus of Nazareth? Art Thou come to destroy us? I know Thee who Thou art; the Holy One of God."

2. Jesus rebuked the spirit, commanding him to be silent, and to go out from the man. Then the devil, throwing the man into the midst of the crowd, went out of him, and left him unharmed. A great fear came upon all who wit-

---

[1] UNCTION, religious fervor and tenderness.

nessed this miracle, and they said one to another: "What word is this? for with authority and power He commandeth the unclean spirits, and they go out."

3. From the synagogue Jesus went to the house of Simon Peter. It so happened that the mother-in-law of Peter was grievously sick, and Jesus was asked to cure her. He drew near her bed, commanded the fever, and it left her. Imme-

THE SICK BROUGHT TO JESUS.

diately she arose, cured of the fever, and waited on them as they sat at table.

4. When the sun was down, the sick and infirm of the city were brought to Jesus, and He laid His hands upon them, and they were healed. Early next morning He left Capharnaum, and retired to a desert place. But the people followed Him in crowds, beseeching Him not to leave them. He said to them: "I must preach the kingdom of God in other cities also; for therefore am I sent."

5. He then preached in the synagogues of Galilee: The

time is accomplished and the kingdom of God is at hand; repent and believe the gospel. He healed all manner of diseases, and the fame of His power and holiness spread over all the country, and people came from far and near to see and hear Him.

QUESTIONS.

1. Where did Jesus go from Nazareth? At what were the people astonished? Who was there in the synagogue? What did the spirit cry aloud? 2. What did Jesus, rebuking him, say? What did the devil then do? What did the people say one to another? 3. From the synagogue, where did Jesus go? Who was grievously sick? What was Jesus asked to do? What did He do? What did she immediately do? 4. When the sun was down, who were brought to Jesus? What did He do to them? Whither did He retire next morning after leaving Capharnaum? What did the people do, following Him in crowds? What did He say to them. 5. Where did He then preach? What else did He do? What spread all over the country?

CHAPTER XIX.

The Miraculous Draught of Fishes.

The blessing of God maketh haste to reward the just; and in a swift hour His blessing beareth fruit.—*Ecclus. 11, 24.*

JESUS preached one day near the lake of Genesareth, which by another name is called the Sea of Galilee. A great crowd came to Him to hear the word of God. He saw moored on the shore two fishing-boats, one of which belonged to Simon Peter; and going into Peter's boat, He desired him to put off a little from the shore. Then seating Himself in the bark, He taught the people.

2. When He had ceased preaching, He told Peter: "Launch out into the deep, and let down your nets for a draught." Peter answered: "Master, we have labored all night, and have taken nothing, but at Thy word I will let down the net." Having done so, they caught so great a multitude of fishes that their net was breaking. They beck-

oned to their partners, James and John, who were in the other bark, to come and assist them.

3. They came, and both barks were so filled with fishes that they threatened to sink. Wonder and terror came upon all that were in the ships. But Simon Peter fell down at the feet of Jesus, saying: Depart from me, for I am a sinful man, O Lord." Jesus said to him: "Fear not, from hence-

THE MIRACULOUS DRAUGHT OF FISHES.

forth thou shalt catch men." Having pushed their ships ashore, they left all things and followed Jesus.

QUESTIONS.

1. Where was Jesus one day preaching? Who came to Him to be instructed? What did He see on the shore? To whom did one of the barks belong? Into which of the barks did Jesus go? What did He desire Peter to do? What did Jesus then do? 2. When He had ceased preaching, what did He tell Peter to do? What did Peter answer? Having done so, what did they catch? To whom did they call to come and assist them? 3. Having come, what did they fill with the fishes? What came upon all that were in the

ships? What did Simon Peter do? What did he say? What did Jesus say to him? Having pushed their barks ashore, what did they do?

CHAPTER XX.

Jesus Heals the Man Sick of Palsy.

The works that I do in the Name of My Father, they give testimony of Me.—*John 10, 25.*

JESUS returned to Capharnaum, and, as He was teaching in a private house, a great multitude of people, coming to hear Him, filled the house and crowded around it. But, behold, four men brought a paralytic[1] on a bed, and as they could not get near to Jesus on account of the throng, they went up on the roof of the house, and, making an opening, let down the paralytic in his bed.

2. Jesus, seeing their faith, said: "Son, be of good heart, thy sins are forgiven thee." Now, there were among the crowd some Scribes and Pharisees, who, hearing these words, thought within themselves: "He blasphemeth. Who can forgive sins but God alone?" Jesus, seeing their thoughts, said to them: "Why do you think evil in your hearts? Which is easier, to say: Thy sins are forgiven thee? or to say: Rise up, take thy bed and walk?

3. "But that you may know that the Son of man hath power on earth to forgive sins, I say to thee: Arise, take up thy bed, and go unto thy house." Immediately the man arose. took up his bed, and went forth in the sight of all. And all the people wondered and glorified God, saying: "We never saw the like."

QUESTIONS.

1. Whither did Jesus return? Where was He teaching? What did four men bring? What did they do when they could not get near to Jesus? 2. What did Jesus say, seeing their faith? What did the Scribes and Pharisees who were among the crowd think within them-

[1] PARALYTIC (pr. para-lit'-ik).

selves? What did Jesus say, seeing their thoughts? 3. What did He say to the paralytic? What did the man do? What did the people do?

CHAPTER XXI.

The Sermon on the Mount.

The declaration of Thy words giveth light; and giveth understanding to little ones.—*Ps. 118, 130.*

ON one occasion, when Jesus saw a very great multitude gathered together to hear Him, He went up into a mountain, and sat down; and His disciples were with Him. The people placed themselves around, and along the sides of the mountain, waiting in respectful silence till He commenced to speak. Then he taught them:

2. *The Eight Beatitudes.*—"Blessed are the poor in spirit, for theirs is the kingdom of heaven. Blessed are the meek, for they shall possess the land. Blessed are they that mourn, for they shall be comforted. Blessed are they who hunger and thirst after justice, for they shall be filled. Blessed are the merciful, for they shall obtain mercy Blessed are the clean of heart, for they shall see God."

3. "Blessed are the peacemakers; for they shall be called the children of God. Blessed are they who suffer persecution for justice's sake, for theirs is the kingdom of heaven. Blessed are you, when men shall revile and persecute you, and shall say all manner of evil against you falsely for My sake; rejoice and be exceeding glad, because your reward is very great in heaven."

4. *The Vocation of the Apostles.*—Then turning to His apostles He said to them: "You are the salt of the earth. But if the salt lose its savor, wherewith shall it be salted? It is good for nothing any more, but to be cast out, and to be trodden upon by men. You are the light of the world. A city seated on a high mountain cannot be hid; neither do men light a candle and put it under a bushel, but upon a candle-

stick, that it may give light to all who are in the house. So let your light shine before men, that they may see your good works, and glorify your Father who is in heaven."

5. *The True Justice of the New Law.*—Again addressing the multitude, He said: "Think not that I am come to destroy the law or the prophets. I am not come to destroy, but to fulfill. Amen, I say unto you, unless your justice abound more than that of the Scribes and Pharisees, you shall not enter the kingdom of heaven."

CHRIST PREACHING ON THE MOUNTAIN.

6. *The Love of our Neighbors and of our Enemies.*—"You have heard that it was said to them of old: 'Thou shalt not kill; and whosoever shall kill, shall be guilty of the judgment.' But I say to you that whosoever is angry with his brother, shall be guilty of the judgment. And whosoever shall say to his brother 'Raca',[1], shall be guilty of the council. And whosoever shall say: 'Thou fool,' shall be guilty of hell-fire."

[1] RACA, a word of contempt.

7. "You have heard that it was said: "Thou shalt love thy neighbor, and hate thy enemy.' But I say to you, love your enemies; do good to those who hate you, and pray for those who persecute and calumniate you, that you may be the children of your Father who is in heaven, who makes His sun rise upon the good and the bad. For, if you love those who love you, what reward shall you have? do not even the publicans the same? And if you salute your brethren only, what do you more? do not the heathens as much? Be you, therefore, perfect, as also your heavenly father is perfect."

8. *About Human Respect*—"Take heed you do not your good works before men in order to be seen by them; otherwise you shall have no reward from your Father who is in heaven. Therefore, when thou doest an alms-deed, sound not a trumpet before thee, as the hypocrites do in the synagogues and in the streets, that they may be honored by men.

9. "Verily, I say unto you, they have received their reward. But when thou givest alms, let not thy left hand know what thy right hand does, that thy alms may be secret; and thy Father, who sees in secret, will repay thee. And when you pray, you shall not be as the hypocrites, who love to stand and pray in the synagogues. But when thou prayest, enter into thy chamber, shut the door, and pray to thy Father in secret; and thy Father, who sees in secret, will repay thee. And when you fast, be not of a sad countenance, as the hypocrites. For they disfigure their faces, that to men they may appear to fast."

10. *Confidence in God.*—Then wishing to show His disciples the danger of riches, He said: "Lay not up for yourselves treasures on earth, where rust and moth consume, and where thieves break through and steal. But lay up for yourselves treasures in heaven, where neither rust nor moth consumes.

11. "Where thy treasure is, there is thy heart also. No man can serve two masters; for either he will hate the one and love the other, or he will cling to the one and slight the

other. You cannot serve God and Mammon. Therefore, I
say to you, be not anxious for your life, what you shall
eat, nor for your body, what you shall put on. Is not
the life more than the food? and the body more than the
raiment?

12. "Behold the fowls of the air, for they sow not, neither
do they reap, nor gather into barns; yet your heavenly
Father feedeth them. And for rainment, why are you solicitous[1]? Consider the lilies of the field, how they grow; they
labor not, neither do they spin. And I say to you, that not
even Solomon, in all his glory, was arrayed as one of these.
Now, if God so clothe the grass of the field, which to-day is,
and to-morrow is cast into the oven, how much more you, O
ye of little faith?

13. "Be not solicitous, therefore, saying: 'What shall we
eat, or what shall we drink, or wherewith shall we be clothed?'
For, after all these things do the heathens seek. For your
Father knows that you have need of all these things. Seek
ye, therefore, first the kingdom of God and His justice, and
all these things shall be added unto you."

14. *Charitable Judgment About our Neighbor.* — "Judge
not, that you may not be judged. For with what judgment
you have judged, you shall be judged; and with what measure
you have measured, it shall be measured to you again. And
why seest thou a mote that is in thy brother's eye, and seest
not a beam in thy own eye? Hypocrite, cast out first the
beam out of thine own eye, and then shalt thou see to cast
out the mote out of thy brother's eye. All things, therefore,
whatsoever you would that men should do to you, do you
also to them; for this is the law and the prophets."

15. *Concluding Remarks.* — After giving instructions on
many other subjects, Jesus said: "Enter ye in at the narrow
gate; for wide is the gate and broad is the way that leadeth
to destruction, and many there are who enter by it. Nar-

[1] SOLICITOUS, anxious, eager to obtain.

row is the gate and strait is the way which leadeth to life, and few there are who find it."

16. "Whosoever heareth these My words, and doeth them, shall be likened to a wise man who built his house upon a rock. And the rain fell, and the floods came, and the winds blew, and they beat upon that house, and it fell not; for it was founded upon a rock. And every one that heareth these My words, and doeth them not, shall be like a foolish man, who built his house upon the sand. And the rain fell, and the floods came and the winds blew, and they beat upon that house, and it fell; and great was the fall thereof."

17. Now it came to pass that when Jesus had fully ended these words, the people were in admiration at His doctrine. For He was teaching them as one having authority, and not as their Scribes and Pharisees.

QUESTIONS.

1. Whither did Jesus go on one occasion, when He saw a great multitude? What did the people do? 2, 3. Say the eight beatitudes. 4. In what does the vocation of the apostles consist? 5. What is the true justice of the New Law? 6, 7. What does our Lord teach about loving our neighbors, and even our enemies? 8, 9. How ought we to guard against human respect? 10, 11, 12, 13. In what words does Jesus invite us to have confidence in God? 14. How ought we to judge our neighbor? 15, 16, 17. What are the concluding remarks of the sermon on the mount?

CHAPTER XXII.

The Cure of the Leper and of the Centurion's Servant.

With the heart we believe unto justice; but with the mouth, confession is made unto salvation.—*Rom. 10, 10.*

AS Jesus descended from the mountain, a leper came, who, falling down, adored Him, saying: "Lord, if Thou wilt, Thou canst make me clean?" Jesus, stretching forth His hand, touched him, saying: "I will, be thou made clean." And immediately his leprosy was cleansed. Then

Jesus spoke to him: "See thou tell no man; but go show thyself to the priests, and offer the gift which Moses commanded as a testimony to them."

2. After this, Jesus returned to Capharnaum. In this city there lived a centurion,[1] a Roman, who was friendly to the Jews and had built them a synagogue. Now the servant of this man was sick and grievously tormented. The centurion therefore, knowing that Jesus had come back to Capharnaum, besought some of the Jewish elders to go and ask our Lord to cure his servant.

3. Jesus went with them. But when the centurion saw our Lord coming with the ancients, he said: "Lord, I am not worthy that Thou shouldst enter under my roof; but only say the word, and my servant shall be healed." Hearing this, Jesus wondered much, and turning to the multitude that followed Him, said: "Amen, I have not found so great faith even in Israel!

4. "And I say unto you that many shall come from the East, and the West, and shall sit down with Abraham, Isaac, and Jacob, in the kingdom of heaven. But the children of the kingdom shall be cast out into exterior darkness; there shall be weeping and gnashing of teeth." Then He said to the centurion: "Go and as thou hast believed, so be it done to thee." The servant was healed at the same hour.

5. As Christ would not have cured the leper, if he had refused to show himself to the priests, so now no one obtains forgiveness of his sins unless he reveals his conscience to a priest in confession.

QUESTIONS.

1. Who came as Jesus descended from the mountain? What did the leper do? Saying what? What did Jesus say, stretching forth His hand? What did He charge him to do? 2. After this, whither did He return? Who lived in this city? Who was sick? What did he beseech some of the ancients of the Jews to do? 3. What did the centurion say, when he saw Jesus coming with the ancients? Hearing this, what did Jesus say to the multitude that followed Him?

[1] CENTURION, a Roman officer, over one hundred men.

4. What did He then say to the centurion? 5. What comparison is there between the leper showing himself to the priest, and the sinner going to confession?

CHAPTER XXIII.

Jesus Raises from the Dead the Son of the Widow of Naim.

I will deliver them out of the hand of death.—*Osee 13, 14.*

NOW it came to pass, after this, that Jesus went into a city called Naim, and there went with Him His disciples and a great multitude. As He drew near the gates of the city, behold, a dead man was carried out, the only son of a widow. The poor mother, plunged in sorrow, walked after the bier,[1] and a number of friends and relatives accompanied her.

2. When the divine Savior saw the bereaved mother, He was moved with compassion, and said to her: "Weep not." Then coming near, He made a sign to the bearers to stop, and, touching the bier, He said: "Young man, I say to thee arise!" Forthwith the young man sat up and began to speak. Then Jesus gave him to his mother. And all who witnessed this grand miracle were afraid, and glorified God saying: "A great prophet is risen up among us, and God hath visited His people."

QUESTIONS.

1. Into what city did Jesus go with His disciples? Who was carried out as He drew near the gates of the city? Who walked after the bier? 2. With what was the divine Savior touched when He saw the bereaved mother? What did He say to her? What did He do, coming near? What did He say? What did the young man do? What did those who witnessed this grand miracle say?

[1] BIER, a frame for bearing the dead.

CHAPTER XXIV.

John the Baptist sends Messengers to Christ.

He that believeth in Me, hath everlasting life.—*John 6, 47.*

HEROD ANTIPAS, the son of that Herod who had ordered the massacre[1] of the innocents, was now king of Galilee and Perea. This Herod was living with Herodias, the wife of his brother Philip, while the latter was still alive. Now John the Baptist said to him: "It is not lawful for thee to have thy brother's wife."

2. This rebuke provoked the wrath of Herod and Herodias. John was apprehended, bound and put in prison. Herod would have put him to death, but he feared the people who considered John as a great prophet. John, being now in prison, and having no other desire but that all should believe in Jesus and follow Him, sent two of his disciples, in order that with their own eyes they might see the miracles wrought by Jesus, and with their own ears they might hear His admirable teachings.

3. These disciples then presented themselves before Jesus, saying: "Art Thou He who is come? or expect we another?" Jesus answered: "Go, and relate to John what you have heard and seen. The blind see, the lame walk, the lepers are made clean, the deaf hear, the dead rise again, to the poor the gospel is preached; and blessed is he that shall not be scandalized[2] in me."

QUESTIONS.

1. Who was king of Galilee and Perea? With whom was he living? What did John the Baptist tell him? 2. What did Herod and Herodias do? Why did he fear to put him to death? What desire had John? Why did he send two of his disciples to Jesus? 3. What did these disciples say to Jesus? How did Jesus answer this question?

[1] MASSACRE, killing with cruelty.   [2] SCANDALIZED, offended.

CHAPTER XXV.

The Penitent Magdalen.

Charity covereth a multitude of sins.—*I. Peter 4, 8.*

IN those days a Pharisee named Simon invited Jesus to eat with him. Jesus went into the house and sat down at table. Now, there was in this city a woman called Mary Mag-

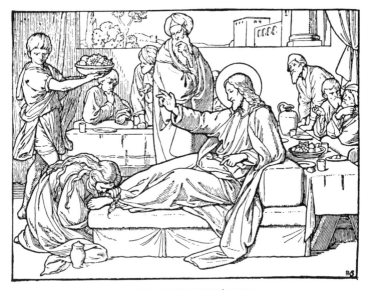

MAGDALEN AT THE SAVIOR'S FEET.

dalen, who, from a great sinner, had recently been converted by the preaching of Jesus. When she heard that our Lord was in the house of Simon, she resolved to honor her divine benefactor.

2. She bought an alabaster box of precious ointment; entered the house, passed through the dining-room unmindful of the guests, fell down before our Lord, without speaking

a word, and breaking the vase, she poured the ointment on His feet. Then, filled with repentance, she began to kiss His feet, and to wash them with her tears, and to wipe them with the hair of her head. And Jesus was pleased. Now Simon seeing this, spoke within himself: "This man, if He were a prophet, would surely know who and what kind of a woman this is who toucheth Him; for she is a sinner."

3. Jesus, reading his thoughts, said to him: "Simon, I have something to say to thee." But he answered: "Master, say it." Then our Lord commenced:"A certain creditor had two debtors; one owed five hundred pence, and the other fifty. And whereas they had not wherewith to pay, he forgave them both. Which, therefore, of the two, loveth his master most?" Simon replied: "I suppose that he to whom he forgave most." Jesus answered: "Thou hast judged rightly."

4. Then pointing to the woman, He said: "Dost thou see this woman? I entered into thy house; thou gavest Me no water for My feet; but she hath washed My feet with tears, and dried them with her hair. Thou gavest Me no kiss; but she, since she came in, hath not ceased to kiss My feet. My head with oil thou didst not anoint; but she, with ointment, hath anointed My feet.

5. "Wherefore, I say to thee, many sins are forgiven her because she hath loved much. But to whom less is forgiven, he loveth less." Then turning to Magdalen, He said: "Thy sins are forgiven thee. Thy faith hath made thee safe. Go in peace." These gracious words, none but a God, and a God of infinite mercy and goodness, could have spoken. They have been, ever since, and will be till the end of time, a source of help and consolation to repentant sinners.

QUESTIONS.

1. Who invited Jesus in those days to eat with him? What did Jesus do? Now, who was there in the city? How had she been converted? What did she do when she heard that our Lord was in the house of Simon? 2. What did she buy? What did she do? What did Simon, seeing all this, say within himself? 3. What did Jesus, reading

his thoughts, say to him? How did Simon answer? How did our Lord commence about the two debtors? How did Simon reply? 4. What comparison did Jesus make between the conduct of Magdalen and that of Simon? 5. What did our Lord say to Magdalen? To whom are the last words of Christ a source of hope and consolation?

CHAPTER XXVI.

Cure of the Man who had been Infirm for Thirty-eight Years.

He hath care of you.—*I. Peter 5, 7.*

AT the time of the Passover, Jesus went up again to Jerusalem. Now, there was at Jerusalem a pond called Probatica, which in Hebrew is named Bethsaida. It was surrounded by a great building which had five porches, under which lay, at all times, a great multitude of the sick, the lame, the blind, and the infirm, waiting for the moving of the water; for at stated times, an angel came down into the pond and moved the water; and he who first went down into the pool, after the angel's visit, was cured of his disease.

2. Among the crowd of those that wished to be healed, there was a man who had been infirm for thirty-eight years. Jesus, seeing him, was moved to pity and said to him: "Wilt thou be made whole?" The infirm man answered: "Sir, I have no one, when the water is troubled, to put me into the pond; for, whilst I am coming, another goeth down before me."

3. Jesus said to him: "Arise, take up thy bed and walk!" Immediately the man was healed, and he took up his bed and went away rejoicing. This took place on the Sabbath. The Jews, therefore, seeing the man carrying his bed, said to him: "It is the Sabbath! It is not lawful for thee to take up thy bed." The man answered. "He who made me whole, He said to me: 'Take up thy bed and walk'."

4. But the Jews asked again: "Who is He that said to thee: Take up thy bed and walk?" Now the man was not able to tell them, for Jesus had withdrawn from the multi-

tude. Soon after, Jesus met this same man in the temple, and said to him: "Behold, thou art made whole; sin no more, lest some worse thing happen to thee." The man then went his way, and told the Jews that it was Jesus who had healed him.

5. Some of the Jews, believing that it was against the law of Moses to heal the sick on the Sabbath, persecuted Jesus for curing the man on that day. But Jesus said to them: "My Father worketh until now; and I work." Thus they became still more angry against Him, because He not only, as they thought, broke the Sabbath, but He said that God was His Father, making Himself equal to God.

6. Jesus then gave them more plainly to understand that He was the Son of God and equal to the Father: "Amen, amen, I say unto you; the Son cannot do anything of Himself, but what He seeth the Father do; for what things soever He doeth, these the Son also doeth in like manner. For the Father loveth the Son, and showeth Him all things which Himself doeth; and greater works than these will He show Him, that you may wonder.

7. "For, as the Father raiseth up the dead, and giveth life; so the Son also giveth life to whom He will. For neither doth the Father judge any man, but hath committed all judgment to the Son, that all men may honor the Son, as they honor the Father. Amen, amen I say unto you, he that heareth My word and believeth Him that sent Me, hath everlasting life."

QUESTIONS.

1. What did Jesus do at the time of the Passover? What pond was there at Jerusalem? Who lay under its five porches? What happened to the pool at stated times? 2. Who was among the crowd of those that wished to be healed? What did Jesus, moved to pity, say to him? What did the infirm man answer? 3. What did Jesus say to him? What followed? What did the man do? What did the Jews, seeing the man carrying his bed, tell him? What did he answer? 4. What did the Jews ask again? Why was he not able to tell them? What did Jesus say to the man when He met him in the temple? What did the man

then tell the Jews?   5.   For what did the Jews persecute Jesus?   What did Jesus say to them?   Why did the Jews seek to kill Jesus?   6, 7. What did Jesus then give them more plainly to understand?   What did He say?

CHAPTER XXVII.

Sin Against the Holy Ghost.—Mary Declared Blessed.

You always resist the Holy Ghost, as your fathers did, so do you also.—*Acts 7, 51.*

WHEN the days of the Pasch[1] were over, Jesus went back again into Galilee, preaching, and doing good as He passed along.   One day, there was brought to Him a man blind and dumb, who was possessed by the devil.   Jesus cured him, and the man spoke and saw.   The multitude who witnessed this miracle said: "Is not this the Son of David?" For never had the like been seen in Israel.

2.   Hearing this, the Pharisees said: "This man casteth out devils by Beelzebub, the prince of devils."   But Jesus answered: "How can Satan cast out Satan?   If a kingdom be divided against itself, that kingdom cannot stand.   But if Satan rise up against himself, he is divided and cannot stand, but hath an end.   But if I, by the Spirit of God cast out devils, then is the kingdom of God come upon you."

3.   "I say to you, whosoever shall speak a word against the Son of Man, it shall be forgiven them; but he that shall speak against the Holy Ghost, it shall not be forgiven him, neither in this world nor the world to come."   Then a certain woman from the crowd, hearing what Jesus said, cried out: "Blessed is the womb that bore Thee, and the breasts that gave Thee nourishment."   But Jesus said: "Yea, rather blessed are they who hear the word of God, and keep it."

4.   Then some of the Scribes and Pharisees asked Him: "Master, we would see a sign from Thee."   Jesus said to

[1] PASCH (pr. Pask), the passover; the feast of Easter.

them: "An adulterous generation[1] seeketh a sign; and a sign shall not be given it, but the sign of Jonas, the prophet. For as Jonas was in the whale's belly three days and three nights; so shall the Son of man be in the heart of the earth three days and three nights. The men of Ninive shall rise in judgment with this generation, and shall condemn it; because they did penance at the preaching of Jonas. And, behold, a greater than Jonas is here. The queen of the south shall rise in judgment with this generation, and shall condemn it; because she came from the ends of the earth to hear the wisdom of Solomon, and, behold, a greater than Solomon is here."

5. The pious woman who praised the mother of Jesus, is a figure of the Catholic Church, whose children love, honor and bless the mother of God. Now our Lord, in answering this holy person, said that all those are blessed who hear the word of God and keep it. But no one, either among angels or men, ever had a faith so great, or virtues so many as the mother of the Redeemer. Hence her throne in heaven is above the thrones of the angels and the saints, and next to that of her divine Son.

QUESTIONS.

1. When the days of the Pasch were over, whither did Jesus go? Who was brought to him? What did Jesus do to him? What did the multitude of people, who witnessed this miracle, say? 2. Hearing this, what did the Pharisees say? What did Jesus answer? 3. What did He say of the sins against the Holy Ghost? What did a certain woman from the crowd cry out? What did Jesus say? 4. What did some of the Scribes and Pharisees say to Jesus? What did Jesus answer? 5. Of whom is the pious woman that praised the Blessed Virgin, a figure? Why is the throne of Mary raised above the thrones of all angels and saints?

[1] GENERATION, an age; a race.

CHAPTER XXVIII.

Jesus Preaching on the Lake of Genesareth.—The Parable of the Husbandman Sowing the Seed.

I will open My mouth in parables.—*Ps. 77, 2.*

ONE day when Jesus was near the Lake of Genesareth, great crowds came to hear Him; and sitting down on the shore, He began to teach. But the multitude still increasing, he went into a boat, and thence spoke to the people. And He taught and spoke to them in parables.

2. *The Parable of the Seed.*—"The sower went out to sow his seed. And as he sowed, some fell by the wayside, and it was trodden down, and the fowls of the air devoured it. And some fell upon a rock; and as soon as it was sprung up, it withered away, because it had no moisture. And some fell among thorns, and the thorns growing up with it, choked it. And some fell upon good ground; and being sprung up, yielded fruit a hundred-fold."

3. Saying these things, He cried out: "He that hath ears to hear, let him hear." And His disciples asked Him what this parable might be. To whom he said: "To you it is given to know the mystery of the kingdom of God; but to the rest in parables, that seeing they may not see, and hearing they may not understand."

4. Now the parable is this: "The seed is the word of God. And they by the wayside are they that hear; then the devil cometh, and taketh the word of God out of their heart, lest believing they should be saved. Now they upon a rock are they who, when they hear, receive the word with joy; and these have no roots; who believe for awhile, and in time of temptation fall away.

5. "And that which fell among thorns, are they who have

heard, and going their way, are choked with cares, and riches, and pleasures of this life, and yield no fruit. But that on the good ground, are they who in a good and perfect heart, hearing the word, keep it, and bring forth fruit in patience."

6. *The Parable of the Seed and the Cockle.*—He proposed another parable to them, saying: "The kingdom of heaven is likened to a man that sowed good seed in his field. But while men were asleep, his enemy came and oversowed cockle among the wheat, and went his way. And when the blade was sprung up, and brought forth fruit, then appeared also the cockle. And the servants of the master of the house came, and said to him: 'Master, didst not thou sow good seed in thy field? From whence, then, hath it cockle?'

7. "He said to them: 'An enemy hath done this.' The servants said to him: 'Wilt thou that we go and gather it up?' And he said: 'No, lest while you gather up the cockle, you root up the wheat, also, together with it. Let both grow until the harvest, and in time of harvest, I will say to the reapers: 'Gather up first the cockle, and bind it in bundles to burn; but the wheat gather into my barn'."

8. Jesus likewise explained this parable, saying that He who sows the good seed is Himself—the Son of man. The field is the world. The good seed represents the children of God, and the cockle those of the devil. The enemy who sowed the cockle is the devil. The harvest time is the end of the world, and the reapers are the angels.

9. As the cockle is plucked up and cast into the fire, so it will happen to the wicked at the end of the world. The Son of man will send His angels, and take away from His kingdom all scandals, and those who are guilty thereof shall be cast into the everlasting flames of hell. But the just, the faithful servants of God, shall be gathered into the eternal granaries of heaven, and they shall shine like the sun in the kingdom of the Father.

QUESTIONS.

1. Who came to Jesus one day when He was near the Lake of Genesareth? What did He do? What parable did He then propose to the people? 2. What became of the seed that fell by the wayside? What became of what fell upon stony ground? What became of that which fell among thorns? What became of that which fell upon good ground? 3. Saying these things, what did He cry out? 4 and 5. Explain the meaning of the parable. 6 and 7. What other parable did He propose to them? 8 and 9. How did Jesus explain this parable?

CHAPTER XXIX.

Christ Stills the Tempest.

Thou rulest the power of the sea; and appeasest the motion of the waves thereof.—*Ps. 88, 10.*

ONE evening Jesus entered into a boat, and His disciples followed Him. A great tempest arose in the sea, so that the boat was covered with waves, and they were in great

CHRIST STILLING THE TEMPEST.

danger. But Jesus was asleep. His disciples came to Him, crying out with fear: "Lord, save us, we perish." Jesus arose and said to them: "Why are ye fearful, O ye of little faith?" Then standing, He rebuked the winds and commanded the sea, and there came a great calm.

2. But the men wondered, saying: "What manner of man is this, for the winds and the sea obey Him?" So it is in all the storms of life. If we have confidence in God, and ask Him to come to our aid, He will not fail us in the hour of our need. He whom the winds and the seas obey. is ever at hand to help those who invoke His name.

QUESTIONS.

1. Who followed Jesus, one evening, into a boat? What arose in the sea? What did the disciples do? What did Jesus say to them? What did Jesus then do? 2. What did the men, wondering, say? With what confidence should this miracle of our Lord inspire us?

CHAPTER XXX.

Jesus Heals the Woman Afflicted with an Issue of Blood, and Raises to Life the Daughter of Jairus.

He is not the God of the dead, but of the living.—*Mark 12, 27.*

WHEN Jesus had reached the opposite shore, a great multitude came to receive Him. Among the people there was one of the rulers of the synagogue, named Jairus. This man threw himself at the feet of Jesus, and besought Him: "Lord, my daughter is at the point of death; but come, lay Thy hand upon her, and she shall live." Now this maiden was twelve years old, and the only child of her parents. Jesus went with Jairus, being followed by His disciples and a great number of people.

2. Among those who followed Jesus and thronged around Him, there was a woman who had been suffering from an is-

sue of blood for twelve years, and had spent all her fortune
paying doctors. But she could not be healed. She now
made her way through the crowd and came close to Jesus;
for she thought within herself: If I shall but touch His garments, I shall be cured. So she walked behind the Savior,
and stretching out her hand, she touched the hem of His garment, and immediately she was healed.

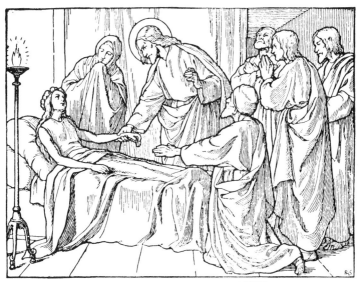

RAISING OF THE DAUGHTER OF JAIRUS.

3. Then Jesus turning round, asked: "Who hath touched
My garment?" The woman, seeing that she could not hide
herself, was trembling with fear, threw herself at His feet,
and confessed for what cause she had touched Him. Jesus
mildly said to her: "Daughter, thy faith hath made thee
whole. Go in peace!"

4. While He yet spoke, a messenger came from the house
of Jairus, saying: "Thy daughter is dead. Do not trouble
the Master any farther." The father groaned in anguish, but
Jesus said to him: "Fear not; believe only, and she shall be

safe." On reaching the house they saw the mourners weeping and lamenting over the dead girl.

5. But Jesus said: "Why make you this ado and wailing? The damsel is not dead, but sleepeth." Going in then with the afflicted father and some of His disciples to where the dead girl lay, and taking her by the hand, He said: "Talitha cumi, that is, Damsel, I say to thee, arise!" Immediately she rose and walked, and they gave her to eat. The fame of this miracle—another splendid proof of His divinity—went abroad through the whole country.

QUESTIONS.

1. Who was there among the multitude that came to receive Jesus on the opposite shore? What did Jairus beseech Jesus to do? What did Jesus do? 2. Who was among those who followed Jesus? What did she think within herself? What did she do? 3. What did Jesus say, turning round? What did the woman do, trembling with fear? What did Jesus mildly say to her? 4. While He yet spoke, who came from the house of Jairus? To tell him what? What did Jesus say to him? What did they see on reaching the house of Jairus? 5. What did Jesus say? What did He do, going in with the father and some of His disciples to where the dead girl lay? What did she do?

CHAPTER XXXI.

Jesus Sends His Apostles.

It is not you that speak, but the Spirit of your Father that speaketh in you.—*Matt. 10, 20.*

THE number of followers and admirers of our Lord, even from distant countries, kept increasing as time went on. One day, when the multitude were around Jesus, eager to hear His teaching, He had compassion on them, for they were as sheep without a shepherd. He said to His disciples: "The harvest indeed is great, but the laborers are few. Pray ye, therefore, the Lord of the harvest, that He send forth laborers into His vineyard."

2. After He had spent the night in prayer, and day being come, He called together His disciples, and chose from among them twelve, that they should be with Him, and that He might send them to preach. Now these twelve He called Apostles, that is, those that are sent. The names of the twelve apostles are these: The first, Simon, who is called Peter, and Andrew his brother; James and John, the sons of Zebedee; Philip and Bartholomew; Thomas and Matthew, the publican; James, son of Alpheus, and Thaddeus; Simon, called the Zealot, and Judas Iscariot.

3. Having chosen His apostles, Jesus commanded them to go to the lost sheep of the house of Israel, and announce to them that the kingdom of heaven was at hand. He also gave them power to heal the sick, raise the dead, cleanse lepers, and cast out devils. He told them not to take anything with them on their journey, because the laborer is worthy of his hire.

4. Jesus spoke: "When you come into a house, say: 'Peace be to this house!' And if that house be worthy, your peace shall come upon it; but if it be not worthy, your peace shall return to you. And whosoever shall not receive you, going forth out of that house, or city, shake off the dust from your feet. Amen, I say to you, it shall be more tolerable for the land of Sodom and Gomorrha in the day of judgment than for that city.

5. "Behold, I send you as sheep in the midst of wolves. Be ye, therefore, wise as serpents and simple as doves. Beware of men; for they will deliver you up in councils, and they will scourge you in their synagogues. And you shall be brought before governors and before kings for My sake. The disciple is not above his master, nor the servant above his lord. Fear not those that kill the body and cannot kill the soul; but rather fear Him that can destroy both soul and body in hell.

6. "Whosoever, therefore, shall confess Me before men, I will also confess him before My Father who is in Heaven.

But whosoever shall deny Me before men, I will also deny him before My Father who is in Heaven. He that loveth father or mother more than Me, is not worthy of Me. And he that loveth son or daughter more than Me, is not worthy of Me. And he that taketh not up his cross and followeth Me, is not worthy of Me.

7. "He that findeth his life shall lose it; and he that shall lose his life for My sake, shall find it. He that receiveth you, receiveth Me; and he that receiveth Me, receiveth Him that sent Me. And whosoever shall give to drink to one of these little ones, only in the name of a disciple, amen, I say to you, he shall not lose his reward." When our divine Lord had thus told His apostles what they had to expect from the world, He sent them, two by two, into every city and place, preaching the word of God, and doing the work that He had commanded them to do.

QUESTIONS.

1. What happened one day when the multitude were around Jesus, eager to hear His words? What did He say to His disciples? 2. After He had spent the night in prayer, day being come, what did He do? How many did He choose from among His disciples? What were the apostles to do? What is the meaning of the word Apostle? What are the names of the Apostles chosen by our Lord? 3. Having chosen His Apostles, what did Jesus command them to do? 4. What did He tell them to say on entering a house? 5. What persecutions did our Lord foretell for His apostles? 6. What does our Lord say of those that deny Him; and of those that love father and mother more than their Savior? 7. What does our Lord say about finding life and losing it? After our Lord had ended these words, what did He do?

CHAPTER XXXII.

John the Baptist is Put to Death.

Blessed are they that suffer persecution for justice' sake.
—*Matt. 5, 10.*

HERODIAS was filled with hatred against John the Baptist, and sought to destroy him. But Herod esteemed John, and for a time obeyed him in many things. Moreover, Herod was still afraid of the people who considered John as a great prophet.

2. Now Herod, on his birthday, gave a banquet to the princes and nobles of his kingdom. And the daughter of Herodias, by her former husband, coming in, danced before the guests, and Herod was pleased; whereupon he promised, with an oath, to give her whatsoever she would ask of him, even if it were the half of his kingdom.

3. But she, being instructed beforehand by her mother, said: "Give me here in a dish the head of John the Baptist!" The king was grieved on hearing these words, but, thinking himself bound to keep the oath which he had sworn before his guests, he sent word to the jailor, who beheaded John, and presented his head on a dish, to the wicked daughter of a still more wicked mother. But the disciples of the holy Baptist took the body of their master and buried it; and came to tell Jesus what had happened.

QUESTIONS.

1. Who was filled with hatred against John? Why was Herod afraid of John? 2. What did Herod do on his birthday? Who, coming in, danced before the guests? What did Herod promise the girl, with an oath? 3. What did she, being instructed beforehand by her mother, say to him? How did the king feel on hearing these words? But what did he think himself bound to do? What did he do? What did the disciples of the holy Baptist do?

CHAPTER XXXIII.

The Miracle of the Loaves and Fishes.

Labor not for the meat which perisheth, but for that which endureth unto life everlasting, which the Son of Man will give you.—*John 6, 27.*

THE Feast of the Passover being at hand, the apostles returned to their divine Master, and gave Him an account of all they had done. But He said to them: "Come ye apart into a desert place, and rest a little." For there were many coming and going, so that they had no time to eat.

So they sailed across the lake and went into a retired spot. But even there the people followed them in large numbers.

2. Jesus, seeing this great multitude, had compassion[1] on them, and, without giving Himself any rest, went up into a mountain.   There He sat with His apostles and disciples, and began to teach them many things.   When He had finished His discourse, He cured the sick that were brought to Him.

3. Now the day was already far spent, and His disciples came to Him and said: "Send them away, that going into the next villages and towns, they may buy themselves meat to eat, for we are here in a desert place."   Jesus said: "They have no need to go.   You give them to eat."   He then inquired how much bread they had.   Andrew replied that there were only five loaves and two fishes.

4. Jesus said: "Bring them hither to Me, and make the men sit down."   When the multitude, numbering five thousand men, besides women and children, had sat down on the grass, Jesus took the loaves and fishes, and, looking up to heaven, blessed them, and gave to His apostles to distribute among the people.

5. Now all the people ate and were satisfied.   And Jesus ordered His disciples to gather up the fragments, lest they should be lost.   They did so, and filled twelve baskets with the remainder of the five loaves and the two fishes.   The multitude, seeing this wonderful miracle, said among themselves: "This is the Prophet indeed, that is to come into the world."

6. Jesus, knowing their thoughts, and fearing that they would make Him king, by force, told His disciples to sail across the water, while He Himself went up to the mountain to pray.   It was dark when the disciples went into the ship. They had rowed about twenty or thirty furlongs in the direction of Capharnaum, and it was now almost the fourth watch of the night, when suddenly a storm arose, and the sea

---

[1] COMPASSION, pity, mercy.

swelled, and the ship was tossed with the waves. But, be-hold, Jesus comes to them walking upon the sea, and draw-ing near the ship, He was going to pass them by. They knew Him not. They were troubled and cried out, and thought it was an apparition. Immediately Jesus spoke to them: "Have a good heart; it is I, fear not." Then they were all astonished. But Peter said: "Lord, if it be Thou, bid me come to Thee upon the waters." Jesus said: "Come."

CHRIST BLESSING THE LOAVES.

7. Peter left the ship and walked upon the water, but see-ing the high waves, he feared, and began to sink. He cried out: "Lord, save me." Jesus stretched forth His hand, took hold of him and said: "O thou of little faith, why didst thou doubt?" They returned to the ship, and the wind ceased. Then those that were in the ship cried out: "Thou art truly the Son of God." Presently the ship was at the place to which they were going. When they had landed, the people

brought the sick to Him and He healed them, and all those that touched His garments were made whole. The great miracle of the loaves and fishes is one of the most striking figures of the Blessed Eucharist, in which the Savior of the world nourishes the souls of countless millions of His faithful people.

CHRIST WALKING UPON THE WATER.

QUESTIONS.

1. What did the apostles do when the Feast of the Passover was at hand? What did Jesus say to them? What did they do? What did the people do? 2. What did Jesus do, seeing this great multitude? When He had finished His discourse, what did He do? 3. When the day was already far spent, what did His disciples, going to Him, say? What did Jesus tell them? What did Jesus ask? What did Andrew answer? 4. What did Jesus say? When the people were seated, what did Jesus do? 5. When all the people were satiated, what did Jesus command His disciples to do? Having done so, what did they fill? What did the multitude say among themselves? 6. What did Jesus fear, knowing their thoughts? What did He do? What did Jesus tell His disciples to do? When did the storm come on? Why were they troubled when Jesus

walked upon the sea? What did Jesus say to them? What did Peter say to Jesus? 7. What happened to Peter? Of what is the miracle of the loaves and fishes a figure?

CHAPTER XXXIV.

Jesus Promises to Give the Bread of Life.

Thou didst feed Thy people with the food of Angels, and gavest them bread from Heaven.—*Wis. 16, 20.*

MANY of those that had miraculously been fed by our Lord, returned next morning to Capharnaum, where they sought Him in the synagogue. Here Jesus addressed them, saying: "Amen, amen, I say to you. You seek Me, not because you have seen miracles, but because you did eat of the loaves and were filled. Labor not for the meat which perisheth, but for that which endureth unto everlasting life, which the Son of man will give you."

2. Then they said to Him: "Lord, give us always this bread." But He answered: "I am the living bread, which came down from Heaven. If any man eat of this bread, he shall live forever. The bread which I will give is My flesh for the life of the world." Hearing this, the Jews who were in the synagogue began to dispute among themselves, saying: "How can this man give us His flesh to eat?"

3. Jesus, far from putting an end to their dispute by giving a figurative[1] meaning to His words, simply repeated what He had spoken: "Amen, amen, I say unto you, unless you eat the flesh of the Son of man, and drink His blood, you shall not have life in you. He that eateth My flesh and drinketh My blood, hath everlasting life, and I will raise him up at the last day."

4. "As the living Father hath sent Me, and I live by the Father, so he that eateth Me, the same also shall live by Me. This is the bread that came down from Heaven. Not

[1] FIGURATIVE, not literal.

as your fathers did eat manna, and died. He that eateth this bread shall live forever."

5. Many of the disciples, hearing these words, did not believe it possible that He could do what He promised; they, therefore, went away, saying: "This word is hard, and who can hear it?" But Jesus, knowing that they murmured at His teaching, asked: "Doth this scandalize you?" It did; and many of them walked no more with Him.

6. Jesus, seeing this, addressed His apostles: "Will you also go away?" Peter answered in the name of all: "Lord, to whom shall we go? Thou hast the words of eternal life. We have believed, and have known that Thou art the Christ, the Son of God." We learn from these words of our Lord that he cannot be saved, who, through his own fault, fails to receive the body of Christ in Holy Communion.

QUESTIONS.

1. Why did those that had been miraculously fed, seek Jesus on the following morning? What did Jesus say to them? 2. What did they then say to him? What did He say? Hearing this, what did the Jews who were in the synagogue begin to do? 3, 4. Did Jesus say that He had spoken figuratively? 5. When His disciples heard this, what did many of them do? 6. How did Jesus then address His apostles? What did Peter answer in the name of all?

CHAPTER XXXV.

The Woman of Chanaan.

Ask, and it shall be given you.—*Matt. 7, 7.*

ON the next Feast of the Passover, Jesus did not go up to Jerusalem on account of the snares laid for Him by the Jews, but retired into Galilee. Immediately He was followed by a great crowd of people bringing the sick, the blind, the lame, the deaf, the dumb, whom they laid at His feet, and He cured them all.

2. Passing, one day, from Galilee to the confines of Tyre

and Sidon, where dwelt the idolatrous[1] descendants of the old Chanaaneans, a woman of that country ran after Him, crying out: "Have mercy on me, O Lord, Thou Son of David; my daughter is grievously troubled by a devil." Jesus made no answer. But she continued to beseech Him that He would have mercy on her daughter.

3. Then the apostles, pitying the woman, and anxious to be rid of her importunity,[2] besought their divine Master to grant her petition. Jesus replied that He was sent only to the lost sheep of the house of Israel. Hearing this, the woman renewed, still more earnestly, her supplications, falling at the Savior's feet and exclaiming: "Lord, help me."

4. Jesus, wishing to try her faith still more, said: "It is not good to take the bread of children, and to cast it to the dogs." But she, nowise discouraged, answered: "Yea, Lord, for the whelps also eat of the crumbs that fall from the table of their master." Jesus was pleased with the humility of her answer, and said: "O woman, great is thy faith. Be it done to thee as thou wilt." At the same moment her daughter was cured.

5. After this, Jesus returned to the sea of Galilee, and they brought to Him a man who was deaf and dumb. He took him aside from the multitude, put His fingers into the man's ears, touched his tongue with spittle, and said: "Ephpheta," that is, be opened; and immediately he was able to speak and hear. The people cried out: "He hath done all things well. He hath made both the deaf to hear and the dumb to speak."

QUESTIONS.

1. What happened on another Feast of the Passover? By whom was He immediately followed? 2. When Jesus went to Tyre and Sidon, who ran after Him? What did she cry? What did Jesus do? What did the woman continue to do? 3. What did the apostles beseech their divine Master to do? What did Jesus reply? Hearing this, what did the woman do? 4. What did Jesus say,

[1] IDOLATROUS, pertaining to the worship of idols.

[2] IMPORTUNITY, urgent request.

wishing to try her faith still more? What did she answer? What did
Jesus, pleased with her humility, say to her? What happened at the
same moment? 5. Whom did they bring to Jesus? What did Jesus
do to him?

CHAPTER XXXVI.

Jesus Promises Peter the Keys of the Kingdom of Heaven.

I will lay the key of the house of David upon his shoulder.
—*Is. 22, 22.*

BEING come to the neighborhood of Cæsarea Philippi
Jesus asked His apostles, as they went along, who the
people said that He was. They replied: "Some, John the

CHRIST GIVING THE KEYS TO PETER.

Baptist; others, Elias; and others, Jeremias, or one of the
prophets." Wishing to hear their own opinion, or, rather,
to draw from them a profession of faith, He asked: "But
who do you say that I am?"

2. Simon Peter answered: "Thou art Christ, the Son of the living God." Jesus said to him: "Blessed art thou, Simon, Bar Jona, because flesh and blood hath not revealed it to thee, but my Father who is in Heaven. And I say to thee that thou art Peter, and upon this rock I will build My church, and the gates of hell shall not prevail against it. And I will give thee the keys of the kingdom of heaven, and whatsoever thou shalt bind upon earth, it shall be bound also in heaven; and whatsoever thou shalt loose upon earth, it shall be loosed also in heaven!"

QUESTIONS.

1. What did Jesus, being come to the neighborhood of Cæsarea Philippi, ask His apostles as they went along? What did they reply? What did He then ask them? 2. What did Simon Peter answer? What did Jesus say to him?

CHAPTER XXXVII.

The Transfiguration.

He will reform the body of our lowness, made like to the body of His glory.—*Phil. 3, 21.*

A SHORT time before His passion, Jesus took with Him Peter, James, and John, and went up to a high mountain to pray. And whilst He prayed, He was transfigured[1] before them. His face shone like the sun, and His garments became white as snow. And, behold, Moses and Elias appeared, discoursing with Him concerning His passion and death, which He was soon to suffer for the redemption of the world.

2. Transported with joy at the sight, Peter exclaimed: "Lord, it is good for us to be here. If thou wilt, let us make here three tabernacles; one for Thee, and one for Moses, and one for Elias." As he was yet speaking, a bright cloud overshadowed them, and the voice of the Eternal Father was

[1] TRANSFIGURED, altogether changed in appearance.

heard, saying: "This is My beloved Son, in whom I am well pleased. Hear ye Him!"

3. The disciples fell prostrate on the ground, terrified by the heavenly voice. Then Jesus came to them, and touched them, saying: "Arise, and be not afraid!" When they arose, they saw no one but Jesus alone. As they went down from the mountain, Jesus said to the three disciples: "Tell

THE TRANSFIGURATION.

the vision to no one till the Son of Man be risen from the dead."

QUESTIONS.

1. Whither did Jesus go a short time before His passion? Whom did He take with Him? What happened while He prayed? Who appeared, discoursing with Him? Concerning what did they discourse? 2. What did Peter exclaim, transported with joy? Whilst he was yet speaking, what happened? What voice was heard? Saying what? 3. What did the disciples do? What did Jesus then do? What did He say? When they arose, who was only to be seen? As they went down from the mountain, what did Jesus say to them?

CHAPTER XXXVIII.

The Tribute for the Temple.

Put not a scandal in your brother's way.—*Rom. 14, 13.*

JESUS having returned with His disciples to Capharnaum, those who collected the annual tribute for the temple, came to Peter and asked: "Doth not your Master pay the didrachma?"[1] Peter replied: "Yes," and went to tell Jesus.

2. But when Jesus saw Peter coming, He said to him: "Of whom do the kings of the earth take tribute or custom? Of their own children, or of strangers?" Peter answered: "Of strangers." Jesus continued: "Then the children are free. But, that we may not scandalize them, go to the sea and cast in a hook, and the fish which shall first come up, take; and when thou hast opened its mouth, thou shalt find a stater[2]; take that, and give it to them for Me and for thee." Peter did as his Master had commanded. Peter being the head of the apostles, paid for all the others by paying for himself.

QUESTIONS.

1. When Jesus returned with His disciples to Capharnaum, who came to Peter? And asked him what? What did Peter reply? What did he do? 2. When Jesus saw Peter coming, what did He ask him? What did Peter answer? What did Jesus say to him? What did Peter do? Did Peter pay for the other apostles?

[1] DIDRACHMA (pr. di-drak'-ma). An ancient Greek silver coin worth about thirty cents.

[2] STATER, an ancient coin.

CHAPTER XXXIX.

Jesus Blesses Little Children.

The Lord is the keeper of little ones.—*Ps. 114, 6.*

ON one occasion, some pious mothers brought their children to Jesus, that He might place His hands upon them and bless them. But the disciples, thinking that He

CHRIST BLESSING CHILDREN.

would not trouble Himself with infants, began to rebuke the mothers, and sent them away. But this conduct of His disciples was not pleasing to our divine Lord, and He said to them: "Suffer little children to come to Me, and forbid them not, for of such is the kingdom of heaven."

2. Then, caressing the children, He placed His hand on their heads and blessed them. Then He said to those who

stood around: "Amen, I say unto you, unless you become as little children, you cannot enter into the kingdom of heaven. But he that shall scandalize one of these little ones that believe in Me, it were better for him that a mill-stone were hanged about his neck and that he were drowned in the depths of the sea."

3. "He that shall receive one such little child in My name, receiveth Me. See that you despise not one of these little ones, for I say to you, that their angels in heaven always see the face of My Father who is in heaven." How touching is the tender affection shown by our blessed Lord for little children, the young ones of His flock. What an encouragement, too, for those who seek to guard them from the dangers of the world, and who train their minds in the ways of God.

QUESTIONS.

1. Why did some pious mothers, on one occasion, bring their children to Jesus? What did the disciples begin to do? Was this conduct of the apostles pleasing to our divine Lord? What did He say to them? 2 and 3. What did He then do? What did He say to those who stood around? Who are especially encouraged by these words of our Lord?

CHAPTER XL.

Fraternal Correction. — Forgiveness of Injuries. — The Unforgiving Servant.

He that stoppeth his ear against the cry of the poor, shall also cry himself and shall not be heard.—*Prov. 21, 13.*

JESUS, continuing His teachings, said: "If thy brother shall offend thee, go and reprove him between thee and him alone. If he shall hear thee, thou shalt gain thy brother. But if he will not hear thee, take with thee one or two more. If he will not hear them, tell the church; and if he will not hear the church, let him be to thee as the heathen and the publican."[1]

2. He then spoke to His apostles: "Amen, I say unto you, whatsoever you shall bind upon earth, shall be bound also in heaven; and whatsoever you shall loose on earth, shall be loosed also in heaven." Whereupon Peter asked Jesus: "Lord, how often shall my brother offend me, and I forgive him? till seven times?" Jesus answered: "I say not to thee till seven times, but till seventy times seven." By this He meant that there is to be no limit to our forgiveness of injuries. Thereupon Jesus related

3. *The Parable of the Unforgiving Servant.*—"The kingdom of heaven is likened to a king who would take an account of his servants. When he had begun to take the account, one was brought to him that owed him ten thousand talents.[2] As he had not wherewith to pay it, his lord commanded that he should be sold, and his wife and children, and all that he had, and payment to be made.

4. "But that servant, falling down, besought him, saying: 'Have patience with me, and I will pay thee all.' Now the lord of that servant, being moved with compassion, let him go, and forgave him the debt. But when that servant was gone out, he found one of his fellow-servants that owed him a hundred pence, and, laying hold of him, he throttled him, saying: 'Pay what thou owest!'

5. "Then his fellow-servant, falling down, besought him, saying: 'Have patience with me, and I will pay thee all.' Yet he would not; but went and cast him into prison till he should pay the debt. Now, his fellow-servants, seeing what was done, were very much grieved; and they came and told their lord all that was done.

6. "Then his lord called him, and said to him: 'Thou

[1] PUBLICAN, an inferior tax-collector of those days among the Jews and Romans. The publicans were held in public odium on account of their cruel oppression of the people.

[2] TALENT, an ancient coin.

wicked servant; I forgave thee all the debt, because thou besoughtest me. Shouldst not thou, then, have had compassion on thy fellow-servant, even as I had compassion on thee?' And his lord, being angry, delivered him to the torturers until he should pay all the debt. So also shall My heavenly Father do to you, if you forgive not every one his brother from your hearts."

QUESTIONS.

1. What did Jesus say about correcting our brother? 2. What did He say to His apostles about binding and loosing? What did Peter ask our divine Lord? What did Jesus answer? 3, 4, 5, and 6. Recite the parable of the unforgiving servant? What is the application of the parable?

CHAPTER XLI.

Jesus sends forth His Seventy-two Disciples.

For Christ therefore we are ambassadors; God, as it were, exhorting by us.—*II. Cor. 5, 20.*

HAVING returned from Galilee to Judea, Jesus selected from among His followers seventy-two, whom He called disciples, that they might assist the twelve apostles in the work of the ministry. He sent them forth, two by two, saying: "He that heareth you, heareth Me, and he that despiseth you, despiseth Me; and he that despiseth Me, despiseth Him that sent Me."

2. A short time after, the seventy-two returned to Him, rejoicing and saying that even the demons were subjected to them. Jesus, fearing that they might become vain of the power that was given them, said: "I saw Satan, as lightning, falling from heaven. Rejoice not because the spirits are subject to you, but rejoice in this, that your names are written in the Book of Life."

3. Then, rejoicing with them, He prayed: "I give thanks to thee, O Father, Lord of heaven and earth, that Thou hast

hid these things from the wise and prudent, and hast revealed them to little ones!" By "little ones" our blessed Lord here meant the lowly, the humble, the unlearned.

QUESTIONS.

1. Jesus having returned from Galilee to Judea, what did He do? How did He send them forth? Saying what? 2. A short time after, when the seventy-two returned to Him rejoicing, what did they say? What did Jesus fear? What did He say? 3. Then what did He say, rejoicing with them? Whom did our Lord mean by the "little ones"?

CHAPTER XLII.

The Doctor of the Law.—The Good Samaritan.

Blessed are the merciful, for they shall obtain mercy.—*Matt. 5, 7.*

ONCE, when Jesus was on His way to Jerusalem, He met a doctor of the law, who, hoping to puzzle our Lord, asked Him, through curiosity: "Master, what must I do to possess eternal life?" Jesus answered: "What is written in the law? how readest thou?" He replied: "Thou shalt love the Lord, thy God, with thy whole heart, and with thy whole soul, and with all thy strength, and with all thy mind, and thy neighbor as thyself."

2. Jesus said to him: "Thou hast answered right; this do, and thou shalt live." But the doctor, wishing to justify himself, asked: "Who is my neighbor?" Then Jesus narrated

3. *The Parable of the Good Samaritan.*—"A certain man went down from Jerusalem to Jericho, and fell among robbers, who also stripped him, and having wounded him, went away, leaving him half dead. Now it happened that a certain priest went down the same way, and seeing him, he passed by. In like manner, also, a Levite, when he was near the place, and saw him, passed by. But a certain Samaritan, being on his journey, came near him, and, seeing him, was

moved with compassion. He, going up to him, bound up his wounds, pouring in oil and wine; and setting him upon his own beast, brought him to an inn and took care of him."

4. The next day he took out two pence and gave to the innkeeper, and said: "Take care of him, and whatever thou shalt spend over and above, I, at my return, will repay thee." Having finished the parable, Jesus asked the doctor:

THE GOOD SAMARITAN.

"Which of these three, in thy opinion, was neighbor to him that fell among the robbers?" The doctor of the law replied: "He that showed mercy to him." Jesus said to him: "Go, and do thou in like manner!"

QUESTIONS.

1. Whom did Jesus once meet when He was going up to Jerusalem? What did the doctor of the law ask Him? What did Jesus answer him? What did the doctor reply? 2 and 3. What did Jesus say to him? What did the doctor ask, wishing to justify himself? What parable did Jesus then relate? 4. What question

did Jesus put at the end of the parable? What did the doctor of the law reply? What advice did Jesus give to the doctor?

CHAPTER XLIII.

Mary and Martha.

Seek ye therefore first the kingdom of God, and His justice; and all these things shall be added unto you.—*Matt. 6, 33.*

WHEN Jesus had returned to Judea, He entered a certain town named Bethania, a short distance from Jerusalem, where He was kindly entertained by two pious sisters, named Mary and Martha. Now, Mary, who is also called Magdalen, sat down at the Savior's feet and listened attentively to the words of wisdom that fell from His divine lips. Martha, on the other hand, busied herself in preparing the repast.

2. Martha, then, seeing that she had to do all the work, complained to the Savior, and said: "Lord, hast thou no care that my sister has left me alone to serve? Speak to her, therefore, that she help me!" But Jesus answered: "Martha! Martha! Thou art careful and troubled about many things; one thing only is necessary. Mary hath chosen the best part, which shall not be taken away from her." The one thing necessary, of which our Lord spoke, is the work of salvation. Jesus does not blame Martha for working, but because she worked in a restless and uneasy state of mind.

QUESTIONS.

1. Where did Jesus go, after He had returned to Jerusalem? By whom was He entertained there? What did Mary do? What did Martha, on the other hand, do? 2. To whom did she complain? What did she say to our Savior? What did Jesus answer? What is "the one thing needful"? Why did Jesus blame Martha?

CHAPTER XLIV.

Jesus the Good Shepherd.

He shall feed His flock like a shepherd; He shall gather together the lambs with His arm.—*Is. 40, 11.*

JESUS having gone back to Jerusalem for the Feast of Tabernacles, went to the temple and taught there, saying: "I am the Good Shepherd. The good shepherd giveth his life for his sheep. But the hireling, and he that is not the shepherd, seeth the wolf coming, and leaveth the sheep, and fleeth. I am the Good Shepherd, and I know mine, and mine know Me, and I lay down My life for My sheep. And other sheep I have, which are not of this fold; them also I must bring, and they shall hear My voice, and there shall be made one fold and one shepherd."

2. The words of our Savior attracted large crowds of people. Even publicans and great sinners were unable to resist the sweetness of His words, and they gathered around Him as He went. Now the Pharisees were scandalized, because Jesus received so kindly those men whom they, puffed up with self-conceit, looked down upon with supreme contempt.

3. But the merciful Savior, seeing their thoughts, said: "What man among you that hath a hundred sheep, and if he shall lose one of them, doth he not leave the ninety-nine in the desert, and go after that which was lost, until he find it? And when he hath found it, doth he not lay it upon his shoulders, rejoicing?

4. "Then coming home, does he not call together his friends and neighbors, saying to them: 'Rejoice with me, because I have found my sheep that was lost.' I say to you, that even so there shall be joy in heaven upon one sinner

that doth penance more than upon ninety-nine just that
need not penance."

1.   Jesus, having gone back to Jerusalem for the Feast of Tabernacles,
what comparison of Himself did He make?   2.   What effect had the
Savior's words?   Who were attracted by the sweetness of His words?
Why were the Pharisees scandalized?   3, 4.   But what did the merciful
Savior say when He saw their thoughts?

CHAPTER XLV.

The Parable of the Prodigal Son.

How great is the mercy of the Lord, and His forgiveness to them that
turn to Him.—*Ecclus. 17, 28.*

ON another occasion, Jesus proposed the following parable to the Jews: "A certain man had two sons.   And
the younger of them said: 'Father, give me the portion of
substance that falleth to me.'   The father did so.   Not many
days after, the younger son, gathering all his property, went
abroad into a far country, and there he spent his substance
living riotously.

2.   "After he had spent all, there came a mighty famine in
that country, and he began to be in want.   Then he went and
joined himself to one of the citizens of that country.   And he
sent him into his farm to feed swine.   Here he would fain have
filled his belly with the husks the swine did eat.   But, entering
into himself, he said: 'How many hired servants in my father's
house have plenty of bread, and I here perish with hunger!'

3.   "'I will arise and will go to my father, and will say to
him: Father, I have sinned against heaven and before thee:
I am not now worthy to be called thy son; make me as one
of thy hired servants!'   Then he rose up and went to his
father.   When he was yet a great way off his father saw him
and was moved with compassion, and ran to him and fell on
his neck and kissed him.

4. "But the son said: 'Father, I have sinned against heaven and before thee; I am not now worthy to be called thy son.' The father said to his servants: 'Bring forth quickly the first robe and put it on him, and put a ring on his hand and shoes on his feet. And bring hither the fatted calf and kill it, and let us eat and make merry; because this my son was dead, and is come to life again; he was lost and is found.'

RETURN OF THE PRODIGAL SON.

5. "Now his elder son was in the field; and when he came and drew nigh to the house, he heard music and dancing. He called one of the servants and asked what these things meant. The servant said to him: 'Thy brother is come, and thy father hath killed the fatted calf, because he hath received him safe.' And he was angry, and would not go in. His father, therefore, coming out, began to entreat him.

6. "But he answering said to his father: 'Behold, for so

many years do I serve thee, and I have never transgressed[1] thy commandment, and yet thou hast never given me a kid to make merry with my friends. But as soon as this thy son is come, who hath devoured his substance, thou hast killed for him the fatted calf.'

7. "But the father replied: 'Son, thou art always with me, and all I have is thine. Yet it was fit that we should make merry and be glad; for this thy brother was dead, and is come to life again; he was lost and is found'." By this beautiful parable our blessed Lord teaches us how willing Almighty God is to receive the penitent sinner, and how rejoiced He is at his return.

QUESTIONS.

1. What parable did Jesus, on another occasion, propose to the Jews? What did the younger son say to his father? How did he spend his substance in the far country? 2. After he had spent all, what did there come in that country? What did the young man do? What did the citizen do? With what would the young man have gladly filled his stomach? What did he say, entering into himself? 3. What did he do? What did his father do when he saw him a great way off, and was moved with compassion? 4. What did the son say? What did the father say to his servants? 5. What did the elder son hear, when he came near to the house? What did he ask one of the servants? What did the servant say to him? What happened then? 6. What did the son say to the father? 7. What did the father then say to him? What does our blessed Lord teach us by this beautiful parable?

CHAPTER XLVI.

The Parable of Dives, the Rich Man, and Lazarus.

In all thy works remember thy last end, and thou shalt never sin.—*Ecclus. 7, 40.*

JESUS, wishing to show the evil effects of riches, when misused, and the advantage of poverty, when borne with patience, said: "There was a certain rich man, who was

---

[1] TRANSGRESS, to break or violate a law.

clothed in purple and fine linen, and fared sumptuously[1] every day. And there was a certain beggar, by name Lazarus, who lay at the rich man's gate, full of sores.

2. "He desired to be filled with the crumbs that fell from the rich man's table, but no one did give him. Moreover, the dogs came and licked his sores. Now it came to pass that the beggar died, and he was carried by the angels into Abra-

DIVES AND LAZARUS.

ham's bosom. But the rich man also died, and he was buried in hell. And lifting up his eyes, when he was in torments, he saw Abraham afar off, and Lazarus in his bosom.

3. "Then he cried and said: 'Father Abraham, have mercy on me, and send Lazarus that he may dip the tip of his finger in water to cool my tongue, for I am tormented in this flame.' Abraham said to him: 'Son, remember that thou didst receive good things in thy lifetime, and likewise Lazarus evil

[1] Sumptuously, expensively, splendidly.

things, but now he is comforted and thou art tormented.

4. "'And besides all this, between us and you there is fixed a great chaos, so that they who would pass from hence to you, cannot; nor from hence come hither.' Thereupon Dives said: Then, father, I beseech thee, that thou wouldst send him to my father's house, for I have five brethren, that he may testify to them, lest they also come into this place of torments.'

5. "But Abraham said to him: 'They have Moses and the prophets; let them hear them.' But he said: 'No, Father Abraham; but if one went to them from the dead, they will do penance!' Abraham said unto him: 'If they hear not Moses and the prophets, neither will they believe if one rise again from the dead'."

QUESTIONS.

1. What did Jesus say, wishing to show the evil effect of riches, when misused, and the advantage of poverty when borne with patience? What certain rich man is mentioned in the parable? Who was the beggar that lay at his gate? 2. What did Lazarus desire? What did the dogs do? Where was the poor man carried when he died? Where was the rich man buried when he died? Where did Dives, looking up, see Lazarus? 3. What did he cry out to Abraham? What did Abraham say? 4. What did Dives say? 5. What did Abraham say to him? What did Dives say about his brothers? What did Abraham reply?

CHAPTER XLVII.

Jesus Gives Sight to the Man Born Blind.

Then shall the eyes of the blind be opened, and the ears of the deaf shall be unstopped.—*Is. 35, 5.*

A S Jesus was one day going out of the temple, He saw a man who had been blind from his birth. The disciples, who were with Jesus, therefore asked Him: "Master, who hath sinned, this man or his parents, that he should be born blind?" Jesus answered: "Neither hath this man sinned, nor his parents; but that the works of God should be made manifest in him."

2. When Jesus had said this, He spat on the ground and made clay with the spittle, and rubbed the clay on the eyes of the man, and said to him "Go, and wash in the pool of Siloe." He went, washed, and came away seeing. Now the neighbors that had known him wondered, and some of them said: "Is not this he that sat and begged?" But the others denied it, saying: "No, but he is like him." The man himself, however, exclaimed: "I am he." Then the Pharisees, perceiving that he saw, asked him how he had received his sight. The man told them how it happened. Then they asked him again: "What sayest thou of Him that hath opened thy eyes?" The man replied: "He is a prophet."

3. But they, still unbelieving, and not satisfied with the man's own testimony,[1] called his parents, and asked them: "Is this your son who you say was born blind? how, then, doth he now see?" The parents replied: "We know that this is our son, and that he was born blind. But how he now seeth, we know not. Ask himself; he is of age, let him speak for himself."

4. The parents said this because they were afraid of the Jews, who had already agreed among themselves that if any man should confess Jesus to be Christ, that man should be put out of the synagogue. Then the Pharisees called again the man who had been blind, and said to him: "Give glory to God. We know that this man is a sinner." But he replied: "Whether he be a sinner, I know not. One thing I know, that whereas I was blind, I now see." Then they inquired again: "What did He do to thee? How did He open thy eyes?" The man answered: "I have told you already, and you have heard. Why would you hear it again? Will you become His disciples?"

[1] TESTIMONY, evidence, proof.

5. Then thy reviled[1] him, saying: "Be thou His disciple, but we are the disciples of Moses. We know that God spoke to Moses. But as to this man we know not from whence He is." The man answered and said to them: "For in this is a wonderful thing, that you know not from whence He is, and He hath opened my eyes. From the beginning of the world it hath not been heard that any man hath opened the eyes of one born blind. Unless this man were God, He could not do anything."

6. Then they, being angry, said to him: "Thou wast wholly born in sins, and dost thou teach us?" Thereupon they cast him out. But Jesus met him and said to him: "Dost thou believe in the Son of God?" He answered: "Who is He, Lord, that I may believe in Him?" Jesus replied: "Thou hast both seen Him, and it is He who talketh with thee." Then the man said: "I believe, Lord!" And falling down he adored Him.

QUESTIONS.

1. Whom did Jesus see as He was one day going out of the temple? As to what did the disciples who were with Jesus question Him? What did Jesus answer? 2. When He had said this, what did He do? What did He then say to the blind man? What was the result? What did the people say who had known the blind beggar? What did the man himself say? What did the Pharisees ask him, perceiving that he saw? What did they then ask him? What did he say? 3. What did they ask the man's parents? What did the parents reply? 4. Why did the parents say this? What did the Pharisees then do? What did they say to the man who had been blind? What did he answer? 5. What did they say, reviling him? What did the man say to them? 6. What did they, being angry, say to him? And what did they do to him? Who met him? What did Jesus say to him? What did he answer and say? What did Jesus say to him? What did the man then say and do?

[1] REVILED, abused.

CHAPTER XLVIII.

The Lord's Prayer.

By prayer and supplication with thanksgiving let your petitions be made known to God.—*Phil. 4, 6.*

JESUS, having gone again to Jerusalem, left the city on one occasion and retired to a desert place to pray. Here one of his disciples said to him: "Lord, teach us to pray, as John also taught his disciples." Then Jesus said to them: "When you pray, say: 'Our father, who art in heaven, hallowed be Thy name; Thy kingdom come; Thy will be done on earth as it is in heaven. Give us this day our daily bread; and forgive us our trespasses as we forgive them who trespass against us. And lead us not into temptation; but deliver us from evil. Amen."

2. He then said to them: "Which of you shall have a friend, and shall go to him at midnight, and shall say to him: 'Friend, lend me three loaves, because a friend of mine is come off his journey to me, and I have not what to set before him;' and he from within should answer and say: 'Trouble me not; the door is now shut, and my children are with me in bed; I cannot rise and give thee.'

3. "Yet if he shall continue knocking, I say to you, although he will not rise and give him, because he is his friend, yet because of his importunity he will rise and give him as many as he needeth. And I say unto you, ask and it shall be given you; seek, and you shall find; knock, and it shall be opened to you.

4. "What father among you, if his son shall ask him for bread, will give him a stone? or if he ask for a fish, will, instead of fish, give him a serpent? If you, then, being evil, know how to give good gifts to your children, how much

more will your Father from heaven give the good spirit to them that ask Him?"

1. Jesus having gone again to Jerusalem, whither did He retire to pray on one occasion? What did one of His disciples say to Him? What prayer did Jesus teach them? 2 and 3. What parable did He relate about two friends? 4. How does He compare God giving good things to men, with a father giving good things to his son?

CHAPTER XLIX.

The Parable of the Rich Man.

Riches shall not profit in the day of revenge; but justice shall deliver from death.—*Prov. 11, 4.*

O N going back into Galilee, Jesus went through that whole country, admonishing[1] the people everywhere and endeavoring to bring them to faith and penance. One day, one of His hearers said to Him: "Master, speak to my brother, that he divide the inheritance with me." Jesus replied: "Man, who hath made me a judge, or a divider over fruits?"

2. Then addressing the multitude, He said: "Take heed, and beware of all covetousness,[2] for a man's life doth not consist in the abundance of things." Then He spoke a parable to them as follows: "The land of a certain rich man brought forth plenty of fruits. So he thought within himself: 'What shall I do, because I have not where to lay up together my fruits?'"

3. "'This will I do: I will pull down my barns, and will build greater ones, and into them I will gather all things that are grown to me, and my goods. Then I will say to my soul: 'Soul, thou hast many goods laid up for many years;

[1] ADMONISHING, reproving, warning.

[2] COVETOUSNESS, strong desire; eagerness to obtain wealth.

take thy rest, eat, drink, make good cheer!' But God said to him: 'Thou fool, this night do they require thy soul of thee, and whose shall those things be which thou hast provided?' " Then the divine Master added: "So is he that layeth up treasure for himself, and is not rich towards God."

QUESTIONS.

1. On going back into Galilee, where did Jesus go? What did one of His hearers one day say to Him? How did Jesus reply? 2. Then addressing the multitude, what did He say? What parable did He speak to them? 3. What did the rich man in the parable say within himself? What did he say to his soul? But what did God say to him? What did the divine Master then add?

CHAPTER L.

The Barren Fig-tree.

How long wilt thou sleep, O sluggard? when wilt thou rise out of thy sleep?—*Prov. 6, 9.*

OUR divine Lord had been now almost three years teaching and admonishing the Jewish people, laboring unceasingly for their salvation; yet His labors and His preaching had produced but little fruit in their souls. He, therefore, compared them to a fig-tree which a certain man had planted in his vineyard, and which, after all his care and trouble, bore no fruit.

2. Then the master of the vineyard said to his vine-dresser: "Behold, for three years I have come seeking fruit on this fig-tree, and I find none. Cut it down, therefore! why doth it take up the ground?" But the vine-dresser, answering, said to him: "Sir, let it alone this year also, until I dig about it, and manure it, if so haply it bear fruit; but if not, then after that thou shalt cut it down." This parable ought to terrify all, but especially those sinners that say: "I will be converted on my death-bed," because they may be stricken down by sudden death.

QUESTIONS.

1. How long had our divine Lord been teaching and admonishing the Jewish people? What fruit had His labors and preachings produced among them? To what did He, therefore, compare them? 2. What did the master of the vineyard then say to his vine-dresser? What did the vine-dresser, answering, say to him? Whom ought this parable especially to terrify?

CHAPTER LI.

The Ten Lepers.

Giving thanks always for all things, in the name of our Lord Jesus Christ.—*Eph. 5, 20.*

AS Jesus drew near to Jerusalem, He was met by ten lepers, who stood afar off, and cried out: "Jesus, Master, have mercy on us!" When He saw them, He said: "Go, show yourself to the priests!" Now it came to pass that as they went, they were cleansed. Then one of them, when he saw that he was cleansed, went back, with a loud voice glorifying God.

2. And he fell on his face before the feet of Jesus, giving thanks. Now this man was a Samaritan.[1] Jesus asked: "Were there not ten made clean? and where are the nine? There is no one found to return and give glory to God, but this stranger." Then He said to the man: "Arise, go thy way, for thy faith hath made thee whole."

QUESTIONS.

1. As Jesus drew near to Jerusalem, by whom was he met? What did the lepers do? Saying what? When He saw them, what did He say? What came to pass as they went? What did one of them do, perceiving that he was healed? 2. Who was this man? What did Jesus say about the others? What did He say to the man?

[1] SAMARITAN, a native or inhabitant of Samaria.

CHAPTER LII.

The Pharisee and the Publican.

I hate arrogance and pride.—*Prov. 8. 13.*

JESUS spoke also the following parable in order that He might convert those who trusted in themselves as just, and despised others. "Two men went up into the temple to pray, the one a Pharisee, and the other a publican. The Pharisee, standing, prayed thus with himself: 'O God, I give Thee thanks that I am not as the rest of men, extortioners,[1] unjust, adulterers, nor such as this publican. I fast twice in the week; I give tithes of all that I possess.'

2. "But the publican, standing afar off, would not so much as lift his eyes towards heaven, but struck his breast, saying: 'O God, be merciful to me, a sinner!' I say to you, this man went down to his house justified, rather than the other. Because every one that exalteth himself shall be humbled, and he that humbleth himself shall be exalted." The Pharisee preferred himself to all other men; this was a sign of great pride; hence his prayers remained unheard.

QUESTIONS.

1. What did Jesus do in order to convert those who trusted in themselves? What did the Pharisee, standing, say? 2. What did the publican, standing afar off, say? What did our Lord say in relation to these two men? Why was the prayer of the Pharisee not heard?

[1] EXTORTIONERS, persons who sell their goods at too high a rate.

CHAPTER LIII.

Jesus at the Feast of the Dedication.

Men loved darkness rather than light, for their works were evil.—
John 3, 19.

JESUS assisted at the feast of the dedication[1] of the temple. As he walked through the porch of Solomon, a number of Jews surrounded Him and said: "How long dost Thou hold our souls in suspense? If Thou be the Christ, tell us plainly." Jesus answered: "I speak to you, and you believe not. The works that I do in the name of My Father, they give testimony of Me. I and the Father are one."

2. The Jews then took up stones to stone him. But He said to them: "Many good works I have shown to you from My Father; for which of those works do you stone Me?" They replied: "For a good work we stone Thee not, but for blasphemy; because that Thou, being a man, makest Thyself God."

3. Jesus said to them: "If I do not the works of My Father, believe Me not. But if I do, though you will not believe Me, believe the works, that you may know and believe that the Father is in Me, and I in the Father." Hearing this, they tried to seize Him, but He escaped out of their hands.

QUESTIONS.

1. At what feast did Jesus assist? By whom was he surrounded as he walked through Solomon's porch? What did they say to Him? What did Jesus answer? 2. What did the Jews then do? And what did He say to them? What did they reply? 3. What did Jesus say to them? Hearing this, what did they try to do? Did they succeed in seizing Him?

[1] DEDICATION, consecrating.

CHAPTER LIV.

The Rich Young Man.

It is easier for a camel to pass through the eye of a needle, than for a rich man to enter into the kingdom of heaven.—*Matt. 19, 24.*

ON one occasion, a young man came to Jesus, and kneeling before Him, said: "Good Master, what good shall I do that I may have life everlasting?" Jesus answered: "If thou wilt enter into life, keep the commandments." He asked: "Which commandments?" Jesus said to him: "Thou shalt not kill; thou shalt not commit adultery; thou shalt not steal; thou shalt not bear false witness; honor thy father and thy mother, and thou shalt love thy neighbor as thyself."

2. The youth replied: "All these I have kept from my youth." Jesus, knowing that this was true, looked tenderly upon him, and said: "If thou wilt be perfect, go, sell what thou hast, and give it to the poor, and thou shalt have treasure in heaven; then come and follow Me." Hearing these words, the young man went away sorrowful, for he was very rich. Had the young man despised his wealth and followed Jesus, he would now be a saint in heaven, and even renowned on earth; as it is, we cannot tell whether he died in the grace of God or not.

QUESTIONS.

1. On one occasion, who came to Jesus? What did the young man say, kneeling before Him? What did Jesus answer? What did he ask? What did Jesus say to him? 2. What did he say? What did Jesus do, knowing that this was true? What did He say? What did the young man ask? What did Jesus reply? Hearing these words, what did the young man do? Why did he go away sorrowful? What might have become of the youth if he had despised his wealth?

CHAPTER LV.

The Laborers in the Vineyard.

Christ died for all.—*II. Cor. 5, 15.*

PETER was greatly rejoiced at the promise which Jesus made to the rich young man, and he asked: "Behold, we have left all things, and followed Thee; what, therefore, shall we have?" Jesus said, addressing all the apostles: "Amen, I say unto you, that you who have followed Me, in the regeneration, when the Son of man shall sit on the seat of His majesty, you also shall sit on twelve seats, judging the twelve tribes of Israel.

2. "And every one that hath left house, or brethren, or sisters, or father, or mother, or wife, or children, or lands, for My name's sake, shall receive a hundredfold in time, and shall possess life everlasting." Then the blessed Savior instructed His hearers by another parable: "The kingdom of heaven is like to a master of a family, who went out early in the morning to hire laborers into his vineyard.

3. "When he had agreed with the laborers for a penny a day he sent them into his vineyard. And he went out about the third hour, and saw others standing idle in the market place. And he said to them: 'Go you, also, into my vineyard, and I will give you what shall be just.' And they went. Again he went out about the sixth and ninth hour, and did in like manner.

4. "But about the eleventh hour he went out and found others standing, and he said to them: 'Why stand you here all the day idle?' They answered: 'Because no man hath hired us.' He said to them: 'Go you also into my vineyard.' Now when evening was come, the lord of the vineyard said to his steward: 'Call the laborers, and pay them their hire, beginning from the last even to the first.'

5. "When, therefore, they came who had come about the eleventh hour, they received every man a penny. But when the first also came, they thought that they should have received more, and they likewise received every man a penny However, when they received it, they murmured against the master of the house, saying: 'These last have worked but one hour, and thou hast made them equal to us, that have borne the burden of the day and the heat.' But he addressed one of them: 'Friend, I do thee no wrong; didst thou not agree with me for a penny?

6. "Take what is thine and go thy way. I will also give to this last even as to thee. Or is it not lawful for me to do what I will? Is thy eye evil because I am good?'" Then Jesus concluded the parable, saying: "So shall the last be first, and the first last; for many are called, but few are chosen."

QUESTIONS.

1. At what was Peter greatly rejoiced? What did he say to Jesus? What did Jesus say, addressing all the apostles? 2. What did the blessed Savior then do? To what did He liken the kingdom of heaven? 3. What did the master agree to pay the laborers? What did he do when he went out about the third, sixth, and ninth hours? 4. What did he do at the eleventh hour? When evening was come, what did the Lord of the vineyard say to his steward? 5 and 6. What did those who came at the eleventh hour receive? What did the others say, murmuring against the master? What did he say to one of them? How did Jesus conclude the parable?

CHAPTER LVI.

The Raising of Lazarus from the Dead.

Thy dead men shall live, awake and give praise, ye that dwell in the dust.—*Is. 26, 19.*

THE two sisters, Martha and Mary Magdalen, who lived in Bethania, had a brother named Lazarus. Now Jesus loved Martha, and Mary, and Lazarus. But Lazarus fell sick, and his sisters sent word to Jesus: "Lord, behold, he whom Thou lovest is sick." Jesus, hearing this, said to His disciples: "This sickness is not unto death, but for the glory of God, that the Son of God may be glorified by it."

2. Two days after, He spoke again to His disciples: "Let us go to Bethania; Lazarus, our friend, sleeps; but I go that I may wake him out of sleep." The disciples answered: "If he sleeps, he shall do well." They thought He spoke of the repose of the body, but Jesus spoke of death. Seeing, however, that they did not understand what He meant, He told them plainly: "Lazarus is dead."

3. When Jesus arrived in Bethania, Lazarus had been four days buried. Now many friends and relatives had come to console the two sisters, who were in great affliction. As soon as Martha heard that Jesus was coming, she left her friends and went forth to meet Him. When she saw Him, she exclaimed: "Lord, if Thou hadst been here, my brother had not died. But now also I know that whatsoever Thou wilt ask of God, God will give it Thee.

4. Jesus said to her: "Thy brother shall rise again." Martha replied: "I know that he shall rise again in the resurrection at the last day." Jesus answered: "I am the resurrection and the life. He that believeth in Me, although he be dead, shall live. Believest thou this?" She said to Him: "Yea, Lord, I have believed that Thou art Christ, the Son of the living God, who art come into this world."

5. Then Martha, going into the house, called her sister secretly, and told her: "The Master is come, and calleth for thee." Mary rose up quickly and went to Him. The Jews who were in the house followed her, saying: "She goeth to the sepulcher to weep there." As soon as Mary came to Jesus, she fell at His feet, exclaiming: "Lord, if Thou hadst been here, my brother would not have died."

6. When Jesus saw her weeping, and the friends who had come with her, He groaned in spirit, and troubled Himself, and said: "Where have you laid him?" They answered: "Come and see!" And Jesus wept. Seeing this, the Jews

exclaimed: "Behold, how He loved him!" Jesus, having come to the vault, or cave, in which the body of Lazarus was laid, said: "Take away the stone!"

7. Martha told him that the body of her brother must be already putrid, seeing that he was four days buried. Jesus said to her: "Did I not say to thee that if thou wilt believe, thou shalt see the glory of God?" They then removed the stone. And Jesus, lifting up His eyes, said: "Father, I give Thee thanks that Thou hast heard me.

THE RAISING OF LAZARUS.

8. "And I know that Thou hearest me always, but because of the people who stand about have I said it, that they may believe that Thou hast sent Me." Then, crying out with a loud voice, He said: "Lazarus, come forth!" And immediately he that had been four days buried came forth, wrapped in the winding-bands. And Jesus said: "Loose him, and let him go!"

QUESTIONS.

1. Who was the brother of Martha and Mary? When he fell sick, what word did the sisters send to Jesus? What did Jesus, hearing it, say to His disciples? 2. What did He say to His disciples two days after? What did the disciples say? Seeing that they did not understand what He meant, what did Jesus tell them? 3. How long had Lazarus been buried when Jesus arrived in Bethania? Who had come to console the sisters of Lazarus? What did Martha do as soon as she heard that Jesus was coming? 4. What did Jesus say to her? What did Martha reply? What did Jesus say to her? What did she say to Him? 5. What did Martha do, going into the house? What did she tell her sister? And what did Mary do? Who followed her? Saying what? What did Mary do when she came where Jesus was? 6. When Jesus saw her weeping, and her friends who came with her, what did He do? What did He say? What did they say? And what did Jesus do? Seeing this, what did the Jews exclaim? What did Jesus do when He came to the vault, or cave, in which Lazarus was laid? 7. What did Martha tell Him? What did Jesus say to her? What did they then do? What did Jesus say, lifting up His eyes? 8. What did He then cry out with loud voice? And immediately, what happened? What did Jesus say?

CHAPTER LVII.

Jesus Foretells His Passion and Death.

The Son of Man shall be betrayed to the chief priests and to the scribes.—*Matt. 20, 18.*

MANY of the Jews who were present when Jesus raised Lazarus from the dead, believed in Him. Some of these went to the Pharisees and told them what Jesus had done. Then the Scribes and Pharisees assembled together, and said one to another: "What do we, for this man doth many miracles? If we let Him alone so, all men will believe in Him." From that day they resolved to put Jesus to death.

2. But Jesus, knowing their thoughts, walked no more openly among the Jews. Six days after He said to the twelve apostles: "Behold, we go to Jerusalem, and the Son of man shall be betrayed to the chief priests, and to the

Scribes and ancients, and they shall condemn Him to death, and shall deliver Him to the Gentiles, and they shall mock Him, and spit on Him, and scourge Him, and kill Him; and the third day He shall rise again."

3. The apostles wondered, not knowing what He meant. Then Jesus drew near to Jericho, in which city there was a rich man named Zacheus, who was the chief of the publicans. Zacheus wished much to see Jesus as He passed, but could not do so on account of the crowd, for he was of low stature.

4. Running, therefore, before the crowd, he climbed into a sycamore-tree. But Jesus, on coming to the tree, looked up, and seeing Zacheus, said to him: "Zacheus, make haste and come down, for to-day I must abide in thy house." Zacheus, coming down, received Him joyfully into his house. Then the Jews who saw this murmured, because they looked on Zacheus as the chief of sinners.

5. But Zacheus said to the Savior: "Behold, Lord, the half of my goods I give to the poor; and if I have wronged any man of anything, I restore him fourfold." Jesus said to him: "This day is salvation come to this house. For the Son of Man is come to seek and to save that which was lost."

QUESTIONS.

1. Many of whom believed in Jesus? What did some of these do? What did the Scribes and Pharisees then do? What did they say one to another? What did they resolve to do from that day? 2. But what did Jesus do, knowing their thoughts? What did He say, six days after, to His apostles? 3. To what city did Jesus draw near? Who was in that city? What did Zacheus wish much? Why could he not do so? 4. What did he do running before the crowd? What did Jesus say when He looked up and saw him? What did Zacheus do? What did the Jews who saw this do? Why? 5. What did Zacheus say to the Savior? What did Jesus say to him?

CHAPTER LVIII.

Jesus is Anointed by Mary.

Many have been brought to fall for gold, and the beauty thereof
hath been their ruin.—*Ecclus. 31, 6.*

AFTER Jesus had departed from Jericho, He returned to
Bethania. A supper was prepared for Him, and Lazarus was one of those who sat at the table with Him. Martha
waited upon the Lord, but Mary Magdalen brought in an
alabaster[1] box, a pound of most precious ointment, and she
poured it on the Savior's head as He was at table.

2. Now the whole house was filled with perfume of the
ointment. But Judas Iscariot said: "Why was not this ointment sold for three hundred pence and given to the poor?"
Then the other disciples, also, had indignation, and said:
"For what purpose is this waste?" Now Judas made this
remark, not because he cared for the poor, but because he
was a thief and carried the purse, and was already possessed
by the love of money, which, a few days later, led him to betray his Master.

3. But Jesus, knowing what was going on among His
disciples, exclaimed: "Why do you trouble this woman?
for she hath wrought a good work upon Me. For the poor
you have always with you, but Me you have not always.
For she, in pouring this ointment upon My body, hath done
it for My burial. Amen, I say to you, wheresoever this gospel shall be preached in the whole world, that also which
she hath done, shall be told for a memory of her."

QUESTIONS.

1. After Jesus had departed from Jericho, where did He go? What
was prepared for Him? Who was one of those who sat with Him at
table? Who waited upon the Lord? What did Mary do? 2. With

[1] ALABASTER, a fine white stone, used for ornamental purposes.

what was the whole house filled? What did Judas Iscariot say? What did the other disciples say? Why did Judas say this? 3. What did Jesus say, knowing what was going on among the disciples?

CHAPTER LIX.

Triumphal Entry of Jesus into Jerusalem.

Out of the mouth of infants and of sucklings Thou hast perfected praise.—*Ps. 8, 3.*

ON the following day, Jesus left Bethania and went to Jerusalem. When He had come to Bethphage, near the Mount of Olives, He sent two of His disciples, saying: "Go ye into the village that is over against you, and immediately you shall find an ass tied, and a colt with her. Loose them, and bring them to Me. And if any man shall say anything to you, say ye that the Lord hath need of them."

2. So the disciples went and found the colt standing, as Jesus had said. They, therefore, brought the colt to Jesus, and, laying their garments upon it, they made Jesus sit thereon. Now many wished to see Jesus, because He had raised Lazarus from the dead. When, therefore, Jesus was near to the city, His disciples and a great multitude spread their garments in the way; while some cut down branches from the trees and strewed them along the road. And a vast multitude went before and followed after, crying: "Hosanna to the Son of David! Blessed is He that cometh in the name of the Lord! Hosanna in the highest!"

3. There were also in the crowd some Pharisees, who, being filled with envy and hatred, never lost sight of Jesus. Seeing the honors that were now paid to Him, they indignantly[1] asked: "Hearest Thou what these say?" Jesus replied: "If these should hold their peace, the stones will cry

[1] INDIGNANTLY, angrily.

out." The nearer He came to the city, the greater the crowd became, and the more the enthusiasm[1] of the people increased.

4.   Then was fulfilled the prophecy[2] of Zachary, that Jerusalem should be visited by her King as a Savior; that He should be poor, and riding on an ass. But, seeing Jerusalem, Jesus wept over it, saying: "If thou hadst known, and that in this thy day, the things that are for thy peace, but now they are hidden from thy eyes!

CHRIST'S TRIUMPHAL ENTRY INTO JERUSALEM.

5.   "For the day shall come upon thee, and thy enemies shall cast a trench about thee, and compass thee round, and straiten thee on every side, and beat thee flat to the ground, and thy children who are in thee; and they shall not leave in thee a stone upon a stone, because thou hast not known the time of thy visitation!"

[1] ENTHUSIASM, excitement.

[2] PROPHECY, something foretold; an inspired foretelling.

6. Jesus rode through the streets directly to the temple. There the sick, the blind, and the lame came to Him from every side, and He cured them all. At this sight the children began to cry out again: "Hosanna to the Son of David!" But the Pharisees, becoming furious,[1] told Him to rebuke them. Jesus answered them: "Have you never read the words: 'Out of the mouth of infants and of sucklings Thou hast perfected praise?' "

QUESTIONS.

1. Where did Jesus go on the following day? Where had He come to? Whom did He send? Saying what? 2. What did the disciples do? What did they bring? What did they lay upon it? Why did many wish to see Jesus? What did the vast multitude cry? 3. Who were also in the crowd? What did they indignantly ask? What did Jesus reply? 4 and 5. What prophecy was then fulfilled? But what did Jesus do, seeing Jerusalem? Saying what? 6. Whither did Jesus ride through the streets? Who came to Him there? What did He do to them? What did the children begin to cry out again? What did the Pharisees tell Jesus to do? What did He answer?

CHAPTER LX.

The Parable of the Marriage Feast.

Many are called, but few are chosen.—*Matt. 20, 16.*

IN the evening Jesus returned from Jerusalem to Bethania. Next morning, however, He went back to the city, and taught in the temple. What grieved Him most was the fickleness of the Jews and their hardness of heart. Wherefore, He spoke to them this parable: "The kingdom of heaven is like to a king who made a marriage for his son.

2. "He sent his servants to call them that were invited to the marriage; and they would not come. Again, he sent other servants, saying: 'Tell them that were invited: Behold, I have prepared my dinner, my beeves and fatlings are killed, and all things are ready; come ye to the wedding.'

[1] FURIOUS, very angry.

But they neglected and went their ways, one to his farm, and another to his merchandise.

3. "And the rest laid hands on his servants, and having treated them contumeliously,[1] put them to death. But when the king heard of it, he was angry, and, sending his armies, he destroyed those murderers and burnt their city. Then he saith to his servants: 'The wedding, indeed, is ready, but they that were invited were not worthy. Go ye, therefore, into the highways, and as many as you shall find, invite to the marriage.'

4. "So his servants, going out into the highways, gathered together all that they found, both bad and good, and the wedding was filled with guests. Then the king went in to see the guests, and he saw there a man who had not on a wedding garment. He saith to him: 'Friend, how camest thou in hither not having on a wedding garment?' But he was silent. Then the king said to the waiters: 'Having bound his hands and feet, cast him into the exterior darkness; there shall be weeping and gnashing of teeth. For many are called, but few are chosen'."

5. The Scribes and Pharisees, understanding that this parable was meant for them, hated our Lord more than ever. They went, therefore, and consulted together, how they could lay hold of some of His words in order to accuse Him publicly. For this purpose they sent some of their disciples, with the Herodians, to ask Him, by way of satisfying their doubts, whether it were lawful to pay tribute to Cæsar, or not. Now, by Cæsar was meant the Roman emperor, to whom Judea was then subject.

6. They thought that if He answered, "Yes," He would make Himself odious[2] to the Jews, and that, on the other hand, if He answered, "No," He would draw down upon Himself the revengeful hatred of Herod and the Romans. But Jesus, knowing their malice, said: "Why do ye tempt

---

[1] CONTUMELIOUSLY, shamefully.
[2] ODIOUS, hateful, offensive.

Me, ye hypocrites? Show Me the coin of the tribute!" They showed Him a penny. And He said to them: "Whose image and inscription[1] is this?" They said: "Cæsar's." Then He said to them: "Render, therefore, to Cæsar the things that are Cæsar's, and to God the things that are God's."

QUESTIONS.

1. In the evening, whither did Jesus return from Jerusalem? What did He do next morning? What was it that grieved Him most? What parable did He, therefore, speak to the people? To what did He liken the kingdom of heaven? 2. Whom did the king send to call those who were invited to the wedding? What did he send other servants saying? But what did the people who were invited do? 3. What did the rest do? What did the king do, when he heard of it, being angry? What did he then say to his servants? 4. And what did the servants do? When the king went in to see the guests, whom did he see there? What did the king say to him? What did he say to the waiters? 5. What did the Pharisees do, understanding that this parable was meant for them? What did they send some of their disciples, with the Herodians, to ask Him? 6. What did they think? But what did Jesus, knowing their malice, say? What did He say when they showed Him a penny? What did they say? What did Jesus say?

CHAPTER LXI.

The Widow's Mite.—Jesus Foretells the Destruction of Jerusalem and the End of the World.

Man seeth those things that appear, but the Lord beholdeth the heart.—*I. Kings 16, 7.*

WHILE Jesus remained in the Temple, He saw many making their offerings, and He noticed the way in which each one made the offering. Several rich persons put much into the treasury, but one poor widow put in two brass mites. Then Jesus called His disciples, and said to them: "Amen, I say to you, this poor widow hath cast in

[1] INSCRIPTION, something written, or engraved, to communicate knowledge.

more than all they who have cast into the treasury: for they all did cast in of their abundance; but she, of her want, has cast in all she had, even her whole living."

2. As He was leaving the temple, some of His disciples called his attention to the rich materials of which it was built. But He told them that the day would soon come when there should not be left one stone upon another of that gorgeous[1] edifice. They asked Him when these things should come to pass, and what signs should precede the end of the world.

3. And He said to them: "When you shall see Jerusalem compassed[2] about with an army, then know that the desolation thereof is at hand. Then let those that are in Judea flee to the mountains. And he that is in the field, let him not go back to take his coat. For there shall be then great tribulation, such as hath not been from the beginning of the world until now, neither shall be. There shall be wrath upon this people. They shall fall by the edge of the sword, and shall be led away captives into all nations.

4. "Jerusalem shall be trodden down by the Gentiles till the time of the nations be fulfilled. Many will come in My name, saying: 'I am Christ,' and they shall seduce many. You shall hear of wars and rumors of wars; nation shall rise against nation, and kingdom against kingdom, and there shall be pestilences, and famines, and earthquakes in places.

5. "These are but the beginning of sorrows. And this gospel of the kingdom shall be preached in the whole world; and immediately after the tribulation of those days, the sun shall be darkened, the moon shall not give her light, the stars shall fall from heaven, and the powers of the heavens shall be moved.

6. "And upon the earth, distress of nations, by reason of the confusion of the roaring of the sea and the waves; men withering away for fear and expectation of what shall come upon the whole world. Then shall appear the sign of

---

[1] GORGEOUS, showy, fine, magnificent.   [2] COMPASSED, encircled.

the Son of Man in heaven, and all the tribes of the earth shall mourn; and they shall see the Son of Man coming in the clouds of heaven with great power and majesty.

7. "He shall send His angels with a trumpet and a great voice, and they shall gather together His elect from the four winds, from the farthest parts of the heaven to the utmost bounds of them. Heaven and earth shall pass away, but My word shall not pass away." The destruction of Jerusalem which took place thirty-seven years after, is a certain proof that the prediction,[1] relating to the end of the world, will undoubtedly be fulfilled.

QUESTIONS.

1. While Jesus remained in the temple, what did He see? What did several rich persons put into the treasury? What did one poor widow put in? What did Jesus then say to His disciples? 2. As He was leaving the temple, to what did some of His disciples call His attention? What did He tell them? What did they ask Him? 3. What did He say to them? What shall there be? 4. What was to happen to Jerusalem? What were people to hear of? 5. What was to take place after the gospel was preached to every creature? 6. What was then to be upon the earth? What sign shall appear in heaven? What shall be seen coming in a cloud in power and majesty? 7. Whom shall He send with a trumpet and a great voice to gather in His elect? What shall pass away? But what shall not pass away? What is a certain proof that the prediction relating to the end of the world shall infallibly be fulfilled?

CHAPTER LXII.

The Parable of the Ten Virgins, and of the Talents.

Watch ye, therefore, because you know not what hour your Lord
will come..—*Matt. 24, 42.*

JESUS warns His followers not to seek the things of this world with too much anxiety, and to make a provision of good works, while they yet have time; for that death will come like a thief in the night, when least expected. To make them better understand this great truth, He gave them the

---

[1] PREDICTION, that which is foretold.

following parable: "Then shall the kingdom of heaven be likened to ten virgins, who, taking their lamps, went out to meet the bridegroom and the bride.

2. "Now, five of them were foolish, and five were wise. But the five foolish, having taken their lamps, took no oil with them; but the wise took oil in their vessels with the lamps. While the bridegroom tarried they all slumbered and slept. And at midnight there was a cry made: 'Behold, the bridegroom cometh; go ye forth to meet him!' Then all those virgins arose and trimmed their lamps.

3. "And the foolish said to the wise: 'Give us of your oil, for our lamps are gone out.' The wise answered, saying: 'Lest there be not enough for us and for you, go you, rather to them that sell, and buy for yourselves.' Now, while they went to buy, the bridegroom came, and they who were ready went in with him to the marriage, and the door was shut.

4. "But at last came also the other virgins, saying: 'Lord, Lord, open to us! But he, answering, said, 'Amen, I say to you, I know you not.' Watch, ye, therefore, because ye know not the day nor the hour." Thereupon He spoke another parable to the same effect, showing the necessity of making good use of the time and the talents confided to us.

5. "Even as a man going into a far country, called his servants, and delivered to them his goods. To one he gave five talents, and to another two, and to another one; to every one according to his proper ability:[1] and immediately he took his journey. Now, he that had received the five talents went his way, and traded with the same, and gained other five."

6. "And in like manner, he that had received the two gained other two. But he that had received the one, going his way, digged in the earth and hid his lord's money. After a long time, the lord of those servants came and reckoned with them. And he that had received the five talents coming, brought other five talents, saying: 'Lord, thou didst de-

---

[1] ABILITY, power, skill.

liver to me five talents; behold, I have gained other five over and above.'

7. "His lord said to him: 'Well done, thou good and faithful servant; because thou hast been faithful over a few things, I will set thee over many things: enter thou into the joy of thy lord'." And to the servant who, having received two talents, came back with four talents, their lord spoke in like manner.

8. "But he that received the one talent came and said: 'Lord, I know that thou art a hard man, and, being afraid, I went and hid thy talent in the earth; behold, here thou hast that which is thine.' Then his lord, answering said: 'Take ye away, therefore, the talent from him, and give it to him that hath ten talents. For to every one that hath, shall be given, and he shall abound; but from him that hath not, that also which he seemeth to have, shall be taken away. And the unprofitable servant cast ye out into exterior darkness."

QUESTIONS.

1. Of what does Jesus warn His followers? Who will come like a thief in the night? What parable did He give them to make them understand this great truth? 2, 3, and 4. Repeat the parable of the wise and foolish virgins. 5. What other parable did He speak to the same effect? 6. When the lord came to reckon with his servants, what did the one who had received the five talents do? What did he say? 7. What did his lord say to him, and to the other who, having received two talents, brought back other two? 8. What did the one who had received the one talent, coming, say? What did his lord, answering say?

CHAPTER LXIII.

The Last Judgment.

God shall judge both the just and the wicked.--*Eccl. 3, 17.*

AFTER Jesus had admonished His disciples to prepare for the last judgment, He described it to them in these words: "When the Son of Man shall come in His majesty, and all the angels with Him, then shall He sit upon the seat of His majesty. All nations shall be gathered together before him; and He shall separate them one from another, as the shepherd separateth the sheep from the goats.

2. "And He shall set the sheep on His right hand, but the goats on the left. Then shall the King say to them that shall be on His right hand: 'Come, ye blessed of My Father, possess the kingdom prepared for you from the foundation of the world. For I was hungry, and you gave Me to eat; I was thirsty, and you gave Me to drink; I was a stranger, and you took Me in; naked, and you clothed Me; sick, and you visited Me; I was in prison, and you came to Me.'

3. "Then shall the just answer Him, saying: 'Lord, when have we done these things to Thee?' The King shall answer, and say to them: 'Amen, I say to you, as long as you did it to one of these, My least brethren, you did it to Me.' Then shall He say to them on His left hand: 'Depart from Me, ye cursed, into everlasting fire which was prepared for the devil and his angels.

4. 'For I was hungry, and you gave Me not to eat; I was thirsty, and you gave Me not to drink; I was a stranger, and you took Me not in; naked, and you clothed Me not; sick, and in prison, and you did not visit Me.' Then shall they also answer Him, saying: 'Lord, when did we see Thee hungry, or thirsty, or a stranger, or naked, or sick, or in prison, and did not minister to Thee?' Then He shall answer them: 'Amen, I say to you, as long as you did it not to one of these least ones, neither did you do it to Me.' And these shall go into everlasting punishment, but the just into life everlasting."

QUESTIONS.

1. After Jesus had admonished His disciples to prepare for the last judgment, what did He do? In what words? 2. Having separated the just from the unjust, what shall the King say to those on His right hand? 3. What shall the just answer Him? What shall the King answer? What shall He then say to those on His left hand? 4. What shall they say? What shall He answer them? Where shall the wicked then go? Where shall the just go?

CHAPTER LXIV.

The Last Supper, and Washing of the Disciples' Feet.

Learn of Me, because I am meek and humble of heart.—*Matt. 11, 29.*

ON the first day of the Azymes, or unleavened bread, when the paschal lamb was to be sacrificed, the disciples went to Jesus and said to Him: "Where wilt Thou that we prepare for Thee to eat the pasch?" He said to Peter and

JESUS WASHING THE DISCIPLES' FEET.

John: "Go ye into the city, and there shall meet you a man carrying a pitcher of water: follow him. And wheresoever he shall go in, say to the master of the house: 'The Master saith, where is my refectory, where I may eat the pasch with my disciples?'

2. "He will show you a large dining-room furnished,

and there prepare ye for us." The disciples went into the city, found all as He had told them, and prepared the pasch. In the evening Jesus came with the other apostles. And when they were at the table, Jesus said to them: "With desire I have desired to eat this pasch with you before I suffer. For I say unto you that I will not eat of it till it be fulfilled in the kingdom of God."

3. He rose from supper and laid aside His garment, and having taken a towel, He girded Himself. After that He poured water into a basin, and began to wash the feet of the disciples, and to wipe them with the towel. But coming first to Peter, the apostle said, in surprise: "Lord, dost Thou wash my feet!" Jesus answered and said: "What I do thou knowest not now, but thou shalt know hereafter."

4. Peter continued to resist, saying that his divine Master should never wash his feet. Then Jesus said to him: "If I wash thee not, thou shalt have no part with Me." Thereupon Peter humbly asked: "Lord, not only my feet, but also my hands and my head." After He had washed the feet of the twelve apostles, He sat down again at the table, and told them that since He, their Lord and Master, had given them such an example, they were to imitate Him in practising humility.

QUESTIONS.

1. On the first day of the Azymes, what did the disciples, going to Jesus, say to Him? What did He tell Peter and John to do? What were they to say to the man with the pitcher of water? 2. What did the disciples do? In the evening, who came? When they were at table, what did Jesus say to them? 3. What did He then do? And what did He begin to do? Coming first to Peter, what did the apostle say in surprise? What did Jesus answer? 4. What did Peter continue to do? Saying what? What did Jesus then say to him? What did Peter then say? After Jesus had washed the apostles' feet, what did He do? What did He tell them?

CHAPTER LXV.

Jesus Institutes the Holy Eucharist, and Foretells the
Treason of Judas.

The bread that I will give, is My flesh for the life of the
world.—*John 6, 52.*

THEN Jesus took bread in His holy and venerable hands,
and, raising his eyes to Heaven, He blessed the bread,
and broke it, and gave it to His apostles, saying: "Take ye

THE LAST SUPPER.

and eat; this is My body, which is given for you; do this for
a commemoration of Me."   In like manner, taking the chalice, He gave thanks and blessed it, saying: "Drink ye all of
this.   For this is My blood of the New Testament, which
shall be shed for many for the remission of sins."

2.   Whilst they were eating, He told the apostles: "Amen,

I say to you, that one of you who eateth with Me shall betray Me." They, being very much troubled, asked Him, with one voice: "Is it I, Lord?" He answered and said: "One of the twelve, who dippeth his hand with Me in the dish." Then he added: "The Son of Man, indeed, goeth, as it is written of Him, but woe to that man by whom the Son of Man shall be betrayed. It were better for that man if he had not been born!"

3. Then Judas, who betrayed Him, said: "Is it I, Rabbi?" But Jesus replied: "Thou hast said it." Then Judas rose from the table, and going immediately to the high-priest, sold his Master for thirty pieces of silver, promising to betray Him into the hands of the high-priest's servants. When he was gone, Jesus said to His disciples: "Now is the Son of Man glorified, and God is glorified in Him."

QUESTIONS.

1. What did Jesus take in His hands? What did He do? What did He say, giving it to His apostles? What did He do, taking the chalice? Saying what? 2. While they were eating, what did He tell His apostles? What did they say, with one voice, being very much troubled? What did He answer and say? What did He then add? 3. What did Judas then say? What did Jesus reply? What did Judas then do? Promising to do what? When Judas was gone, what did Jesus say to His disciples?

CHAPTER LXVI.

Jesus tells Peter that he shall Deny Him, and Bids Farewell to His Disciples.

Watch ye, and pray that ye enter not into temptation.—*Matt. 26, 41.*

HAVING given His apostles this great proof of His love, —His own body and blood, Jesus vouchsafed to give them also a new commandment of love. "Little children," said He, "yet a little while I am with you. I give you a new commandment: That you love one another, as I have loved you. By this shall all men know that you are My disciples, if you have love one for another."

2. Simon Peter said to Him: "Lord, whither goest thou?" Jesus answered: "Whither I go thou canst not follow Me now, but thou shalt follow Me afterwards." Peter said to Him: "Why cannot I follow Thee now? I will lay down my life for Thee." Jesus answered him: "Wilt thou lay down thy life for Me? Amen, amen, I say unto thee, the cock shall not crow twice till thou deny Me thrice!"

3. Then the Lord addressed Peter: "Simon, Simon, behold, Satan hath desired to sift you as wheat. But I have prayed for thee that thy faith fail not; and thou, being once converted, confirm thy brethren. All of you shall be scandalized in Me this night. For it is written: 'I will strike the shepherd, and the sheep of the flock shall be dispersed[1].'"

4. Jesus, seeing that they were sad at what He had said, consoled them, saying: "In My Father's house there are many mansions; I go to prepare a place for you. I will come again and will take you to Myself, that where I am you also may be. And where I go you know, and the way you know." But Thomas said to Him: "Lord, we know not whither Thou goest, and how can we know the way?"

5. Jesus replied: "I am the Way, the Truth, and the Life, no man cometh to the Father but by Me. And I will ask the Father, and He shall give you another Paraclete, that He may abide with you forever—the Spirit of Truth, the Comforter, the Holy Ghost, whom the Father will send in My name—He will teach you all things, and bring all things to your mind whatsoever I shall have said to you.

6. "Peace I leave with you, My peace I give to you, not as the world giveth do I give to you. But now I will not speak many things with you. For the prince of this world cometh, and in Me he hath not any thing. But that the

[1] DISPERSED, scattered.

world may know that I love the Father, and as the Father
hath given Me commandment, so do I. Arise, let us go
hence!" As on a previous occasion the Lord had made
Peter the head of His church, so now He promises to him a
faith that shall never fail and never err.

QUESTIONS.

1. Having given His apostles this great proof of His love, what did
Jesus vouchsafe also to give them? What did He say? 2. What did
Simon Peter then say to Him? What did Jesus answer? What did
Peter say to Him? What did Jesus answer? 3. What did the Lord
say to Peter? 4. Jesus, seeing that they were sad at what He had
said, what did He say to console them? What did Thomas say to Him?
5, 6. What did Jesus reply? What did the Lord on this occasion promise
to Peter, whom He had already made the head of His church?

CHAPTER LXVII.

The Agony of Jesus in the Garden.

He hath borne our infirmities, and carried our sorrows.—*Is. 53, 4.*

WHEN Jesus had said these things, He went forth with
His disciples over the brook Cedron, to a place
called Gethsemani, on the Mount of Olives, where there was
a garden, into which He entered. Then He said to His disciples: "Sit you here till I go yonder and pray." And taking with Him Peter, James, and John, He advanced into the
garden. He began to be sorrowful, and said to them: "My
soul is sorrowful even unto death; stay ye here, and watch
with Me."

2. Then going a little farther, He fell upon His face and
prayed, saying: "My Father, if it be possible, let this
chalice pass from Me. Nevertheless, not as I will, but as
Thou wilt." And, standing up, He came to His disciples,
and finding them asleep, He said to Peter: "Could you not
watch one hour with Me? Watch ye and pray, that ye enter

not into temptation. The spirit, indeed, is willing, but the flesh is weak."

3. And going a second time, He prayed, saying: "My Father, if this chalice cannot pass away, except I drink it, Thy will be done!" He came again and found His disciples sleeping; and, leaving them, He went away again, and prayed a third time, in the same words as before. Then He fell into an agony, and His sweat became as drops of blood,

THE AGONY IN THE GARDEN.

trickling down to the ground. And behold, an angel came and strengthened and consoled Him.

4. Then going a third time to His Apostles, He found them still asleep. He said to them: "Sleep now, and take your rest. Behold, the hour is at hand, and the Son of Man shall be betrayed into the hands of sinners. Rise, let us go. Behold, he is at hand that will betray me!"

QUESTIONS.

1. When Jesus had said these things, what did He do? Where did they go? What did He then say to His disciples? Whom did He take with Him? What did He begin to be? What did He say? 2. Going a little farther, what did He do? Saying what? Standing up then, what did He do? Finding them asleep, what did He say to Peter? 3. Going a second time, and praying, what did He say? When He came again, how did He find His disciples? Leaving them, what did He do? Into what did He then fall? What did His sweat become? What did an angel come to Him and do? 4. Going a third time to His apostles, how did He find them? What did He then say to them?

CHAPTER LXVIII.

Jesus is Seized.

He was offered because it was His own will.—*Is. 53, 7.*

WHILE Jesus was yet speaking, Judas came with a great crowd of soldiers and servants from the chief-priests and the ancients. Now the traitor had given them a sign, saying: "Whomsoever I shall kiss, that is He; hold Him fast!" As soon as he saw Jesus, he approached Him, saying: "Hail, Rabbi!" And he kissed Him. Jesus said to him: "Friend, whereto art thou come? Judas, dost thou betray the Son of Man with a kiss?"

2. Then advancing towards the troop, He said: "Whom seek ye?" They answered: "Jesus of Nazareth." He said to them, with a look of majesty: "I am He!" At the sound of His voice they started back and fell to the ground as though they had been struck by lightning. When they had raised themselves up, He asked them again: "Whom seek ye?" They spoke as before: "Jesus of Nazareth." He answered: "I have told you that I am He. If, therefore, you seek Me, let these go their way." They then laid hold of Him.

3. The apostles, seeing this, asked their Lord if they might

not strike with the sword in His defense. But Peter, without waiting for permission, struck a servant of the high-priest, called Malchus, and cut off his right ear. Then Jesus said to Peter: "Put up thy sword into the scabbard. Thinkest thou that I cannot ask My Father, and He will give Me presently more than twelve legions of angels?"

4. "How, then, shall the Scriptures be fulfilled, that so it must be done?" So saying, He touched the ear of Malchus and healed him. He then held out His hands, and they bound Him, and led Him away. Then the disciples all fled, leaving Him alone in the hands of His enemies.

QUESTIONS.

1. While Jesus was yet speaking, who came? What sign had the traitor given? As soon as he saw Jesus, what did he do? Saying what? What did he do? What did Jesus say to him? 2. What did He say, advancing towards the troop? What did they answer? What did He say, with a look of majesty? At the sound of His voice what happened? When they had raised themselves, what did He again ask them? What did they say? What did He answer? What did they then do? 3. What did the apostles, seeing this, ask their Lord? What did Peter do? What did Jesus say to Peter? 4. So saying, what did He do? What did He then do? What did the disciples then do?

CHAPTER LXIX.

Jesus Before Annas and Caiphas.

They have bent their tongue, as a bow, for lies, and not for truth.—
Jer. 9, 3.

THE troop of soldiers and servants first led Him before Annas, a former high-priest, and the father-in-law of Caiphas, the high-priest of that year. Annas questioned Jesus concerning His disciples and His doctrine. Jesus calmly told him that He had spoken openly, and he might question those who had heard Him. Then one of the servants who stood by gave Jesus a blow, saying: "Answerest Thou the high-priest so?"

2. Jesus meekly replied: "If I have spoken ill, give testimony of the evil; but if well, why strikest thou Me?" Annas, having bound Jesus with cords, sent Him to Caiphas, who, meanwhile, had assembled the grand council of the Jews. Now he and the whole council would willingly have found some pretext for putting Jesus to death; but they could find none, although many false witnesses had appeared against Him.

3. At last there came two false witnesses who affirmed that they had heard Jesus saying He would destroy the temple, and after three days build it up again. But they still contradicting each other, the high-priest arose and said to Jesus: "Answerest Thou nothing to the things which these witness against Thee?" Jesus was silent. Then the high-priest said to Him: "I adjure Thee, by the living God, that Thou tell us if Thou be the Christ, the Son of God!"

4. Jesus answered: "Thou hast said it. I say to you, hereafter you shall see the Son of Man sitting at the right hand of the power of God, and coming in the clouds of heaven." Then the high-priest rent his garments, saying: "He hath blasphemed; what further need have we of witnesses? Behold, now you have heard the blasphemy: what think you?" They answered: "He is guilty of death."

QUESTIONS.

1. Where did the troop first lead Him? Who was Annas? Who was Caiphas? On what did Annas question Jesus? What did Jesus calmly tell him? Then what did one of the servants do, who stood by? Saying what? 2. What did Jesus meekly reply? To whom did Annas send Jesus? What had Caiphas, meanwhile, done? What would he and the whole council willingly have done? 3. Who came at last? What did they say? What did the high-priest, rising, then say to Jesus? Jesus being silent, what did the high-priest say to Him? 4. What did Jesus answer? Then what did the high-priest do? Saying what? What did they answer?

CHAPTER LXX.

Peter Denies Jesus.

The Spirit, indeed, is willing, but the flesh is weak.—*Matt. 26, 41.*

PETER and John had followed Jesus at a distance, even to the house of the high-priest, in order to see the end. In the court-yard there was a fire, to which Peter went to warm himself. While there, Peter was noticed by one of the maid-servants of the high-priest. She looked at him and said: "This man also was with Jesus of Nazareth." Peter denied it, saying: "Woman, I know Him not." Immediately the cock crew.

2. After a little while a man coming to Peter, exclaimed: "Thou also art one of them." But Peter said: "O man, I am not." Now after the space of an hour, a certain servant saw Peter, and pointing him out to the others affirmed: "Surely thou art also one of them, for even thy speech doth discover thee!" But Peter swore that he knew not the man. Then the cock crew a second time.

3. And the Lord, turning, looked at Peter. That look pierced his heart. Remembering the words of his divine Master: "Before the cock crow twice thou shalt deny Me thrice," he went out and wept bitterly. During all that fearful night, Jesus was guarded in the court by the soldiery, who amused themselves by inflicting upon Him all manner of insult; they spat upon Him, blindfolded Him, and struck Him in the face.

4. Early in the morning, the council assembled to pronounce sentence of death upon Jesus. Then Judas began to be sorry for having betrayed his divine Master, and going to the chief priests, he would have given back the thirty pieces of silver he had received as the price of his treason, saying: "I have sinned in betraying innocent blood." But they re-

plied: "What is that to us? Look thou to it." Then, being filled with remorse, and losing all hope, he cast down the pieces of silver in the temple, and, in despair, went and hanged himself with a halter.

QUESTIONS.

1. Who had followed Jesus to the house of the high-priest in order to see the end? What was there in the court-yard? Who went to warm himself there? While there, by whom was Peter addressed? What did she say to him? What did Peter say? What happened immediately? 2. Who came, soon after, to Peter? What did the man say? What did Peter again do? After a while, what did a certain servant say to Peter? What did Peter answer? What happened a second time? 3. What did the Lord do? What effect had that look on Peter? What did he remember? What did he do? Where was Jesus all that fearful night? How did the soldiery amuse themselves? 4. What was done early in the morning? Then what did Judas begin to do? What did he do, going to the chief-priests? Saying what? But what did they say? What did Judas, filled with remorse, then do?

CHAPTER LXXI.

Jesus before Pilate and Herod.

They have sharpened their tongues like a serpent; the venom of asps is under their lips.—*Ps. 139, 4.*

THE great council of the Jews, called the Sanhedrim, could not pronounce the sentence of death without the permission of the Roman governor. Therefore the chief-priests and the ancients of the people led Jesus before Pontius Pilate, who then governed Judea for the Roman emperor. Pilate went out to the excited crowd and asked: "What accusations bring you against this man?"

2. They answered: "We have found Him perverting the nation, and forbidding to give tribute to Cæsar, saying that He is Christ, the King." Hearing this, Pilate went into the hall where Jesus was, and asked Him: "Art Thou the King of the Jews?" Jesus replied: "My kingdom is not of

this world.' Then Pilate went out again to the Jews, and said that he found no cause for condemning the person whom they had brought before him.

3. But they insisted that Jesus was guilty of sedition, stirring up the people from Galilee even to Jerusalem. To this charge Jesus made no answer. Then Pilate, seeing that He remained silent, asked Him: "Answerest Thou nothing? Behold, in how many things they accuse Thee?" Still Jesus was silent, and His silence surprised the governor exceedingly.

4. But as soon as Galilee was mentioned, Pilate asked if the accused were a Galilean, and being told that He was, he remembered that Herod, king of Galilee, was then in Jerusalem. Now, Pilate wished to rid himself of a case in which he was obliged either to go against his conscience or to displease the Jews. He, therefore sent the Savior to Herod, that Herod might set Jesus free or condemn Him.

5. Herod was glad to see Jesus, of whom he had heard many wonderful things. He hoped to witness some great miracle. When Jesus was brought before him he asked many questions, prompted by idle curiosity. But our Lord, knowing his motive, made no answer to any of his questions. Then Herod and his court mocked Jesus, and treated Him as a fool, and, clothing Him in a white garment, sent Him back to Pilate.

QUESTIONS.

1. Without whose permission could the great council of the Jews not pronounce sentence of death? Before whom, therefore, did the chief-priests and the ancients accuse Jesus? What did Pilate ask the crowd? 2. What did they answer? What did Pilate, going back to Jesus, ask Him? What did Jesus reply? What did Pilate then, going out again, tell the Jews? 3. But what did they insist? Did Jesus make any answer to this charge? What did Pilate then ask Him? 4. To whom did Pilate then send Jesus? Why did he send Him to Herod? 5. Was Herod glad to see Jesus? What did he hope? What did he do when Jesus was brought before him? Did our Lord answer any of his questions? What did Herod and his court then do? To whom did Herod send Jesus?

CHAPTER LXXII.

Jesus is Scourged, Crowned with Thorns, and Condemned to Death.

He was wounded for our iniquities, He was bruised for our sins.—*Is. 53, 5.*

PILATE well knew that it was through envy that the chief-priests and the ancients had brought the Savior before him, and therefore, he wished to save Jesus from their hands. He therefore went out to the people again and said: "You have a custom that I should release to you one of the prisoners at the pasch. Will you, therefore, that I should release to you Jesus or Barabbas?" Now this Barabbas was a murderer who had been taken captive in a sedition of the people.

2. Immediately the crowd, instigated[1] by the chief-priests and the ancients, cried out: "Away with this man, and release unto us Barabbas!" Then Pilate said to them in amazement: "What shall I do then with Jesus, that is called Christ?" They cried out with savage fury: "Crucify Him! Crucify Him!" Pilate, still endeavoring to save Jesus, asked again: "Why, what evil hath He done? I find no cause of death in Him. I will chastise Him, therefore, and let Him go."

3. He then caused Jesus to be scourged. Immediately the whole cohort[2] was assembled. They stripped Jesus of His clothes, tied Him to a pillar, and scourged Him. Then, covering Him, in derision, with a purple garment, they platted a crown of sharp thorns, placed it upon His head, and pressed it down so that the thorns pierced the flesh, and entered into the sacred head.

[1] INSTIGATE, to tempt, to incite.
[2] COHORT, one of the divisions of the Roman army.

4. Then placing a reed in His right hand, by way of scepter, they bent the knee before Him in mockery, saying: "Hail, King of the Jews!"   Others spat upon Him, and took the reed that was in His hand, and with it struck His head, driving the thorns still deeper into the flesh and bone. Every torment and every insult that malice could invent was then inflicted on His sacred person. At last they

THE SCOURGING AT THE PILLAR.

blindfolded Him, and then they renewed all manner of insult and injury.

5. By this time the Savior was reduced to a state so pitiable that Pilate thought the sight of Him would inspire the mob with compassion. He, therefore, took Jesus out on a balcony and showed Him to the crowd, saying: "Behold the man." But they cried out: "Crucify Him! Crucify Him!" Pilate exclaimed: "Take Him you, and crucify

Him, for I find no cause in Him." The mob cried out:
"We have a law, and according to the law He ought to die.
because He made Himself the Son of God."

6. Pilate, fearing still more, entered the hall and said to
Jesus: "Whence art Thou?" Jesus gave him no answer.
Then Pilate continued: "Speakest Thou not to me; knowest
Thou not that I have power to crucify Thee, and that I have

BEHOLD THE MAN.

power to release Thee?" Jesus answered: "Thou shouldst
not have any power against Me, unless it were given thee
from above." Now, Pilate sought to release Jesus, but the
high-priests, seeing that Pilate was disposed to favor Him,
gave the governor to understand that he could be no friend
of Cæser if he released this man.

7. Hearing this, Pilate was afraid, lest he should lose the
emperor's favor. But being still convinced of the innocence
of Jesus, he took water in a basin and washed his hands be-

fore the whole people, saying: "I am innocent of the blood
of this Just Man; look you to it." The mob cried out:
"His blood be upon us, and upon our children." Then
Pilate released Barabbas, and delivered Jesus to be crucified.

QUESTIONS.

1. Why did Pilate wish to save Jesus from the hands of the chief-
priests? What did Pilate say to the people? Who was Barabbas?
2. What did the crowd, instigated by the chief-priests, immediately
cry out? What did Pilate then say to them in amazement? What did
they cry out with savage fury? What did Pilate ask again? What did
he say he would do? 3. What did he then cause to be done? What did
they do to Jesus? With what did they cover Him, in derision? What did
they put upon His head? 4. What did they place in His right hand?
What insults were heaped upon Him? 5. What did Pilate think and
do, when he saw Jesus in so pitiable a state? What did the mob cry
out, when Pilate said to them: "Ecce Homo"? Repeat what was said
by Pilate and the crowd. 6. Fearing, still more, what did Pilate say to
Jesus? What did Jesus answer? 7. Was Pilate willing to give up the
friendship of Cæsar? Was he still convinced of the innocence of Jesus?
What did he say? What did the Jews cry out?

CHAPTER LXXIII.

Jesus Carries His Cross to Mount Calvary.—He is Crucified.

He humbled Himself, becoming obedient unto death; even to the death
of the cross.—*Phil. 2, 8.*

THEN the soldiers of the governor, tearing from the
body of Jesus the purple robe, clothed Him again in
his own garments, and laid the cross, whereon He was to be
crucified, upon His bruised and mangled shoulders. Bearing
this heavy burden, He advanced through the streets of Jerusalem towards the place of punishment, which was called
Golgotha, or Calvary. Two robbers were also led out to be
crucified with Him.

2. But Jesus, exhausted by long fasting and loss of blood,
fell three times under the weight of the cross. Then the
Jews, fearing that Jesus might die on the way, forced a cer-

tain man, who was passing by, named Simon of Cyrene, to help Him carry the cross to the place of execution.

3. Among the vast crowd that followed Jesus there were some pious women, who shed tears of compassion on seeing Him reduced to such a state. But Jesus, turning towards them, said: "Daughters of Jerusalem, weep not over Me, but weep for yourselves and for your children. For, behold, the

JESUS FALLING UNDER THE CROSS.

day shall come when they shall say to the mountains: 'Fall upon us,' and to the hills: 'Cover us.' For if in the green wood they do these things, what shall be done in the dry?"

4. When Jesus reached the top of the hill of Calvary, the soldiers offered Him wine mingled with myrrh, but He refused to drink. Then they tore the clothes from His badly mangled body, and nailed His hands and feet to the cross. And they crucified with Him two thieves, one on the right, the other on the left. Naked and bleeding He hung

upon the cross, raised aloft between heaven and earth. Pilate wrote a title in Hebrew, Greek, and Latin, and put it on the cross. The writing was: "JESUS OF NAZARETH, THE KING OF THE JEWS." Many of the Jews were dissatisfied; they came to Pilate and said: "Write not, the King of the Jews, but that He said: 'I am the king of the Jews'." But Pilate answered: "What I have written, I have written." And the soldiers cast lots for His garments, even as the prophets had foretold.

QUESTIONS.

1. What did the soldiers of the governor then do? How did Christ advance through the streets of Jerusalem? What was the place of punishment called? Who were also led out to be crucified with Him? 2. What did Jesus do, exhausted by long fasting and loss of blood? What did the Jews then do? Why did they force Simon of Cyrene to help Him to carry the cross? 3. Who were amongst the vast crowd that followed Jesus? What did they do on seeing Jesus reduced to such a state? What did Jesus, turning to them, say? 4. When Jesus reached the top of the hill of Calvary, what did the soldiers offer Him? Did He drink it? What did they then do? Whom did they crucify with Him? What did Pilate write? Were the Jews satisfied with it? What was Pilate's answer? What did the soldiers do?

CHAPTER LXXIV.

Jesus Speaks Seven Words on the Cross and Dies.

All they that saw Me have laughed Me to scorn; they have spoken with the lips, and wagged the head.—*Ps. 21, 8.*

MANY of those who passed that way, and saw Jesus hanging on the cross, blasphemed and said: "Thou that destroyest the temple of God, and in three days buildest it up again, save Thyself. If Thou be the Son of God, come down from the cross." The chief-priests also, and the scribes, and the ancients mocked Him, saying: "He saved others, Himself He cannot save."

2. But Jesus prayed: "Father, forgive them, for they know not what they do." And one of the thieves who was

crucified with Him, blasphemed like the others, saying: "If
thou be Christ, save Thyself and us!"　But the other rebuked him, saying:　"Neither dost thou fear God, seeing thou
art under the same condemnation.　We, indeed, justly,
for we receive the due reward for our deeds; but this
man hath done no evil."　Then he said to Jesus: "Lord,
remember me when Thou shalt come into Thy kingdom!"

THE CRUCIFIXION.

3.　Jesus replied:　"Amen, I say to thee, this day thou
shalt be with Me in paradise."　Near the cross stood Mary,
the mother of Jesus, and John, His beloved disciple, and
Mary Magdalen.　Looking upon them with tender affection,
He said to His mother:　"Woman, behold thy son!"　Then
addressing John, He said:　"Behold thy mother!"　Now from
the sixth hour there was darkness over the whole earth until
the ninth hour, while Jesus was in His agony.

4.　That He might drink the chalice of sorrow even to the

dregs, our divine Lord was abandoned at that awful moment by His Eternal Father. This was the crowning point of His terrible agony; for He exclaimed: "Eli, Eli, Lamma Sabacthani," that is: "My God, my God, why hast Thou forsaken Me?" After a few moments' silence, He said: "I thirst."

5. Then one of the soldiers took a sponge, and steeping it in vinegar and gall, put it on the end of a reed and presented it to His lips. But when he had tasted the vinegar, He said: "It is consummated!"[1] Then He cried out with a loud voice: "Father, into Thy hands I commend My spirit!" And bowing down His sacred head, He expired. How great must have been the sufferings of the Blessed Virgin who witnessed all the torments of her Divine Son without being able to give Him relief!

QUESTIONS.

1. What did many of those do who passed that way, and saw Jesus hanging on the cross? What did they say? What did the chief-priests and the scribes and the ancients do? Saying what? 2. But what did Jesus, praying, say? What did one of the thieves do who was crucified with Him? Saying what? What did the other say, rebuking him? 3. What did Jesus reply? Who stood near the cross? What did Jesus say to His mother? What did He say to John? What was there from the sixth to the ninth hour? 4. Why was our divine Lord abandoned at that awful moment by His Eternal Father? What did He exclaim? After a few moments' silence, what did He say? 5. What did one of the soldiers then do? When Jesus had tasted the vinegar, what did He say? What did He cry out with a loud voice? What did He then do? Was the grief of the Blessed Virgin great?

[1] CONSUMMATED, completed, finished.

CHAPTER LXXV.

Jesus is Laid in the Sepulcher.

His sepulcher shall be glorious.—*Is. 11, 10.*

IN order that the bodies of those who were crucified might not remain on the cross during the Sabbath, the soldiers came and broke the legs of the two thieves; but coming to

JESUS IS LAID IN THE SEPULCHER.

Jesus, they found Him already dead. Hence there was no need to break His legs. Fearing, nevertheless, that some vestige of life might still remain in Him, one of the soldiers pierced His side with a spear, and immediately blood and water came forth.

2. There was among the secret disciples of Jesus a rich man, named Joseph of Arimathea, a member of the council.

He went to Pilate and asked for the body of Jesus, that he might bury it. Pilate granted his request. Then Joseph, together with Nicodemus, took down the sacred body from the cross, and wrapped it up, with costly aromatic[1] spices, in a linen shroud.

3. It so happened that Joseph had a garden near the place where Jesus was crucified, and in the garden was a new sepulcher, hewn from the rock, wherein no one had yet been buried. In this they laid the body of Jesus, and rolled a great stone to the door of the sepulcher.

4. On the following day, the chief-priests and the Pharisees went to Pilate, and said: "Sir, we have remembered that that seducer said, while He was yet alive: 'After three days I will rise again.' Command, therefore, the sepulcher to be guarded until the third day, lest His disciples come and steal Him away, and say to the people: 'He is risen from the dead'." Pilate gave them guards to watch the sepulcher, and they, moreover, sealed the stone. The water and the blood that flowed from the side of Jesus, are figures of two great sacraments, namely: the blood refers to the Holy Eucharist and the water to Baptism.

QUESTIONS.

1. Why did the soldiers break the legs of the two thieves who were crucified? Why did they not break those of Jesus? Fearing that some vestige of life might still remain in Him, what did they do? What came forth from His side? 2. Who was amongst the secret disciples of Jesus? What did Joseph do? Pilate having granted his request, what did Joseph, with Nicodemus, do? 3. What had Joseph near the place where Jesus was crucified? What was in the garden? Where did they lay the body of Jesus? What did they roll to the door? 4. On the following day, what did the chief-priests and the Pharisees do? What did they say? What did Pilate give them? What did they, moreover, do? Of what were the water and the blood that flowed from the side of Jesus a figure?

[1] AROMATIC, fragrant, sweet-smelling.

CHAPTER LXXVI.

Jesus Rises from the Dead

Nor wilt Thou give Thy Holy One to see corruption.—*Ps. 15, 10.*

EARLY in the morning, on the third day, there was a great earthquake. At the same moment Jesus came forth from the tomb, glorious and immortal. And an angel

THE RESURRECTION.

came down from heaven. His face shone like lightning, and his garments were white as snow. So terrified[1] were the guards at his appearance that they swooned away, and became as dead men.

2. But the angel rolled the stone from the door of the sepulcher, and sat upon it. As soon as the guards recovered

1 TERRIFIED, frightened.

from their terror, they ran in great haste to the city to tell what they had seen. Towards sunrise, Mary Magdalen, and Salome, and Mary Cleophas brought spices to the sepulcher, intending to embalm the body of Jesus. As they drew near the sepulcher they said one to another: "Who shall roll us back the stone from the door of the sepulcher?"

3. When they came to the place, they found that the stone had already been rolled away. Surprised and alarmed, they entered in, and behold, the body of Jesus was not there! Great, then, was their sorrow and distress, for they knew not what had become of the body of their Lord. But, immediately, two men in shining garments stood before them.

4. Seeing this, the women were afraid. But one of the angels said to them: "Be not affrighted. You seek Jesus of Nazareth, who was crucified. He is risen. He is not here. Go. tell His disciples and Peter!" The women joyfully went and told the disciples what they had seen and heard. In the meantime the chief-priests consulted with the ancients, and then gave the soldiers that had been at the sepulcher a great sum of money, and told them: "Say you that His disciples came by night and stole Him away when we were asleep." The soldiers took the money and did as they were told.

QUESTIONS.

1. What was there early in the morning on the third day? What did Jesus do at the same moment? Who came down from heaven? What was his appearance? What effect had his appearance on the guards? 2. What did the angel do? What did the guards do as soon as they recovered from their terror? What did three devout women bring, about sunrise, to the sepulcher? As they drew near the sepulcher, what did they say one to another? 3. When they came to the place, what did they find? What did they do? Who stood immediately before them? 4. What did one of the angels say to the women? What did the women joyfully do? What did the chief-priests and the ancients give and say to the soldiers that had been at the sepulcher?

CHAPTER LXXVII.

Jesus Appears to Mary Magdalen and Peter.

This Jesus hath God raised again, whereof all we are witnesses.
—*Acts 2, 32.*

NOW, Mary Magdalen, seeing that the stone was rolled away from the sepulcher, and noticing that the body was not there, went in all haste to Jerusalem to tell the news to the apostles. But immediately she returned weeping to the grave, and there she saw the two angels. One of them said to her: "Woman, why weepest thou?"

2. Mary sorrowfully replied: "Because they have taken away my Lord and I know not where they have laid Him!" When she had said this, she turned back and saw Jesus standing. But she knew not that it was Jesus. He said to her: "Whom seekest thou?" She, thinking that it was the gardener, replied: "Sir, if thou hast taken Him, tell me where thou hast laid Him, and I will take Him away." Jesus said to her: "Mary!"

3. Immediately recognizing Him she fell down at His feet, and exclaimed: "Rabboni!" that is to say, "Master." He said to her: "Go to My brethren, and say to them: I ascend to My Father and to your Father, to My God and to your God." He instantly disappeared. The same day Jesus appeared also to the other women and to Simon Peter.

QUESTIONS.

1. Seeing the stone rolled away from the sepulcher, what did Mary Magdalen do? What did she afterwards do? What did she see there? What did one of them say to her? 2. What did Mary sorrowfully reply? When she had done this, whom did she see standing? Did she know Jesus? What did Jesus say to her? What did she reply? 3. Immediately recognizing Him, what did she do? What did she exclaim? What did He say to her? What happened then? The same day, to whom did Jesus also appear?

CHAPTER LXXVIII.

Jesus Appears to Two of His Disciples on the way to Emmaus.

They shall obtain joy and gladness; sorrow and mourning shall
flee away.—*Is. 51, 11.*

ON the evening of the resurrection, two of the disciples
went to Emmaus, and talked together of the events
that had taken place in Jerusalem. Jesus suddenly joined
them under the form of a stranger. He walked on with
them, but they knew Him not. He asked them what these
events were of which they spoke, and why they appeared so
sad.

2. Then one of them, whose name was Cleophas, answered:
"Art Thou alone a stranger in Jerusalem, and hast not known
the things that have been done there in these days?" Then
Jesus asked: "What things?" They replied: "Concerning
Jesus of Nazareth, who was a prophet, and concerning our
chief-priests and rulers who crucified Him. Now to-day it
is the third day since these things were done. Yea, some
women, also of our company, who have been at the sepulcher,
say that He is alive." When Jesus had heard these words,
He said to them: "O foolish and slow of heart to believe all
the things which the prophets have spoken! Ought not
Christ to have suffered these things, and so enter into His
glory?"

3. Then, beginning with Moses and the prophets, He explained to them everything in the scriptures that was said in
relation to Himself. When they reached Emmaus, He was
about to take leave of them, but they pressed Him to remain
with them, as the day was far spent. He remained accordingly.

4. But when they sat down to table, He took bread and
blessed it, and gave it to them. And immediately their eyes

were opened, and they knew Him. But He vanished from their sight. They then said to one another: "Was not our heart burning within us whilst He was speaking in the way?" The same evening they returned to Jerusalem, where they found the eleven gathered together, who exclaimed: "The Lord is risen indeed, and hath appeared to Simon." The two disciples now told the apostles how they also had seen the Lord, and how they knew Him in the breaking of bread.

QUESTIONS.

1. Who suddenly joined the two disciples who were going to Emmaus on the evening of the resurrection? The disciples not recognizing Him, what did He do? And what did He ask them? 2. What did Cleophas then say to Him? What did they tell Him? When Jesus had heard these words, what did He say? 3. Beginning with Moses and the prophets, what did He explain to them? When they reached Emmaus, what was He about to do? But what did they do? And what did He do? 4. When they sat down to table, what did He do? And immediately what happened? But what did He do? What did they then say to one another? Whither did they return the same evening? What did they tell the apostles?

CHAPTER LXXIX.

Jesus Appears to the Assembled Apostles, and Institutes the Sacrament of Penance.

Confess, therefore, your sins one to another.—*James 5, 16.*

WHEN the apostles were assembled together in a room in Jerusalem, the doors of which were closed, Jesus came and stood in their midst, saying to them: "Peace be to you! It is I, fear not!" They trembled with fear, thinking it was a spirit. But He said to them: "Why are you troubled? See My hands and feet! A spirit hath not flesh and bones as you see Me to have."

2. Then He showed them His hands, His feet, and His side. But they still wondered, and were scarcely able to believe

their own eyes, when Jesus asked: "Have ye here anything to eat?" They gave Him broiled fish and some honey-comb. And when He had eaten in their presence, He took what remained and gave it to them, saying: "Peace be to you! As the Father hath sent Me, I also send you."

3.   When He had said this, He breathed upon them, saying: "Receive ye the Holy Ghost. Whose sins you shall forgive, they are forgiven them; and whose sins you shall retain, they are retained." Now, it so happened that Thomas was not with the other apostles when Jesus appeared to them. Therefore, they told Thomas afterwards that they had seen the Lord.

4.   But Thomas declared that he would not believe, unless he saw in His hands and in His feet the print of the nails. Eight days after, the apostles were again assembled, Thomas being in their midst. And Jesus suddenly appeared to them, saying: "Peace be to you!"

5.   Then He told Thomas to put his finger in the print of the nails in His hands and feet, and to put his hand into His side. Thomas did so, and exclaimed with fervor: "My Lord and my God!" Jesus replied: "Because thou hast seen Me, Thomas, thou hast believed. Blessed are they that have not seen and have believed."

QUESTIONS.

1.   When the apostles were assembled together in a room, the doors of which were closed, who came and stood in their midst? What did He say to them? What did they think, trembling with fear? But what did He say to them? 2.   What did He then show them? But they still wondering, what did Jesus ask? What did they give Him? And when He had eaten, what did He do? Saying what? 3.   When He had said this, what did He do? What did He say? Now, what had so happened? What did the others say to Thomas afterwards? 4. But what did Thomas declare? What took place eight days after? Who was with them? Who suddenly appeared in the midst of them? Saying what? 5. What did He then tell Thomas? Thomas having done so, what did he exclaim? What did the Lord say to him?

CHAPTER LXXX.

Jesus Bestows on Peter the Supreme Pastorship.

I will set up one shepherd over them and he shall feed
them.—*Ezechiel 34, 23.*

AT the command of their Lord, the apostles left Jerusalem and went into Galilee. There Jesus appeared to
them one day on the banks of the lake of Genesareth, and

JESUS BESTOWING THE SUPREME PASTORSHIP ON PETER.

having blessed them, He ate with them. And after they had
eaten, the Lord said to Simon Peter: "Simon, son of John,
lovest thou Me more than these?" Peter answered: "Yea,
Lord, Thou knowest that I love Thee."

2. Jesus said to him: "Feed My lambs." Then the Lord
said to him again: "Simon, son of John, lovest thou Me?"
Peter again replied: "Yea, Lord, Thou knowest that I love

Thee." And Jesus spoke to him again: "Feed My lambs!"
Then Jesus, as though to try His apostle still further, asked
him a third time: "Simon, son of John, lovest thou Me?"
Peter was grieved because his divine Master seemed to doubt
his love, and he answered warmly and earnestly: "Lord,
Thou knowest all things, Thou knowest that I love Thee!"
Then the Lord said to him: "Feed My sheep."

3. On a previous occasion the Lord had chosen Peter as
the foundation of the church; later on Christ bestowed on
Peter the gift of unerring faith for himself and for his brethren; and now Jesus confides to him the lambs and the sheep
—that is, the whole flock. But the flock of Christ is the
True Church. Hence, if it is the duty of Peter to govern the
whole church of Christ, it must also be the duty of the members of the church to obey Peter. Whosoever, therefore,
does not obey Peter, or his successors, he cannot enter into
the friendship of Christ.

QUESTIONS.

1. At the command of their Lord, what did the apostles do? There,
what did Jesus one day do? After they had eaten, what did the Lord
say to Simon Peter? What did Peter answer? 2. What did Jesus say
to him? What did the Lord say to him again? What did Peter again
reply? What did Jesus say to him again? What did Jesus ask him
a third time? Why was Peter grieved? What did he answer warmly
and earnestly? What did the Lord then say to him? 3. What three
privileges did the Lord bestow on Peter and his successors? If it is the
duty of Peter and his successors to govern the Church, what must the
duty of the faithful be?

CHAPTER LXXXI.

The Ascension of Jesus Christ.

Lift up your gates, O ye princes, the King of Glory shall enter in.—*Ps. 23, 9.*

THUS it was that Jesus often appeared to His apostles after His resurrection, and spoke to them of the kingdom of God; that is to say, of all that was requisite for the

THE ASCENSION.

foundation and government of His Church. On the fortieth day after His resurrection, He manifested Himself to them for the last time. He then commanded them to wait in Jerusalem until they had received the Holy Ghost, and then He added:

2. "All power is given to Me in heaven and in earth. As the Father hath sent Me, I also send you. Go ye, therefore, and teach all nations, baptizing them in the name of the

Father, and of the Son, and of the Holy Ghost; teaching them to observe all things whatsoever I have commanded you. And, behold, I am with you all days, even to the consummation[1] of the world.

3. "He that believeth, and is baptized, shall be saved; but he that believeth not, shall be condemned. And these signs shall follow them that believe: In My name they shall cast out devils; they shall speak with new tongues; they shall take up serpents; and if they shall drink any deadly thing, it shall not hurt them." He then took them to Mount Olivet, raised up His hands and blessed them.

4. Then He began to ascend, and soon a cloud hid Him from their sight. Whilst they stood looking sorrowfully after Him, two angels appeared to them in shining white garments, saying: "Ye men of Galilee, why stand you looking up to heaven? This Jesus who is taken up from you into heaven, so shall He come, as you have seen Him going into heaven."

5. Hearing these words, the apostles fell down and adored God, and returned to Jerusalem, praising and blessing God. Many other things which Jesus did are not related in the Gospel; for St. John thinks that if they were all written, the world would not be able to contain all the books. But this much has been written, that we may believe that Jesus is the Son of God; and that, believing, we may have life in His name.

QUESTIONS.

1. What did Jesus often do after His resurrection? Of what did He speak to them? On what day did He manifest Himself for the last time to His apostles? What did He command them to do? 2 and 3. Whither did He take them? What did He then say to them? What did He then do? 4. What did He then begin to do? What soon hid from their sight? Whilst they stood looking up after Him, who appeared to them? What did the angels say? 5. Hearing these words, what did the apostles do? What are not related in the gospel? For what reason does St. John think so? But why has this much been written?

[1] CONSUMMATION, termination, end.

SECOND SECTION.

THE ACTS OF THE APOSTLES.

CHAPTER LXXXII.

The Election of Matthias.—Descent of the Holy Ghost.

You shall receive the power of the Holy Ghost coming upon
you.—*Acts 1, 8.*

DESCENDING from Mount Olivet, the apostles repaired
to the upper chamber, or supper-room of the house
in which they usually assembled. There they remained in
prayer for ten days, with Mary the mother of Jesus, several
other holy women, and a great number of disciples, the
number of persons being about one hundred and twenty.
During those days of prayer, Peter, rising up, said that it
was expedient[1] that a new apostle should be chosen instead
of the traitor Judas.

2. Two of the disciples were then proposed: Joseph,
called Barsabas, and Matthias. After praying for light from
above, they cast lots, and the lot fell upon Matthias, who
was numbered with the eleven apostles, and filled the place
left vacant by the lamentable fall of Judas. Ten days after
the ascension, the Jews celebrated the Feast of Pentecost.

3. On that day the apostles were assembled together, persevering in prayer, when suddenly there came a sound from
heaven as of a mighty rushing wind, and it filled the whole
house where they were sitting. There appeared to them
cloven tongues, as it were of fire, and it sat upon every one
of them. And they were filled with the Holy Ghost, and
began to speak in divers tongues.

4. Now, there were at that time, in Jerusalem, Jews from

[1] EXPEDIENT, advisable, proper.

every nation under heaven, who had come for the celebration of the feast. These, having heard of what had taken place, hastened with a great number of the inhabitants of Jerusalem, to the house wherein the apostles were assembled. Each one was astonished to hear them speak in his own tongue.

5. But some of the people mocked them, saying that they were full of new wine. Then Peter, going forth from the

THE DESCENT OF THE HOLY GHOST.

house with the other apostles, lifted up his voice, and spoke, "These are not drunk, as you suppose, but this is that which was spoken of by the prophet Joel: 'In the last days I will pour out of My Spirit upon all flesh, and your sons and your daughters shall prophesy.'

6. "Ye men of Israel, hear these words: Jesus of Nazareth, a man approved of God among you by miracles, and wonders, and signs, which God did by Him in the midst of you, as you also know; Him you have crucified and put to

death by the hands of wicked men. God hath raised Him up, whereof we all are witnesses. Being exalted, therefore, by the right hand of God, and having received of the Father the promise of the Holy Ghost, He hath poured forth this which you see and hear.

7. "Therefore, let all the house of Israel know most assuredly that God hath made Him Lord and Christ, this same Jesus whom you have crucified." The words of Peter had a divine power that penetrated all hearts, and many, repenting of their sins, asked Peter and the other apostles what they ought to do. Peter said to them: "Do penance, and be baptized, every one of you, in the name of Jesus Christ for the remission of your sins, and you shall receive the gift of the Holy Ghost." They received his words with joy, and on that day about three thousand persons were baptized.

QUESTIONS.

1. Descending from Mount Olivet, where did the apostles go? What did they do there? During those days of prayer, what did Peter say, rising up? 2. What was then done? Upon whom did the lot fall? What did the Jews celebrate ten days after the ascension? 3. What took place on that day when the apostles were assembled together, persevering in prayer? What then appeared to them? With what were they filled? And began to do what? 4. Who were at that time in Jerusalem? What did these do when they heard of what had taken place? At what was each one astonished? 5 and 6. What did some of the people, mocking them, say? What did Peter, going forth from the house, say? 7. What power had his words? What effect had they? What did they ask Peter and the other apostles? What did Peter say to them? How did they receive his words? How many of them were baptized on that day?

CHAPTER LXXXIII.

A Lame Man Cured by Peter and John. They are brought before the Council.

The works that I do, he also shall do, and greater than these shall he do.—*John 14, 12.*

ONE day, Peter and John were going up to the temple to pray. There was at the gate called the Beautiful, a man who was lame from his birth, and who was carried every day to the gate of the temple to beg alms from those who went in. Seeing Peter and John he asked them for an alms. But Peter said to him: "Silver and gold I have none, but what I have I give thee: In the name of Jesus Christ of Nazareth, rise up and walk!"

2. Then having taken the man by the right hand, Peter lifted him up, and immediately his feet and soles became firm. Then, leaping up, he stood and walked, and entered with them into the temple, praising and blessing God. All the people were filled with amazement to see the lame man walking and leaping.

3. But Peter said to them: "Ye men of Israel, why wonder you at this? or why look you upon us as if by our strength we had made this man to walk. The God of our fathers hath glorified His Son Jesus, whom you delivered up to death. The faith which is by Him has given this perfect soundness in the sight of you all. I know that you did it through ignorance. Be penitent, therefore, and be converted, that your sins may be blotted out!"

4. Many of those who heard these words were converted. But while the apostles were yet speaking to the people, the priests and the officers of the temple came and laid hands on them, and cast them into prison, where they remained till the following day.

5. Then the chief-priests and the ancients had the apostles

brought before them, and asked: "By what power, or in whose name have you done this?" Peter answered: "Be it known to you all, and to all the people of Israel, that in the name of our Lord Jesus Christ of Nazareth, whom you crucified, whom God hath raised from the dead, even by Him, doth this man stand here before you whole."

6. The chief-priests and the ancients ordered Peter and John to be taken out, and said one to another: "What shall we do to these men? for a miracle, indeed, hath been done by them, conspicuous[1] to all the inhabitants of Jerusalem; it is manifest, and we cannot deny it. But that it may be no further divulged[2] among the people, let us threaten them, that they speak no more in this name to any man."

7. Then, calling the two apostles, they charged them not to speak at all in the name of Jesus. But they answered them, saying: "If it be just in the sight of God to hear you rather than God, judge ye, for we cannot but speak the things which we have seen and heard."

QUESTIONS.

1. Whither were Peter and John one day going up? Who was there at the Beautiful gate? Seeing Peter and John what did he do? But what did Peter say to him? 2. What did Peter then do? And what happened immediately? And what did the man do? With what were all the people filled? 3. What did Peter say to them? 4. But while the apostles were yet speaking to the people, who came? What did they do to the apostles? 5. What did the chief-priests and the ancients then do? What did they ask them? What did Peter answer? 6. What did the chief-priests and the ancients say to one another? 7. What did they then charge the two apostles? But what did they answer?

[1] CONSPICUOUS, clearly seen, prominent.

[2] DIVULGED, made known, spread.

CHAPTER LXXXIV.

Ananias and Saphira.

Lying lips are an abomination to the Lord.—*Prov. 12, 22.*

WHEN Peter and John told the disciples all that had taken place, they were excited to great fervor, and prayed that God might strengthen them in the faith, and work signs and wonders by their hands. Whilst they thus prayed, the place wherein they were, was shaken, and the Holy Ghost coming upon them, imparted to them the gift of courage and the spirit of concord.

2. They persevered in the doctrine of the apostles, in prayer and in the breaking of the bread; that is, the apostles celebrated the holy sacrifice of the mass, and the faithful received Holy Communion. Thus they became so perfect that, of their own accord, they sold all they had, and brought the price thereof to the apostles to distribute among the poor. It so happened that a certain man, named Ananias, with his wife Saphira, sold a piece of land, and brought a portion of the price to the apostles. They acted as if they had given the whole price; yet they concealed a part for themselves.

3. But Peter said: "Ananias, why hath Satan tempted thy heart that thou shouldst lie to the Holy Ghost, and by fraud keep part of the price of the field? Whilst it remained, did it not remain to thee? And being sold, was it not in thy power? Why hast thou conceived this thing in thy heart? Thou hast not lied to men, but to God." Ananias, hearing these words, fell down and expired.

4. Great fear came upon all who heard it, and the young men, rising up, carried away the body. About three hours after, Saphira, the wife of Ananias, came in, and Peter addressed her, saying: "Tell me whether you sold the land for so much?" She answered: "Yea, for so much." Then

Peter rebuked her sharply: "Why have you agreed together to tempt the Spirit of the Lord?

5. "Behold, the feet of those who have buried thy husband are at the door, and they shall carry thee out!" Immediately she was struck dead at his feet, and the young men, coming in, carried her out also, and buried her with her husband. This terrible punishment of Ananias and Saphira ought to inspire us with a salutary[1] fear of sinning against the truth.

QUESTIONS.

1. When Peter and John told the disciples all that had taken place, to what were they excited? And what did they pray? Whilst they thus prayed, what happened. What did the Holy Ghost impart to them? 2. What is meant by "the breaking of the bread"? When they became so perfect, what did they do? Who sold a piece of land? What did they bring to the apostles? What did they conceal? 3. But what did Peter say? What did Ananias do when he heard these words? 4. What came upon all who heard it? What did the young men do? About three hours after, who came in? What did Peter say to her? What did she say? What did Peter then do? Saying what? 5. What happened immediately? What did the young men, coming in, do? With what ought this terrible punishment of Ananias and Saphira to inspire us?

CHAPTER LXXXV.

The Twelve Apostles in Prison.—Gamaliel's Counsel.

If you partake of the suffering of Christ, rejoice, that when His glory shall be revealed, you may also be glad with exceeding joy.—*I. Pet. 4, 13.*

THE apostles wrought many signs and wonders among the people. The sick were brought forth into the streets on beds or couches, so that at least the shadow of Peter might fall upon them, and they might be cured. By the daily repetition of these prodigies, the number of believers was wonderfully increased. Wherefore, the high-

[1] SALUTARY, beneficial, useful.

priest caused all the twelve apostles to be seized and cast into prison.

2. But an angel of the Lord came by night, and opening the doors of the prison, led them forth saying: "Go, and, standing, speak in the temple to the people the words of life!" Hearing this, they went into the temple, at the dawn of day, and taught. The chief-priests were enraged when they heard that the apostles were again teaching in the temple.

3. They gave orders to have them immediately arrested and put in prison. Then the apostles were again brought before the council, and the elders said: "We commanded you that you should not teach in this name. Behold, you have filled Jerusalem with your doctrine." Peter and the apostles answered: "We ought to obey God rather than men. The God of our fathers hath raised up Jesus, whom you put to death, hanging him upon a tree.

4. "This Prince and Savior, God hath exalted with His right hand, to give penitence to Israel, and remission of sins." When the priests and ancients heard these things they were filled with anger, and thought to put the apostles to death. But one of the council, a Pharisee named Gamaliel, a doctor of the law, and respected by all the people, rising up, commanded the men to be removed for a little while.

5. He then addressed the council, saying: "Ye men of Israel, consider with yourselves what you are about to do with these men. If this work be of men, it will fall to nothing. But if it be of God, you are not able to destroy it, lest, perhaps, you be found to oppose God." They agreed with Gamaliel, and calling in the apostles, they scourged them, and charged them to speak no more in the name of Jesus.

6. But the apostles went forth from the presence of the council rejoicing that they were accounted worthy to suffer reproach for the name of Jesus. They went daily to the temple, and from house to house, teaching and preaching to

the people, proclaiming everywhere the glory and power of the crucified Savior of the world.

QUESTIONS.

1. What did the apostles work among the people? Who were brought forth into the streets? By what, falling upon them, were they cured? What did the sight of these prodigies do? What did the high-priest, therefore, cause to be done? 2. But what did an angel of the Lord do? Saying what? Hearing this, what did they do? 3, 4. What orders did the chief-priests give? When the apostles were again brought before them, what did they say? What did the apostles answer? When the chief-priests and ancients heard this, with what were they filled? What did they think? What did Gamaliel, one of the council, command to be done? 5. What did he say, addressing the council? Did they agree with Gamaliel? What did they do to the apostles? 6. But what did the apostles do? What did they do daily?

CHAPTER LXXXVI.

Election of the Deacons.—Stephen the First Martyr.

Take heed to the ministry which thou hast received in the Lord, that thou fulfill it.—*Coll. 4, 17.*

AS the number of the disciples increased, it happened that some poor widows were neglected in the daily distribution. Hence it was that the apostles, calling together the multitude of the disciples, said: "It is not fit that we should leave the word of God, and serve tables. Therefore, brethren, look out among you seven men of good reputation, full of the Holy Ghost and wisdom, whom we may appoint over this business."

2. This proposal was pleasing to the disciples. They chose Stephen, a man full of faith and of the Holy Spirit, with Philip and five others. These they presented to the apostles, who prayed over them, and imposed hands upon them. Stephen, full of grace and power, did great wonders amongst the people. Some of the most learned of the doctors, envying his fame, began to dispute with him, but even

they could not equal the marvelous[1] wisdom with which he
spoke.

3. Ashamed of their defeat, they stirred up the people
against him. He was seized and brought before the council.
They then brought up false witnesses, who testified that he
ceased not to speak against the holy place and the law. All
the members of the council looked angrily upon him, but

THE MARTYRDOM OF ST. STEPHEN.

they saw his face shining like that of an angel. Filled with
divine love and the Spirit of God, Stephen reminded them of
the wonders which God had wrought for their fathers in
Egypt and other places.

4. After showing them how ungrateful their fathers had
been, he concluded with these words: "With a stiff neck
and uncircumcised heart and ears, you always resist the
Holy Ghost, as your fathers did. Which of the prophets

[1] MARVELOUS, wonderful, astonishing.

have not your fathers persecuted? And they have slain those who foretold the coming of the Just One, of whom you have been now betrayers and murderers!"

5. When they heard him speak thus, they raged, and gnashed their teeth with fury. But Stephen, being filled with the Holy Ghost, looked up steadfastly into heaven, and saw the glory of God, and Jesus standing at the right hand of God. When Stephen told them of his vision, they cried out with a loud voice and stopped their ears, and rushing upon him with one accord, drove him out of the city, and stoned him.

6. Whilst Stephen was being put to death, a young man named Saul held the garments of the murderers. But Stephen, falling on his knees, cried with a loud voice: "Lord, lay not this sin to their charge!" When he had said these words, he expired. The prayer of St. Stephen for his enemies was very pleasing to God, and some say that through this prayer, Saul received, later on, the grace of conversion.

QUESTIONS.

1. As the number of the disciples increased, what happened? Hence, what did the apostles do? Saying what? 2. Whom did the disciples choose? What did the apostles do when the seven were presented? What did Stephen do among the people? What did some of the most learned of the Jewish doctors, envying his fame, do? What followed? 3. Ashamed of their defeat, what did they do? What was done to Stephen? Whom did they bring up? What did they testify? When the members of the council looked angrily upon him, what did they see? Of what did Stephen remind them? 4. What did he show them? In what words did he conclude? 5. When they heard him speak thus, what did they do? But what did Stephen do? What did he see? When Stephen told them of his vision, what did they do? 6. Whilst Stephen was being put to death, who held the garments of the murderers? What did Stephen, falling on his knees, cry out? What happened then? Was the prayer of Stephen for his enemies pleasing to God?

CHAPTER LXXXVII.

The Sacrament of Confirmation.—Baptism of the Officer of
Queen Candace.

He that believeth and is baptized, shall be saved.—*Mark 16, 16.*

AFTER the death of Stephen, the disciples of Jesus Christ
were grievously afflicted in Jerusalem. Among the
worst of the persecutors was Saul, the same who had held the
garments of those who put Stephen to death. He went from
house to house, dragging out men and women who professed
to be followers of Christ, and threw them into prison.

2. On account of this fierce oppression, the disciples were
scattered abroad through all Judea and Samaria, preaching
everywhere the gospel of Jesus Christ. The deacon Philip
went to Samaria, where he cured all manner of diseases.
The inhabitants of that city received the gospel with joy, believed and were baptized.

3. When the apostles in Jerusalem heard this they sent
Peter and John to confirm the newly baptized. The two apostles
went to Samaria and prayed for the new Christians. Then they
imposed hands upon them, and they received the Holy Ghost.
After Peter and John had preached the gospel in Samaria,
and the country round about it, they returned to Jerusalem.

4. But an angel appeared to Philip, saying: "Arise, and
go towards the south, to the way that goeth from Jerusalem
down to Gaza!" Philip went immediately. While journeying along, he was overtaken on the road by an officer of Candace, Queen of Ethiopia, who was returning from Jerusalem,
where he had gone to worship.

5. As he rode along, sitting in his chariot, he read aloud
the prophecy of Isaias. Then the spirit said to Philip: "Go
near, and join thyself to that chariot!" He did so, and
heard the officer reading the words: "As a sheep, He was led

to the slaughter; and, like a lamb, without a voice, before His shearer, so opened He not His mouth." Philip asked him: "Thinkest thou that thou understandest what thou readest?" The officer replied: "How can I, unless some one show me?"

6. He then requested Philip to come up into the chariot and sit with him. Philip did so, and, beginning with the text which had puzzled the officer, he explained to him all the Scriptures relating to Jesus Christ, instructing him in the mystery of redemption. As they rode on, they came to a stream, and the stranger said to Philip: "See, here is water, what hindereth me from being baptized?"

7. Philip replied: "If thou believest with thy whole heart, thou mayest!" He answered: "I believe that Jesus Christ is the Son of God." He then stopped the chariot, and they both went down into the water, and Philip baptized the officer. But when they came up out of the water, the Spirit of the Lord took away Philip, and the officer saw him no more. Praising and glorifying God, he went back joyfully to his own country.

QUESTIONS.

1. After the death of Stephen, what happened? Who was amongst the worst of the persecutors? What did he do? 2. What was the result of this fierce persecution? Who went to Samaria? What did he do there? What did the inhabitants of that city do? 3. What did the apostles in Jerusalem do when they heard this? What did these two apostles, being come, do? After they had preached the gospel in Samaria, what did Peter and John do? 4. Who appeared to Philip? Saying what? By whom was Philip overtaken on the road? 5. What was the officer reading aloud as he rode along in his chariot? What did the spirit say to Philip? What words did he hear the officer reading? What did Philip ask him? What did the officer reply? 6. What did he then request Philip to do? Having done so, what did Philip do? What did the officer say when they came to a stream? 7. What did Philip say? What did he then do? What did they both do? But when they came out of the water, what happened? What did the officer do?

CHAPTER LXXXVIII.

The Conversion of Saul.—(About A. D. 37.)

By the grace of God, I am what I am; and His grace in me has not been void.—*I. Cor. 15, 10.*

SAUL, still breathing threats and slaughter against the disciples of our Lord Jesus Christ, went to the high-priest and asked him for letters to Damascus, that he might bring the disciples whom he found there prisoners to Jerusa-

SAUL STRUCK DOWN ON THE ROAD TO DAMASCUS.

lem. As he journeyed on the road to Damascus, suddenly a great light from heaven shone around him. Struck as if by lightning, he fell to the ground.

2. At the same moment, he heard a voice saying: "Saul, Saul, why dost thou persecute Me?" Saul asked: "Who art Thou, Lord?" The voice replied: "I am Jesus, whom thou dost persecute." Trembling with fear, and much astonished,

Saul said: "Lord, what wilt Thou have me to do." The Lord spoke to him: "Arise, and go into the city, and there it shall be told thee what thou must do."

3. Saul rose up from the ground, and opened his eyes, but he had lost his sight. His companions then took him by the hand and led him into the city. There he remained three days without eating and drinking. Now, there dwelt in Damascus a certain disciple of Jesus, named Ananias. The Lord appeared to him in a vision, saying: "Arise, and go into the street that is called Strait, and seek, in the house of Judas, Saul of Tarsus, for behold, he prayeth."

4. Ananias answered: "Lord, I have heard, from many, of this man, how great evils he hath done to Thy saints at Jerusalem." The Lord said to him: "Go, for this man is a vessel of election to Me, to carry My name before the Gentiles, and kings, and the children of Israel. For I will show him how great things he must suffer for the sake of My name."

5. Ananias went, and entering into the house where Saul was, he laid his hands upon him, and said: "Saul, brother, the Lord Jesus hath sent me; He who appeared to thee in the way as thou camest, that thou mayest receive thy sight, and be filled with the Holy Ghost." And suddenly there fell from the eyes of Saul, as it were scales, and he received his sight, and, rising up, was baptized. Immediately he began to preach in the synagogues that Jesus was the Son of God.

QUESTIONS.

1. What did Saul do, still breathing threats and slaughter against the disciples of our Lord Jesus Christ? Why did he ask for letters to Damascus? What happened to him as he journeyed on the road to Damascus? 2. What did he hear a voice saying to him? What did Saul say? What did the voice reply? What did Saul say, trembling with fear? What did the Lord say to him? 3. What did Saul do? What had he lost when he rose from the ground? What did his companions do? How long did he remain without eating and drinking? Who dwelt in Damascus? Who appeared to him in a vision? Saying what? 4. What did Ananias answer? What did the Lord say to him? 5. What did Ananias do? What did he say to Saul? What fell from the eyes of Saul? What followed? What did he immediately begin to do?

CHAPTER LXXXIX.

Peter's Journey.—He Raises Tabitha to Life. (*A. D. 39.*)

They shall lay their hands upon the sick, and they shall recover.—*Mark 16, 18.*

AFTER the conversion of Saul, the Church enjoyed peace for a while throughout Judea and Samaria. Peter went about among the faithful encouraging and confirming them in the faith. During this time he performed two great miracles. At Lydda there was a man named Eneas, who had kept his bed for eight years, being afflicted with palsy.

2. Peter said to him: "Eneas, the Lord Jesus Christ healeth thee. Arise, and make thy bed." Immediately he arose. Seeing this great miracle, all the inhabitants of Lydda were converted to the Lord. While Peter remained at Lydda, he was sent for in haste by some of the disciples in Joppe, not far distant, because a certain holy woman named Tabitha had just died there.

3. Peter, rising quickly, went to Joppe. They brought him to an upper chamber, where Tabitha lay dead. Many poor widows stood around weeping, and showed him the garments which Tabitha had made for them. Peter was touched at the sight, and, ordering all to leave the room, he knelt down and prayed. Then turning to the corpse, he said: "Tabitha, arise!" She opened her eyes, and when she saw Peter, sat up. The fame of this miracle converted very many to the Lord Jesus Christ.

QUESTIONS.

1. After the conversion of Saul, what did the Church enjoy for awhile? And what did Peter do? During this time, what did he perform? Who was Lydda? 2. What did Peter say to Eneas? What did he do? Seeing this great miracle, what happened? By whom was Peter sent for in haste? Why? 3. What did Peter do? Where did they bring him? Who stood around weeping? What

did they show Peter? What did Peter do? What did he say, turning to the corpse? What did she do? What did the fame of this miracle do?

CHAPTER XC.

The Conversion of Cornelius.

In one Spirit were we all baptized into one body, whether Jews or Gentiles.—*I. Cor. 12, 13.*

THERE lived in Cæsarea a man named Cornelius, a Roman centurion, a devout and God-fearing man, who gave much to the poor, and prayed continually. One day an angel appeared to him and said: "Thy prayers and thy alms have ascended for a memorial in the sight of God. Send men to Joppe, and call hither Simon, who is surnamed Peter. He shall tell thee what thou must do."

2. Then the angel disappeared, but Cornelius sent three men, who feared the Lord, to Joppe. On the following day as these men were drawing near the city, Peter, waiting for his midday meal, went up to the house-top to pray. During his prayer, he was wrapt in ecstasy. He saw heaven opened, and behold, a great sheet, as it were, was let down by the four corners from heaven to earth.

3. In the sheet were all manner of four-footed beasts, and creeping things of the earth, and birds of the air. Then a voice came from heaven, saying: "Arise, Peter, kill and eat!" Peter replied: "Far be it from me, Lord, for I have never eaten any common and unclean thing." But the voice spoke to him again. "That which God hath purified, do not thou call common!" This was done three times, after which the vision disappeared.

4. Whilst Peter was wondering what this vision might signify, the Spirit of God spoke within him, saying: "Behold, three men seek thee; arise, therefore, go down, and go with

them, doubting nothing, for I have sent them." Immediately Peter went down and met the men whom Cornelius had sent. Next day he set out with them, and with some of his own disciples, for Cæsarea. He was met by Cornelius, who, bowing down before Peter, told his vision, and all that the angel had said.

5. Peter then understood his own vision about clean and unclean animals; that is to say, that the Gentiles, who had hitherto been considered as unclean, were thenceforth to be received into the Church of Christ. Whereupon he announced to Cornelius and his household the doctrine of Jesus Christ.

6. Whilst Peter was yet speaking, the Holy Ghost came upon all who heard him. Peter and his disciples were astonished to hear these Gentiles speak in divers tongues, even as the apostles had done on the day of Pentecost. Then Peter commanded them all to be baptized in the name of the Lord Jesus Christ.

7. From that time forth, the gospel was preached to the Gentiles in various other places. Paul, as Saul was now called, and Barnabas, his companion, preached, especially at Antioch, the ancient capital of Syria. There the number of the faithful increased very much; and there, for the first time, the believers in Christ were called Christians, after the name of their divine Founder and Master Jesus Christ.

QUESTIONS.

1. Who lived in Cæsarea? Who appeared to him one day? What did the angel say? 2. When the angel had disappeared, what did Cornelius do? On the following day, in Joppe, while Peter waited for his midday meal, what did he do? Whilst he prayed, what happened? And what did he see? 3. What were in the sheet? What did a voice, coming from heaven, say? What did Peter say? What did the voice say again? 4. Whilst Peter was wondering what this vision might mean, what did the spirit of God say within him? Whom did Peter meet on going down? Next day, what did he do? By whom was he met in Cæsarea? What did Cornelius tell him? 5. What did Peter then understand? What was the meaning of the strange vision he had had? What did Peter announce? 6. Whilst Peter was yet speaking, what happened? What did Peter and his disciples hear that astonished them? What did Peter then

command to be done?   7. What was done from that time forth?
What was Saul now called? Who was his companion? Where did they
especially preach? What name was given to the faithful there? After
whom were they called Christians?

CHAPTER XCI.

Peter in Prison. (*A. D. 42.*)

The Lord is good to them that hope in Him.—*Lam. 3, 25.*

HEROD AGRIPPA, grandson of that Herod who had
caused the little children of Bethlehem to be slaugh-
tered, was now reigning in Judea. Wishing to find favor
with the Jews, he began to persecute the disciples of Jesus;
and, having put James, brother of John, to death, he caused
Peter to be arrested and thrown into prison.

2. Now, it was the time of the Jewish Passover; so Herod
gave the apostle in charge to four files of soldiers, that they
might guard him till after the festival-time, when he meant to
put him to death publicly. But prayer was made unceasingly
by the infant Church for Peter. Now, the night preceding the
day on which he was to be put to death had already come.

3. That night, being bound with two chains, Peter slept between two soldiers. The other soldiers kept watch at the door
of the prison. And behold, an angel of the Lord appeared
to Peter, and a bright light shone all around. The angel
struck Peter on the side, and awakened him, saying: "Arise,
quickly!" He did so, and the chains fell from off his hands.

4. Then the angel spoke to him: "Gird thyself and put on
thy sandals, and follow me!" Peter obeyed, not knowing, however, whether it was a dream, or a reality. Going out, they
passed through the first and the second ward, or watch, and
came to the iron gate leading to the city, which opened, of itself, before them. But when they came out of the prison-yard,
and had passed along one street, the angel disappeared.

5. Then Peter, coming to himself, found it was not a dream, and he exclaimed: "Now I know in very deed that the Lord hath sent His angel, and hath delivered me out of the hand of Herod, and from all the expectation of the people of the Jews!" He went then to the house of Mark, where many Christians were assembled in prayer. When Peter knocked at the door a young girl named Rhode came to listen.

ST. PETER'S DELIVERY FROM PRISON.

6. On hearing and recognizing Peter's voice, the girl was so delighted that she forgot to open the door, and ran in haste to tell the others. But they supposed that she had lost her mind. Yet she insisted that Peter was really at the gate. They then said that it must be his angel. Meanwhile Peter continued knocking. When the door was at length opened, and they saw it was indeed Peter, every one was struck with amazement.

7. Their wonder increased when they heard how the angel of the Lord had delivered him from prison. When morning came, and Peter was not to be found, the guards were filled with consternation.[1] And well they might, for Herod hearing of Peter's escape, caused them all to be put to death. But Herod himself did not long escape the punishment which his impiety and cruelty had deserved.

8. He had gone to Cæsarea, and was seated on his throne in kingly state to receive some foreign ambassadors. He delivered an oration which drew from the people the wildest acclamation.[2] They said he spoke as a god and not as a man. This absurd and senseless flattery was very acceptable to the tyrant. He was well pleased to be considered as a god. But immediately the angel of the Lord struck him with a terrible and loathsome disease, and he expired in fearful torments.

QUESTIONS.

1. Who was now reigning in Judea? Wishing to find favor with the Jews, what did he do? Whom did he put to death? Whom did he cause to be arrested and thrown into prison? 2. To whom did Herod give the apostle in charge? When did he mean to put him to death publicly? But what was done by the infant Church? What had already come? 3. How was Peter sleeping? Who appeared to Peter? What did the angel do? Saying what? When he did so, what happened? 4. Then what did the angel say to him? What did Peter and the angel do, going out? When they had passed along one street, what happened? 5. What did Peter, coming to himself, find? What did he say? Where did he then go? Who were assembled there? When Peter knocked at the door, who came to listen? 6. On hearing Peter's voice, what did the girl do? What did they suppose? But what did she answer them? What did they then say? Meanwhile, what did Peter do? 7. When did the wonder of the people within increase? What did Herod cause to be done when he heard of Peter's escape? 8. Whither had Herod gone? Why had he gone? What did he deliver? What did it draw from the people? What did they say? Was this flattery acceptable? But what happened then?

[1] CONSTERNATION, alarm, horror.

[2] ACCLAMATION, a shout of applause.

CHAPTER XCII.

Paul's First Mission. (*A. D. 45 to 48.*)

The Lord is my Helper; I will not fear what man can do unto me.—*Ps. 117, 6.*

THE Holy Ghost commanded the chief men of the Christians of Antioch to set apart Paul and Barnabas for the work to which they were called. Then after they had prayed and fasted, they imposed hands upon both of them, and sent them forth to preach the gospel. Then it was that Paul began in all earnest to labor for the conversion of the pagan world.

2. He preached first to the Jews. But they still refusing to receive the divine gift of faith, he betook himself to the Gentiles. Many of these heard with delight the word of life, and were baptized, so that the Church of Jesus Christ increased from day to day. Then Paul and Barnabas went to Cyprus, the native country of Barnabas. After they had preached throughout the whole island, the pro-consul, Sergius Paulus, sent for them, that he might hear from their mouth the word of God.

3. There was with Sergius a Jew, a false prophet named Bar-Jesus. This man resisted them to his utmost, and endeavored to dissuade Sergius from becoming a Christian. But Paul, full of the Holy Ghost, looked at him, and said: "O thou, full of all guile and of all deceit, son of the devil, enemy of all justice; thou dost not cease to pervert the right ways of the Lord. And now behold, the hand of the Lord is upon thee, and thou shall be blind, not seeing the sun for a time!"

4. Immediately a thick mist came before his eyes, and he went about groping for some one to take him by the hand. The pro-consul, seeing this miracle, believed in the Lord Jesus Christ. From Cyprus, Paul and Barnabas sailed for

Asia Minor. Having come to Antioch, in Pisidia, they entered into the synagogue on the Sabbath-day, and preached to the people Jesus crucified and risen again from the dead, with the remission of sins through Him alone.

5. Paul's discourse pleased the people so much that he was requested to come on the following Sabbath and preach again. But the Jews were filled with envy, seeing the multitude that came on that second Sabbath to hear Paul, and they contradicted all he said. Then Paul and Barnabas spoke boldly: "To you it behooved us to speak first the word of God; but seeing that you reject it, and judge yourselves unworthy of eternal life, behold, we turn to the Gentiles."

6. The Gentiles, hearing this, rejoiced, and the gospel was proclaimed throughout the whole land. The Jews, however, incited a persecution against Paul and Barnabas, and they were expelled from that country. The two apostles, shaking the dust from their feet, went to Iconium, where Paul preached the gospel.

7. Among those who heard him was a man who had been a cripple from his birth, and had never walked. Paul, looking at him, perceived that he had faith, and said with a loud voice: "Stand upright on thy feet!" The cripple leaped up and walked. The multitude, seeing this, cried out: "The gods, in the likeness of men, are coming down to us!" And they called Barnabas, on account of his height, Jupiter; and Paul they called Mercury, because of his eloquence.

8. Even the priest of Jupiter, bringing oxen, with garlands of flowers, to the gate, would have offered sacrifice, with the people, to Paul and Barnabas. But they, seeing what was going on, rent their garments, and ran among the people, crying out: "O men, why do ye these things? We also are mortals, men like unto you, preaching to you to be converted from these vain things to the living God, who made heaven and earth and the sea, and all things that are in them.

9. "Who, in past generations, suffered all nations to walk in their own way. Nevertheless, He left not Himself without testimony, doing good from heaven, giving rains and fruitful seasons, filling our hearts with food and gladness." Hearing this, many believed in the word of God. But some Jews, who had come from Antioch and Iconium, stirred up the people against Paul. They stoned him until they thought he was dead, and cast him out of the city.

10. But while the disciples of the city, who had gone out, stood weeping around him, he arose and went back with them to the city. Then he and Barnabas, having announced the gospel in Derbe, returned to the cities where they had already preached. They exhorted the disciples to persevere, ordained priests for them in every church, and, with fasting and prayer, commended them to the Lord. Finally, they returned to Antioch and related the great things which God had done to them, and through them, and how He had opened the door of faith to the Gentiles.

QUESTIONS.

1. What did the Holy Ghost command the chief men of the Christians of Antioch to do? After they had prayed and fasted, what did they do? What did Paul then begin to do in all earnest? 2. To whom did he first preach? But they still refusing to receive the divine gift of faith, to whom did they betake themselves? Did many of them receive the word of life? Where did Paul and Barnabas then go? After they had preached throughout the whole island, who sent for them? 3. Who was with Sergius? What did this man do? But what did Paul, looking at him, say? 4. And immediately, what happened to him? What did the pro-consul, seeing this miracle, do? From Cyprus, whither did Paul and Barnabas sail? Having come to Antioch, where did they preach on the Sabbath-day? 5. What was Paul requested to do on the next Sabbath-day? But what did the Jews do? Then what did Paul and Barnabas say? 6. What did the Gentiles do, hearing this? What did the Jews do? Whither did the two apostles go? 7. Who was amongst Paul's hearers? What did Paul say to him with a loud voice? What did the cripple do? What did the multitude, seeing this, cry out? What did they call Barnabas? What did they call Paul? 8. What did the priest of Jupiter do? But what did the

apostles, seeing this, do?   Crying what?   9. Hearing this, what did many do?   But what did some Jews do?   What did the people do? 10. But while the disciples stood weeping around him, what did Paul do?   Then what did he and Barnabas do?   What did they exhort the disciples to do?   Finally, what did they do?

CHAPTER XCIII.

The Council of Jerusalem.   (About A. D. 50.)

He saith to him: Feed My lambs; feed My sheep.—*St. John 21, 15-17.*

SOME disciples, who were formerly Jews, came to Antioch, and said to the Christians there: "Unless you be circumcised after the manner of Moses, you cannot be saved."   Paul and Barnabas opposed this doctrine.   But, in order to settle the question, they went up to Jerusalem to consult with Peter and the other apostles.

2.   When Paul and Barnabas arrived in Jerusalem, the apostles and the priests assembled in council to consider the matter.   After much discussion,[1] Peter rose up and said: "Men, brethren, you know that in former days God made choice among us, that the Gentiles, by my mouth, should hear the word of the gospel, and believe.

3.   "And God, who knoweth the hearts, gave them testimony, giving to them the Holy Ghost as well as to us, and made no difference between us and them, purifying their hearts by faith.   Now, therefore, why tempt you God to put a yoke upon the necks of the disciples, which neither our fathers nor we were able to bear.   But by the grace of the Lord Jesus Christ, we believe to be saved, even as they."

4.   James, bishop of Jerusalem, spoke to the same effect. It was then decreed by the whole council of Jerusalem that the Christians at Antioch, or elsewhere, were no longer bound to observe the law of Moses.   This decree commenced with these remarkable words: "It hath seemed good to the

[1] DISCUSSION, reasoning, examination by argument.

Holy Ghost and to us to lay no further burden upon you."
We see that even in the first council, in which the apostles
were assembled, the word and voice of Peter finished the
doubt and the dispute. But as the doctrine of Peter was in-
fallible, so the teaching of his successors in Rome is also in-
fallible.

QUESTIONS.

1. Who came to Antioch? What did they say to the Christians there?
Who opposed this doctrine? What did they do in order to settle the
question? 2. When Paul and Barnabas arrived in Jerusalem, what did
the apostles and priests do? 3. After much discussion, what did Peter,
rising up, say? 4. Who spoke to the same effect? What was then
decreed by the whole council of Jerusalem? With what remarkable
words did this decree commence? What did the word of Peter finish
in this first council? Why? What is the teaching of his successors in
Rome?

CHAPTER XCIV.

The Second Mission of St. Paul. (A. D. 51 to 54.)

For Thy sake we are put to death all the day long; we are accounted as
sheep for the slaughter.—*Rom. 8, 36.*

SOME time after, St. Paul set out on another apostolic
journey. He preached with great zeal in Syria, Cili-
cia, Phrygia, Lycaonia, Galatia, Mysia, and nearly all Asia
Minor. At last he came to Troas. There he doubted where he
should go next: but God made it known to him in a vision.
During the night he saw, as it were, a man of Macedonia,
who said to him: "Pass over into Macedonia and help us!"

2. Immediately, Paul set out for Europe, with his com-
panions Silas, Luke, and Timothy, and landed safely in
Philippi, the capital of Macedonia. On the Sabbath-day
Paul preached the Gospel of Christ. Among his hearers was
a God-fearing woman named Lydia, a seller of purple.
Opening her ears and her heart to the divine word, she re-

ceived it with joy, and was baptized with her whole family.

3. Very soon, however, a storm was raised against the apostles. As Paul and Silas were going, as usual, to the place of prayer, they were met by a certain girl, who had a spirit of divination,[1] and was, therefore, a source of great gain to her masters. She persisted in following the apostles, crying out: "These men are the servants of the Most High God, who show to you the way of salvation!"

4. Paul, turning round, said to the spirit that possessed her: "I command thee, in the name of Jesus Christ, to go out of her." And the spirit left her. Then her masters, seeing that the hope of their gain was gone, seized Paul and Silas, and brought them into the market-place before the magistrates, saying: "These men, being Jews, disturb our city."

5. Then the people rose against them, their garments were torn off, and the magistrates commanded them to be beaten with rods, and then to be thrown into prison. At midnight, Paul and Silas were praying and praising God, and suddenly there was a great earthquake, so that the walls of the prison were shaken to their foundations. Immediately the doors flew open, and the bonds of the prisoners were rent asunder.

6. The keeper of the prison awaking in terror from his sleep, and seeing the doors open, drew his sword to kill himself, because he thought that the prisoners had fled. But Paul cried out to him: "Do thyself no harm, for we are all here!" Then the jailer, calling for a light, went in trembling, and fell down at the feet of Paul and Silas.

7. Then he brought them out, and said to them: "Masters, what must I do that I be saved?" They answered: "Believe in the Lord Jesus, and thou shalt be saved." That same hour he took them and washed their wounds; and he and all his household were baptized. Next morning the magistrates sent orders to the jailer to release Paul and Silas, but when they learned that the two apostles were Ro-

[1] DIVINATION, foretelling.

man citizens, they came themselves to ask pardon for having ill-treated them.

8. After this, Paul and his companion visited many cities of Macedonia. From there Paul went to Athens, the most celebrated city of Greece. Seeing that city wholly given up to idolatry, his heart was stirred within him; he disputed publicly in the synagogues with the Jews, and in the market-place every day with all who were present.

ST. PAUL PREACHING TO THE ATHENIANS.

9. Then came to Paul certain philosophers, who conducted him to the Areopagus,[1] saying: "May we know what this new doctrine is, which thou speakest of?" And Paul, standing in the midst of the Areopagus, said: "Ye men of Athens, passing, and seeing your idols, I found an altar on which was written: *'To the unknown God.'*

10. "What, therefore, you worship without knowing it,

[1] AREOPAGUS (pr. Ar-e-op'-a-gus), a sovereign tribunal at Athens.

this I preach to you." He then preached to them the doctrine of Jesus Christ, but only a few of them believed. Among these few was Dionysius the Areopagite, one of the most learned men of his time. After Paul had preached the gospel at Athens, he went to Corinth.

11. There he preached first to the Jews, but they would not hear him, but rather blasphemed and contradicted all that he said. Then Paul, filled with a holy indignation, spoke to them: "Your blood be upon your own heads; I am clean. From henceforth I will go to the Gentiles." He then preached to the pagans of Corinth, many of whom were converted. Having remained in Corinth a year and six months, teaching and preaching, he returned to Antioch.

QUESTIONS.

1. What did St. Paul do soon after? Where did he preach with great zeal? Where did he at last come to? What did God make known to him in a vision? What did he see during the night? What did the man of Macedonia say to him? 2. With whom did Paul set out for Europe? Where did he land? What did Paul do on the Sabbath-day? Who was amongst his hearers? What did she do? 3. What was soon raised? By whom were Paul and Silas met? What did she cry out, following the apostles? 4. What did Paul say to the spirit that possessed her? What did her masters then do? Saying what? 5. What did the people then do? What did the magistrates command to be done to them? What happened at midnight when Paul and Silas were praying and praising God? 6. What did the keeper of the prison do, seeing the doors open, and supposing that the prisoners had fled? But what did Paul cry out to him? What did the jailer then do? 7. What did he say to them? What did they answer him? What did the magistrates do next morning? 8. What did Paul and his companion do after this? From Macedonia, where did Paul go? What did he do there? 9. Who came to Paul? Whither did they conduct him? Saying what? What did Paul, standing in the midst of the Areopagus, say? 10. Who was amongst the few converts made then by St. Paul? From Athens, where did Paul go? 11. To whom did he there preach first? Did they hear him? What did Paul say to them? To whom did he then preach? Were many of them converted? How long did Paul remain in Corinth?

CHAPTER XCV.

St. Paul's Third Mission. (A. D. 55 to 58.)

I have fought a good fight, I have finished my course, I have kept
the faith; as to the rest, there is laid up for me a
crown of justice.—*II. Tim. 4, 7 and 8.*

AFTER Paul had remained some time at Antioch, he
passed a second time through the greater part of Asia
Minor, and came to Ephesus, the capital of the Roman province of Asia. Here he met some twelve disciples, and said to
them: "Have you received the Holy Ghost?" They answered him: "We have not so much as heard whether there
be a Holy Ghost."

2. Paul asked them again: "In what then were you baptized?" They replied: "In John's baptism." Then Paul said:
"John baptized the people with the baptism of penance, saying that they should believe in Him who was to come after
him, that is to say: Jesus." Hearing this, they were baptized
in the name of the Lord Jesus. Then Paul laid his hands
upon them, and they received the Holy Spirit.

3. Paul remained two years at Ephesus, so that all those
who dwelt in the Roman province of Asia heard the word of
the Lord. Moreover, God was pleased to work many wonderful miracles by the hand of the holy apostle, and no
sooner were handkerchiefs or aprons, that had touched his
body, applied to the sick than they were instantly cured.
Seeing these things, a great fear came upon all the people,
and they magnified the name of Jesus.

4. Many of those who had dealt in the magic art brought
their books, which were of great value, and burned them before the apostle and the whole people. But a certain man
named Demetrius, a silversmith, who made little idols and
miniature[1] models in silver of the famous temple of Diana.

[1] MINIATURE, a representation on a small scale.

called together his fellow-craftsmen and told them that Paul, by his preaching, was destroying their trade, turning the people away from the worship of Diana, on which their living depended.

5. When the silversmiths heard this, they cried out: "Great is Diana of the Ephesians!" And a tumult was raised throughout the whole city. The people were about to lay hold on Paul and his disciples, with intent to kill them; but, happily, the town clerk, by wise persuasions, succeeded in appeasing[1] their wrath, so that peace was speedily restored.

6. The tumult being quelled, Paul assembled the Christians of Ephesus, and having exhorted them to persevere, sailed for Macedonia. Thence he went to Troas, where he remained seven days. On Sunday, he assembled all the faithful in an upper chamber, where he offered up the Holy Sacrifice and preached to the people till midnight.

7. The sermon being so long, a young man named Eutychus, who sat in the window, having fallen asleep, fell from the third story to the ground, and was taken up dead. Paul, hearing of the accident, immediately went down and restored the young man to life.

8. From Troas, Paul repaired to Lesbos, Chios, Samos, and Miletus. From the latter place he sent for the clergy of Ephesus, and bade them a last tender farewell, saying: "Now, behold, bound in the spirit, I go to Jerusalem, not knowing the things that shall befall me there." He then told them that he feared nothing, but was willing to lay down his life for his divine Master.

9. To the bishops he said: "Take heed to yourselves, and to all the flock over which the Holy Ghost has placed you bishops to rule the Church of God, which He hath purchased with His own blood. I know that after my departure, ravenous wolves will enter in among you, not sparing the flock." Then, kneeling down, he prayed with them all.

[1] APPEASING, satisfying.

And there was much weeping among them; and, falling on Paul's neck, they embraced him, and accompanied him to the ship, sorrowing that they should see his face no more.

QUESTIONS.

1. After Paul had remained some time at Antioch, what did he do? Whom did he there meet? What did he say to them? What did they answer him? 2. What did Paul ask them again? What did they reply? What did Paul then say? Hearing this, what was done to them? 3. How long did Paul remain in Ephesus? What was God pleased to work by the hands of the holy apostle? 4. What did many of those who had dealt in the magic art do? Who was Demetrius? What did he do? What did he tell them? 5. What did the silversmiths cry out, hearing this? What was raised throughout the city? What were the people about to do? Who succeeded in appeasing their wrath? 6. The tumult being quelled, what did Paul do? Where did he then go? What did he do on Sunday? 7. What happened during the long sermon? What did Paul do, hearing of the accident? 8. From Troas, whither did Paul repair? For whom did he send from the latter place? What did he say, bidding them farewell? 9. What did he say to the bishops? What did he then do? And what did they do?

CHAPTER XCVI.

Last Years of the Life of the Apostles.

Their sound hath gone forth into all the earth, and their words unto the ends of the world.—*Ps. 18, 5.*

WHEN Paul had returned to Jerusalem, he was seized by the Jews and cast into prison. After two years' imprisonment he was sent, at his own request, to Rome, to be judged by the emperor. On his way to the great city he was shipwrecked at Malta, but was saved in a miraculous manner.

2. Arrived in Rome, he was kept two years more in prison, but having then obtained his freedom, he began to preach the gospel. At the same time the other apostles were journeying in various countries, preaching as they went, and working all manner of signs and prodigies. Peter, in his capacity of

head of the Church, visited the different churches, confirming them in the faith.

3.   It was with that intention that he had gone before Paul
to the capital of the ancient world, and had there established
his episcopal see; thither he returned after each of his apostolic journeys, or visitations, and in his last years he remained there permanently.

QUESTIONS.

1.   What happened to Paul when he returned to Jerusalem?   After
two years' imprisonment, whither was he sent?   What happened to him
on his way to the great city?   2.   What happened to him on his arrival
in Rome?   Having obtained his freedom, what did he do?   At the same
time, what were the other apostles doing?   What did Peter do?   3.
What had he done with that intention?   What did he establish in the
capital of the ancient world?

APPENDIX.

But Thou, O Lord, shalt remain forever; Thy throne from generation
to generation.—*Lam. 5, 19.*

PETER and the other apostles everywhere established
bishops as their successors.   These bishops were to
govern the faithful, and to teach them the same doctrine that
they had learnt from the apostles.   As to the scriptures of
the New Testament, we must bear in mind that they were
written later, and collected later still.   Hence the apostles
and the first followers of the apostles had no written books
wherewith to convert the world.   It was all done by preaching.   The apostles preached what they had seen with their
own eyes, and their successors preached what they had learnt
from the apostles.   Much of what the apostles preached
was written down in the books of the New Testament, but
not all.   Yet even the unwritten teaching has come down to
us, and it is called tradition.

2.   All the apostles, with one exception, sealed with their
blood the gospel which they announced to the world.   In the

year of our Lord 67, Paul returned to Rome, where he and
Peter gloriously suffered martyrdom under Nero. Paul, being a Roman citizen, was beheaded; Peter died on a cross,
with his head downwards. James the Greater suffered under
Herod, about the year 42 of the Christian era.

3. John, the beloved disciple, who had been thrown into a
cauldron of boiling oil, and was miraculously preserved, was

the only one who died a natural death, which event took
place about the year 100. The successors of the apostles
were no less zealous for the truth than their masters had
been; most of them sealed their faith with their blood. Yet
the Church was not abandoned.

4. The bishops continued with unwearying zeal the work
which the holy apostles had commenced. And as the faithful were obedient to their bishops, so the bishops were obedient to the successor of St. Peter, that is, the Pope of Rome,

who is the chief pastor of the Church. In this manner there was a bond of union and unity between the faithful and their priests, between the priests and their bishops, and between all the bishops and the Pope.

5. Thus was established the One, Holy, Catholic, and Apostolic Church, which, built by Christ upon the rock of Peter, and guided by the Holy Ghost, has now existed for nearly nineteen centuries, and shall exist till the end of time, in spite of all that the infernal[1] powers can do against it. Happy are they that belong to that Church, who believe as she believes, and who do the works which she prescribes.

QUESTIONS.

1. What did Peter and the other apostles everywhere establish? What had the bishops to do and to teach? Was the New Testament then already written? Hence what did the apostles preach? What their successors? Was the whole doctrine of the apostles written down? Is the unwritten teaching lost? 2. What did all the apostles, with one exception, do? In what year did Paul return to Rome? Under what emperor did he and Peter gloriously suffer? How did Paul die? How did Peter die? Under whom did James the Greater suffer? 3. Who was the only one of the apostles that died a natural death? About what year did he die? What had been done to him? What did most of the successors of the apostles do? 4. To whom were the faithful obedient, and to whom the bishops? What bond of unity was there in the Church? 5. What was thus established? On what was the Church built? By whom? By whom guided? How long has it existed? How long shall it exist? Who are happy?

[1] INFERNAL, hellish, relating to the lower regions.

THE END

PRONOUNCING VOCABULARY OF PROPER NAMES

No attention has been paid to variant pronunciations; for each entry, only one pronunciation has been adopted. Secondary accents have not been indicated.

ā as in āce.
â as in câre.
ă as in ăm.
ä as in ärm.
ạ as in ạll.
á as in ásk and in sofá.

ē as in ēve.
ĕ as in ĕnd.

ē as in makēr.
ė as in novėl.

ī as in īce.
ĭ as in ĭll.

ō as in ōld.
ô as in nôr.
ŏ as in nŏt.
ó as in dragón.

ōō as in fōōl.
ŏŏ as in fŏŏt.
ou as in foul.

ū as in ūse.
û as in ûrn.
ŭ as in cŭp.
ụ as in circụs.

Aar'on (âr'ón)
Ab-di'as (ăb-dǐ'ás)
A'bel (ā'bĕl)
A-bi'a (ă-bī'á)
A-bi'as (ă-bī'ás)
A-bi-li'na (ă-bĭ-lī'ná)
A-bi'ron (ă-bī'rón)
A-bis'a-i (ă-bĭs'á-ī)
Ab'ner (ăb'nẽr)
A'bra-ham (ā'bráhăm)
A'bram (ā'brám)
Ab'sa-lom (ăb'sálóm)
A'chab (ā'kăb)
A-cha'ia (á-kā'yá)
A'chaz (ā'kăz)
Ad'am (ăd'ám)
A-dri-at'ic (ā-drĭăt'ĭc)
Ae-ge'an (ē-jē'án)
Af'ri-ca (ăf'rĭ-cá)
A'gag (ā'găg)
Ag-ge'us (ăg-gē'ùs)
A-grip'pa (á-grĭp'á)
Aj'a-lon (ăj'á-lón)
Al-ex-an'der (ăl-ĕgzăn'dẽr)

Al-ex-an'dri-a (ăl-ĕgzăn'drĭ-á)
Al-phe'us (ăl-fē'ùs)
Am'a-lec (ăm'á-lĕk)
A-mal'e-kite (ă-măl'ė-kīt)
A'man (ā'măn)
Am'mon-ite (ăm'ónīt)
Am'or-rhite (ăm'ôrīt)
An-a-ni'as (ăn-á-nī'ás)
An'drew (ăn'drōō)
An'na (ăn'á)
An'nas (ăn'ás)
An'ti-och (ăn'tĭ-ŏk)
An-ti'o-chus (ăntī'ō-kùs)
An'ti-pas (ăn'tĭ-păs)
A-ra'bi-a (á-rā'bĭ-á)
A-ra'bi-an (á-rā'bĭán)
Ar'a-rat (ăr'á-răt)
Ar-e-o'pa-gite (ăr-ēŏ'pá-jīt)
Ar-e-o'pa-gus (ăr-ēŏ'pá-gùs)

Ar-i-ma-the'a (ăr-ĭmá-thē'á)
Ar-me'ni-a (ärmē'nĭ-á)
As'ca-lon (ăs'ká-lón)
A'ser (ā'sēr)
A'sia (ā'shá)
As-su-e'rus (ăs-sōōē'rùs)
As-syr'i-a (ă-sĭr'ĭ-á)
As-syr'i-an (ă-sĭr'ĭán)
Ath'ens (ăth'ĕnz)
Au-gus'tus (ạ-gŭs'tùs)
Az-a-ri'as (ăz-á-rī'ás)
Az'ymes (ăz'ĭmz)

Ba'al (bā'ál)
Ba·a-lim (bā'á-lĭm)
Ba'bel (bā'bĕl)
Bab'y-lon (băb'ĭ-lón)
Bab-y-lon'i-a (băbĭ-lōn'ĭ-á)
Bab-y-lon'i-an (băbĭ-lōn'ĭ-án)
Ba'laam (bà'lám)
Ba'lac (bā'lăk)

1

Bal-tas'sar (băl-tăs'är)
Bar-ab'bas (bär-ăb'ás)
Bar'ac (băr'ák)
Bar Jo'na (bär jō'ná)
Bar'na-bas (bär'ná-bás)
Bar'sa-bas (bär'sá-bás)
Bar-thol'o-mew (bär-thŏl'ŏ-mū)
Ba-thu'el (bá-thū'él)
Be-el'ze-bub (bē-ĕl'zē-bŭb)
Bel (bĕl)
Ben'ja-min (bĕn'já-mĭn)
Be-tha'ni-a (bĕ-thä'nĭ-á)
Beth'a-ny (bĕth'á-nĭ)
Beth'el (bĕth'ĕl)
Be-thes'da (bē-thĕz'dá)
Beth'le-hem (bĕth'lĕ-hĕm)
Beth'pha-ge (bĕth'fá-jē)
Beth-sa'be-e (bĕth-sā'bé-ē)
Beth-sa'i-da (bĕth-sā'ĭ-dá)
Beth-sa'mes (bĕth-sā'mĕz)
Beth-u-li'a (bĕth-ŏŏ-lī'á)
Bo'oz (bō'óz)

Cae'sar (sē'zēr)
Caes-a-re'a (sĕs-á-rē'á)
Cain (kān)
Ca'i-phas (kā'ĭ-fás)
Ca'leb (kā'lĕb)
Cal'va-ry (kăl'vá-rĭ)
Ca'na (kā'ná)
Can'da-ce (kăn'dá-sē)
Ca-phar'na-um (ká-fär'ná-ùm)
Ca'rith (kā'rĭth)
Car'mel (kär'mĕl)

Ce'dron (sē'drŏn)
Ce'phas (sē'fás)
Chal-de'a (kăl-dē'á)
Chal-de'an (kăl-dē'án)
Cham (kăm)
Cha'naan (kā'nán)
Cha-naan-e'an (kă-nán-ē'án)
Cha'naan-ite (kā'nán-īt)
Cher'u-bim (chĕr'ŏŏ-bĭm)
Chi'os (kī'ŏs)
Ci-li'ci-a (sĭ-lĭsh'ĭ-á)
Cle'o-phas (klē'ŏ-fás)
Co're (kŏ'rē)
Cor'inth (kŏr'ĭnth)
Cor-ne'li-us (kôr-nē'lĭ-ùs)
Cy'prus (sī'prŭs)
Cy-re'ne (sī-rē'nē)
Cy'rus (sī'rùs)

Da'gon (dā'gón)
Dal'i-la (dăl'ĭ-lá)
Da-mas'cus (dá-măs'kús)
Dan (dăn)
Dan'iel (dăn'yĕl)
Da-ri'us (dá-rī'ùs)
Da'than (dā'thán)
Da'vid (dā'vĭd)
De-me'tri-us (dē-mē'trĭ-ùs)
Di-an'a (dī-ăn'á)
Di-o-nys'i-us (dī-ō-nĭsh'ĭ-ùs)

Eb-en-e'zer (ĕb-ĕn-ē'zēr)
Ec-cle-si-as'ti-cus (ĕ-klē-zĭ-ăs'tĭ-kùs)
E'den (ē'dĕn)
E'dom (ē'dòm)
E'gypt (ē'jĭpt)
E-gyp'tian (ē-jĭp'shán)
El'ca-na (ĕl'ká-ná)
El-e-a'zar (ĕl-ē-ā'zár)
E-li'ab (ē-lī'áb)
E-li'as (ē-lī'ás)

El-i-e'zer (ĕl-ĭ-ē'zēr)
E-lim'e-lech (ē-lĭm'ĕ-lĕk)
El-i-se'us (ĕl-ĭ-sē'ùs)
E-liz'a-beth (ē-lĭz'á-bĕth)
Em-man'u-el (ĕ-măn'ū-ĕl)
Em-ma'us (ĕ-mā'ùs)
E-ne'as (ē-nē'ás)
Eph'e-sus (ĕf'ē-sùs)
E'phra-im (ē'frá-ĭm)
Eph'ra-ta (ĕf'rá-tá)
E'sau (ē'sạ)
Es'dras (ĕz'drás)
Es'ther (ĕs'tēr)
E-thi-o'pi-a (ē-thĭ-ō'pĭ-á)
E-thi-o'pi-an (ē-thĭ-ō'pĭ-án)
Eu-phra'tes (ū-frā'tēz)
Eu'rope (ū'rŏp)
Eu'ty-chus (ū'tĭ-kùs)
Eve (ēv)
Ez-e-chi'as (ĕz-ē-kī'ás)
E-ze'chi-el (ē-zē'kĭ-él)

Gab'a-on (găb'á-òn)
Gab'e-lus (găb'ē-lùs)
Ga'bri-el (gā'brĭ-èl)
Gad (găd)
Ga-la'ti-a (gá-lā'shĭ-á)
Gal-i-le'an (găl-ĭ-lē'án)
Gal'i-lee (găl'ĭ-lē)
Ga-ma'li-el (gá-mā'lĭ-él)
Gar'i-zim (găr'ĭ-zĭm)
Ga'za (gā'zá)
Ged'e-on (gĕd'ē-òn)
Gel-bo'e (gĕl-bō'ē)
Ge-nes'a-reth (gē-nĕs'á-rĕth)
Ges'sen (gĕs'én)
Geth (gĕth)
Geth-sem'a-ni (gĕth-sĕm'á-nĭ)
Gi-e'zi (gī-ē'zī)

Gol'go-tha (gŏl'gō-thá)

Go-li'ath (gō-lī'áth)

Go-mor'rha (gō-mŏr'á)

Greece (grēs)

Hab'a-cuc (hăb'á-kŭk)

Ha-cel'da-ma (há-sĕl'dá-má)

Ha'ran (hā'rán)

Hav'i-lah (hăv'ĭ-lä)

He'brew (hē'brōō)

He'bron (hē'brŏn)

He'li (hē'lī)

He'noch (hē'nŏk)

Her'od (hĕr'ŏd)

He-ro'di-as (hē-rō'dĭ-ás)

Hev'i-la (hĕv'ĭ-lá)

Hol-o-fer'nes (hŏl-ō-fĕr'nēz)

Hor (hôr)

Ho'reb (hō'réb)

Hur (hûr)

I-co'ni-um (ī-kō'nĭ-ùm)

I'saac (ī'zák)

I'sai (ī'sī)

I-sa'ias (ī-zā'yás)

Is-car'i-ot (ĭs-căr'ĭ-ŏt)

Is'ra-el (ĭz'rā-ĕl)

Is'ra-el-ite (ĭz'rā-ĕl-īt)

Is'sa-char (ĭs'á-kär)

Ja'cob (jā'kŏb)

Ja'i-rus (jā'ĭ-rùs)

James (jāmz)

Ja'phet (jā'fĕt)

Je-ho'vah (jē-hō'vä)

Je'hu (jē'hū)

Jeph'te (jĕf'tē)

Jer-e-mi'as (jĕr-è-mī'ás)

Jer'i-cho (jĕr'ĭ-kō)

Jer-o-bo'am (jĕr-ō-bō'ám)

Je-ru'sa-lem (jē-rōō'sá-lèm)

Jes'se (jĕs'ē)

Je'sus (jē'zùs)

Jeth'ro (jĕth'rō)

Jew (jōō)

Jez'a-bel (jĕz'á-bĕl)

Jez'ra-hel (jĕz'rá-hĕl)

Jez'ra-hel-ite (jĕz'rá-hĕl-īt)

Jo'ab (jō'áb)

Jo'a-kim (jō'á-kĭm)

Job (jŏb)

Jo'el (jō'ĕl)

John (jŏn)

Jo'nas (jō'nás)

Jon'a-than (jŏn'á-thán)

Jop'pe (jŏp'ē)

Jor'dan (jôr'dán)

Jo'seph (jō'zĕf)

Jos'u-e (jŏs'ōo-ē)

Ju'da (jōō'dá)

Ju'das (jōō'dás)

Ju-de'a (jōō-dē'á)

Ju'dith (jōō'dĭth)

Ju'pi-ter (jōō'pĭ-tĕr)

La'ban (lā'bán)

Laz'a-rus (lăz'á-rùs)

Leb'a-non (lĕb'á-nón)

Les'bos (lĕz'bŏs)

Le'vi (lē'vī)

Le'vite (lē'vīt)

Lot (lŏt)

Lu'ci-fer (lōō'sĭ-fĕr)

Luke (lōōk)

Lu'za (lū'zá)

Lyc-a-on'i-a (lĭk-á-ōn'ĭ-á)

Lyd'da (lĭd'á)

Lyd'i-a (lĭd'ĭ-á)

Mac'e-don (măs'ē-dŏn)

Mac-e-do'ni-a (măs-ē-dō'nĭ-á)

Mach'a-bees (măk'á-bēz)

Mach-a-be'us (măk-á-bē'ùs)

Ma'di-an (mā'dĭ-án)

Ma'di-an-ite (mā'dĭ-án-īt)

Mag'da-len (măg'dá-lèn)

Ma'gi (mā'jī)

Ma-ha-na'im (mā-há-nā'ĭm)

Mal-a-chi'as (măl-á-kī'ás)

Mal'a-chy (măl'á-kē)

Mal'chus (măl'kùs)

Mal'ta (mạl'tá)

Ma-nas'ses (má-năs'ēz)

Ma'ne (mä'nā)

Man'hu (män'hōō)

Ma-nu'e (má-nū'ē)

Mar'do-chai (mär'dō-kī)

Mark (märk)

Mar'tha (mär'thá)

Ma'ry (mā'rĭ)

Math-a-thi'as (măth-á-thī'ás)

Ma-thu'sa-la (má-thōō'zá-lá)

Mat'thew (măth'ū)

Mat-thi'as (má-thī'ás)

Medes (mēdz)

Me'di-a (mē'dĭ-á)

Mel-chis'e-dech (mĕl-kĭz'ē-dĕk)

Mer'cu-ry (mĕr'kū-rĭ}

Mes-o-po-ta'mi-a (mĕs-ō-pō-tā'mĭ-á)

Mes-si'as (mĕ-sī'ás)

Mi'chael (mī'kĕl)

Mi-che'as (mī-kē'ás)

Mi-le'tus (mī-lē'tùs)

Mir'i-am (mĭr'ĭ-ám)

Mis'a-el (mĭs'á-ĕl)

Mo'ab (mō'áb)

Mo'loch (mō'lŏk)

Mo-ri'a (mō-rī'á)

Mo'ses (mō'zĕz)

Mys'i-a (mĭsh'ĭ-á)

Na'a-man (nā'á-mán)

Na'both (nā'bŏth)

Nab-u-cho-don'o-sor (năb-ū-kō-dŏn'ō-sôr)

Na'chor (nā'kôr)

Na'im (nā'ĭm)
Na'than (nā'thán)
Na-than'a-el (ná-thăn'á-ĕl)
Naz-a-rene' (năz-á-rēn')
Naz'a-reth (năz'á-rĕth)
Naz'ar-ite (năz'ár-īt)
Ne'bo (nē'bō)
Neph'ta-li (nĕf'tá-lī)
Ne'ro (nē'rō)
Nic-o-de'mus (nĭk-ō-dē'mùs)
Nile (nīl)
Nin'i-ve (nĭn'ĭ-vè)
Ni'san (nī'sán)
No'e (nō'è)
No'e-mi (nō'è-mī)

O'bed (ō'bĕd)
Ol'i-vet (ŏl'ĭ-vĕt)
O-ni'as (ō-nī'ás)
Oph'ni (ŏf'nĭ)
Or'pha (ŏr'fá)
O-zi'as (ō-zī'ás)

Pal'es-tine (păl'ĕs-tīn)
Par'a-dise (păr'á-dīs)
Par'thi-ans (pär'thĭ-ánz)
Pasch (pásk)
Pass'o-ver (pás'ō-vĕr)
Paul (pạl)
Pau'lus (pạ'lùs)
Pen'te-cost (pĕn'tē-kŏst)
Per-e'a (pĕr-ē'á)
Per-e'ans (pĕr-ē'ánz)
Per'sia (pĕr'shá)
Per'sian (pĕr'shán)
Pe'ter (pē'tĕr)
Pha-nu'el (fá-nū'ĕl)
Pha'ran (fā'rán)
Pha'ra-o (fā'rá-ō)
Pha'res (fā'rēz)
Phar'i-see (făr'ĭ-sē)
Phil'ip (fĭl'ĭp)
Phi-lip'pi (fĭ-lĭp'ī)
Phi-lis'tines (fĭ-lĭs'tĭnz)
Phin'e-es (fĭn'ē-ĕs)

Phryg'i-a (frĭj'ĭ-á)
Pi'late (pī'lát)
Pi-sid'i-a (pī-sĭd'ĭ-á)
Pon'tius (pŏn'shús)
Pro-bat'i-ca (prō-băt'ĭ-cá)
Pu'ti-phar (pū'tĭ-fár)

Rab'bi (răb'ĭ)
Rab-bo'ni (rá-bō'nĭ)
Ra'ca (rā'ká)
Ra'chel (rā'chĕl)
Ra'ges (rā'jēz)
Rag'u-el (răg'ū-ĕl)
Ra'ma (rā'má)
Ra'pha-el (rā'fá-ĕl)
Re-bec'ca (rē-bĕk'á)
Reu'ben (rōō'bĕn)
Ro-bo'am (rō-bō'ám)
Rome (rōm)
Ruth (rōōth)

Sa'ba (sā'bá)
Sad'du-cee (săd'ū-sē)
Sa'lem (sā'lĕm)
Sal-ma-na'sar (săl-má-nā'sár)
Sa-lo'me (sá-lō'mē)
Sam-a-ri'a (săm-á-rī'á)
Sa-mar'i-tan (sá-mär'ĭ-tán)
Sa'mos (sā'mòs)
Sam'son (săm'sṵ
Sam'u-el (săm'ū-ĕl)
San'he-drim (săn'hē-drĭm)
Sa-phi'ra (sá-fī'rá)
Sa'ra (sā'rá)
Sa'rai (sā'rī)
Sa-rep'ta (sá-rĕp'tá)
Sa'tan (sā'tán)
Saul (sạl)
Scribe (skrīb)
Se'gor (sē'gôr)
Sem (sĕm)
Sem'e-i (sĕm'ē-ī)
Sen-nach'e-rib (sĕ-năk'ē-rĭb)
Se-pho'ra (sē-fō'rá)
Ser'gi-us (sĕr'jĭ-ùs)
Seth (sĕth)
Si'char (sī'kár)

Si'chem (sī'kĕm)
Si'don (sī'dón)
Si-do'ni-a (sī-dō'nĭ-á)
Si-do'ni-an (sī-dō'nĭ-án)
Si'las (sī'lás)
Si'lo (sī'lō)
Sil'o-e (sĭl'ō-ē)
Sim'e-on (sĭm'ē-ón)
Si'mon (sī'món)
Si'nai (sī'nī)
Si'on (sī'ón)
Si'rach (sī'rák)
Sod'om (sŏd'óm)
Sol'o-mon (sŏl'ō-món)
Ste'phen (stē'vĕn)
Sur (soōr)
Su-san'na (sōō-zăn'á)
Syn'a-gogue (sĭn'á-gŏg)
Syr'i-a (sĭr'ĭ-á)

Tab'i-tha (tăb'ĭ-thá)
Ta'bor (tā'bôr)
Tar'sus (tär'sùs)
Thad-de'us (thád-dē'ùs)
Thar'sis (thär'sĭs)
The'cel (tā'kĕl)
Thom'as (tŏm'ás)
Ti-be'ri-as (tĭ-bē'rĭ-ás)
Ti-be'ri-us (tĭ-bē'rĭ-ùs)
Ti'gris (tī'grĭs)
Tim'o-thy (tĭm'ō-thĭ)
To-bi'as (tō-bī'ás)
Tro'as (trō'ás)
Tyre (tīr)

U-ri'as (ū-rī'ás)

Zab'u-lon (zăb'ū-lón)
Zach'a-ry (zăk'á-rĭ)
Za-che'us (zá-kē'ùs)
Zeb'e-dee (zĕb'è-dē)
Ziph (zĭf)
Zo-ro'ba-bel (zō-rō'bá-bĕl)

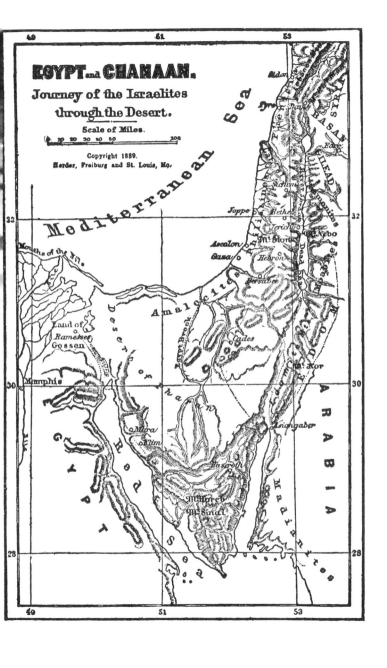

EGYPT and CHANAAN.

Journey of the Israelites through the Desert.

Scale of Miles.

Copyright 1889.
Herder, Freiburg and St. Louis, Mo.

Mediterranean Sea

Mouths of the Nile

Memphis

Land of Ramesses
Gossen

Desert of Than

EGYPT

Red Sea

Mara
Elim
Haseroth
M:Horeb
M:Sinai

Amalecites

Desert of Kadesh

Cades

M:Hor

Asingaber

ARABIA

Madianites

Joppe
Ascalon
Gasa
Bethel
Jericho
M:Stone
M:Nebo
Hebron
Bersabe
Dead Sea

GALILEE
SAMARIA
Sichem
JUDEA

BASAN
GILEAD
Edom

Aldon
Jordan

Jordan

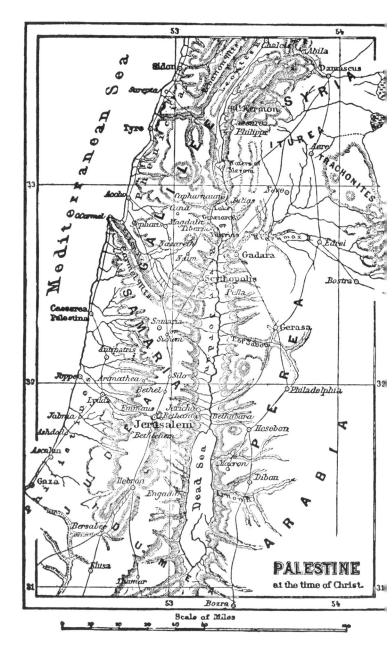

PALESTINE

at the time of Christ.

Scale of Miles

If you have enjoyed this book, consider making your next selection from among the following . . .

The Guardian Angels 2.00
Eucharistic Miracles. *Joan Carroll Cruz* 15.00
The Incorruptibles. *Joan Carroll Cruz* 13.50
Padre Pio—The Stigmatist. *Fr. Charles Carty* 15.00
Ven. Francisco Marto of Fatima. *Cirrincione,* comp. 1.50
The Facts About Luther. *Msgr. P. O'Hare.* 16.50
Little Catechism of the Curé of Ars. *St. John Vianney* 6.00
The Curé of Ars—Patron St. of Parish Priests. *O'Brien* 5.50
The Four Last Things: Death, Judgment, Hell, Heaven 7.00
Pope St. Pius X. *F. A. Forbes* 8.00
St. Alphonsus Liguori. *Frs. Miller & Aubin* 16.50
Confession of a Roman Catholic. *Paul Whitcomb.* 1.50
The Catholic Church Has the Answer. *Paul Whitcomb* 1.50
The Sinner's Guide. *Ven. Louis of Granada* 12.00
True Devotion to Mary. *St. Louis De Montfort* 8.00
Life of St. Anthony Mary Claret. *Fanchón Royer* 15.00
Autobiography of St. Anthony Mary Claret. 13.00
I Wait for You. *Sr. Josefa Menendez* 75
Words of Love. *Menendez, Betrone, Mary of the Trinity.* 6.00
Little Lives of the Great Saints. *John O'Kane Murray* 18.00
Prayer—The Key to Salvation. *Fr. Michael Müller.* 7.50
The Victories of the Martyrs. *St. Alphonsus Liguori* 10.00
Canons and Decrees of the Council of Trent. *Schroeder.* 15.00
Sermons of St. Alphonsus Liguori for Every Sunday 16.50
A Catechism of Modernism. *Fr. J. B. Lemius* 5.00
Alexandrina—The Agony and the Glory. *Johnston.* 6.00
Life of Blessed Margaret of Castello. *Fr. Bonniwell* 7.50
The Ways of Mental Prayer. *Dom Vitalis Lehodey* 14.00
Fr. Paul of Moll. *van Speybrouck* 12.50
Abortion: Yes or No? *Dr. John L. Grady, M.D.* 2.00
The Story of the Church. *Johnson, Hannan, Dominica.* 16.50
Hell Quizzes. *Radio Replies Press* 1.50
Purgatory Quizzes. *Radio Replies Press.* 1.50
Virgin and Statue Worship Quizzes. *Radio Replies Press* 1.50
Moments Divine before/Bl. Sacr. *Reuter* 8.50
Meditation Prayer on Mary Immaculate. *Padre Pio* 1.50
Little Book of the Work of Infinite Love. *de la Touche.* 3.00
Textual Concordance of/Holy Scriptures. *Williams.* PB. 35.00
Douay-Rheims Bible. *Paperbound* 35.00
The Way of Divine Love. (pocket, unabr.). *Menendez* 8.50
Mystical City of God—Abridged. *Ven. Mary of Agreda* 18.50

Prices subject to change.

Prices subject to change.

Forty Dreams of St. John Bosco. *Bosco* 12.50
Blessed Miguel Pro. *Ball* 6.00
Soul Sanctified. *Anonymous* 9.00
Wife, Mother and Mystic. *Bessieres* 8.00
The Agony of Jesus. *Padre Pio* 2.00
Catholic Home Schooling. *Mary Kay Clark* 18.00
The Cath. Religion—Illus. & Expl. *Msgr. Burbach* 9.00
Wonders of the Holy Name. *Fr. O'Sullivan* 1.50
How Christ Said the First Mass. *Fr. Meagher* 18.50
Too Busy for God? Think Again! *D'Angelo* 5.00
St. Bernadette Soubirous. *Trochu* 18.50
Passion and Death of Jesus Christ. *Liguori* 10.00
Life Everlasting. *Garrigou-Lagrange* 13.50
Confession Quizzes. *Radio Replies Press* 1.50
St. Philip Neri. *Fr. V. J. Matthews* 5.50
St. Louise de Marillac. *Sr. Vincent Regnault* 6.00
The Old World and America. *Rev. Philip Furlong* 18.00
Prophecy for Today. *Edward Connor* 5.50
Bethlehem. *Fr. Faber* 18.00
The Book of Infinite Love. *Mother de la Touche* 5.00
The Church Teaches. *Church Documents* 16.50
Conversation with Christ. *Peter T. Rohrbach* 10.00
Purgatory and Heaven. *J. P. Arendzen* 5.00
Liberalism Is a Sin. *Sarda y Salvany* 7.50
Spiritual Legacy/Sr. Mary of Trinity. *van den Broek* 10.00
The Creator and the Creature. *Fr. Frederick Faber* 16.50
Radio Replies. 3 Vols. *Frs. Rumble and Carty* 42.00
Convert's Catechism of Catholic Doctrine. *Geiermann* 3.00
Incarnation, Birth, Infancy of Jesus Christ. *Liguori* 10.00
Light and Peace. *Fr. R. P. Quadrupani* 7.00
Dogmatic Canons & Decrees of Trent, Vat. I. 9.50
The Evolution Hoax Exposed. *A. N. Field* 7.50
The Priest, the Man of God. *St. Joseph Cafasso* 13.50
Christ Denied. *Fr. Paul Wickens* 2.50
New Regulations on Indulgences. *Fr. Winfrid Herbst* 2.50
A Tour of the Summa. *Msgr. Paul Glenn* 18.00
Spiritual Conferences. *Fr. Frederick Faber* 15.00
Bible Quizzes. *Radio Replies Press* 1.50
Marriage Quizzes. *Radio Replies Press* 1.50
True Church Quizzes. *Radio Replies Press* 1.50
Mary, Mother of the Church. *Church Documents* 4.00
The Sacred Heart and the Priesthood. *de la Touche* 9.00
Blessed Sacrament. *Fr. Faber* 18.50
Revelations of St. Bridget. *St. Bridget of Sweden* 3.00

Prices subject to change.

Saint Michael and the Angels. *Approved Sources* 7.00
Dolorous Passion of Our Lord. *Anne C. Emmerich*. 16.50
Our Lady of Fatima's Peace Plan from Heaven. *Booklet*. 75
Three Ways of the Spiritual Life. *Garrigou-Lagrange* 6.00
Mystical Evolution. 2 Vols. *Fr. Arintero, O.P.* 36.00
St. Catherine Labouré of the Mirac. Medal. *Fr. Dirvin* 13.50
Manual of Practical Devotion to St. Joseph. *Patrignani* 15.00
The Active Catholic. *Fr. Palau* 7.00
Ven. Jacinta Marto of Fatima. *Cirrincione* 2.00
Reign of Christ the King. *Davies* 1.25
St. Teresa of Ávila. *William Thomas Walsh* 21.50
Isabella of Spain—The Last Crusader. *Wm. T. Walsh* 20.00
Characters of the Inquisition. *Wm. T. Walsh* 15.00
Philip II. *William Thomas Walsh*. HB. 37.50
Blood-Drenched Altars—Cath. Comment. Hist. Mexico 20.00
Self-Abandonment to Divine Providence. *de Caussade* 18.00
Way of the Cross. *Liguorian* 1.00
Way of the Cross. *Franciscan* 1.00
Modern Saints—Their Lives & Faces, Bk. 1. *Ann Ball*. 18.00
Modern Saints—Their Lives & Faces, Bk. 2. *Ann Ball*. 20.00
Divine Favors Granted to St. Joseph. *Pere Binet*. 5.00
St. Joseph Cafasso—Priest of the Gallows. *St. J. Bosco* 5.00
Catechism of the Council of Trent. *McHugh/Callan*. 24.00
Why Squander Illness? *Frs. Rumble & Carty* 2.50
Fatima—The Great Sign. *Francis Johnston* 8.00
Heliotropium—Conformity of Human Will to Divine 13.00
Charity for the Suffering Souls. *Fr. John Nageleisen* 16.50
Devotion to the Sacred Heart of Jesus. *Verheylezoon* 15.00
Sermons on Prayer. *St. Francis de Sales*. 4.00
Sermons on Our Lady. *St. Francis de Sales* 10.00
Sermons for Lent. *St. Francis de Sales*. 12.00
Fundamentals of Catholic Dogma. *Ott* 21.00
Litany of the Blessed Virgin Mary. (100 cards) 5.00
Who Is Padre Pio? *Radio Replies Press* 2.00
Child's Bible History. *Knecht*. 5.00
The Life of Christ. 4 Vols. H.B. *Anne C. Emmerich* 60.00
St. Anthony—The Wonder Worker of Padua. *Stoddard*. 5.00
The Precious Blood. *Fr. Faber* 13.50
The Holy Shroud & Four Visions. *Fr. O'Connell* 2.00
Clean Love in Courtship. *Fr. Lawrence Lovasik* 2.50
The Secret of the Rosary. *St. Louis De Montfort*. 5.00

At your Bookdealer or direct from the Publisher.
Call Toll Free 1-800-437-5876

Prices subject to change.

NOTES